# Part of the Family

# Part of the Family

*Christadelphians, the Kindertransport,
and Rescue from the Holocaust*

*Volume 1*

### JASON HENSLEY

"Part of the Family" is an ongoing project attempting to catalogue the lives and experiences of the Jewish refugees who lived with Christadelphians during the 1930s and 1940s. To that end, if readers know of anyone who could possibly be included in a further work, or if they or their family were Jewish refugees who were sheltered by Christadelphians and would like to have their story published, please contact the author at iwaspartofthefamily.com

Grateful acknowledgment is made to the following for permission to reprint previously published material:

Excerpts from the Glossary in *Echoes and Reflections Teacher's Resource Guide* (New York: Anti-Defamation League, 2005, 2014), www.echoesandreflections.org. All rights reserved.

Library of Congress Cataloging-in-Publication Data
Hensley, Jason, author.
Part of the family : Christadelphians, the Kindertransport, and rescue from the Holocaust / Jason Hensley. -- First edition.
volumes cm
Includes bibliographical references and index.
LCCN 2016907794
ISBN 978-1-5327-4053-4 (volume 1)

1. Kindertransports (Rescue operations)--Great Britain. 2. Jewish children in the Holocaust--Biography. 3. Refugee children--Great Britain--Biography. 4. Holocaust survivors--Great Britain--Biography. 5. Christadelphians--Great Britain--Biography. 6. Holocaust, Jewish (1939-1945)--Personal narratives. 7. World War, 1939-1945--Jews--Rescue--Great Britain. 8. World War, 1939-1945--Children--Great Britain.   I. Title.
D804.6.H46 2016          940.53'1835083
QBI16-600075

*To Dante, Kezia, Leah, Moriah, and Rachel*

I know not whether the men, who at present contrive the foreign policy of Britain, entertain the idea of assuming the sovereignty of the Holy Land, and of promoting its colonization by the Jews; their present intentions, however, are of no importance one way or the other; because they will be compelled, by events soon to happen, to do what, under existing circumstances, heaven and earth combined could not move them to attempt. . . . The finger of God has indicated a course to be pursued by Britain which cannot be evaded, and which her counsellors will not only be willing, but eager, to adopt when the crisis comes upon them. . . . To Britain, then, the prophet calls as the protector of the Jewish nation in the evening-tide trouble, and commands it to send its messengers in swift vessels because the crisis is urgent, and to plant Israel as 'an ensign upon the mountains' (Isa. 18:3).

JOHN THOMAS
*Elpis Israel*
1849

# CONTENTS

# Part of the Family

## Volume 1

# PREFACE

In 2014, I received an invitation from a friend to attend the Belfer National Conference for Educators at the United States Holocaust Memorial and Museum in July of 2015. Our family already had plans to visit the East Coast that year, and as the dates coincided, attending the conference was feasible. A few months later, I found myself in Washington, D.C.

This book is a direct result of that conference.

The Belfer National Conference for Educators is a three-day training program for English and history teachers. The instructors are also English and history teachers, ones who have been specifically trained in a museum fellowship program to teach about the Holocaust. The idea behind the conference is to educate educators on how to appropriately teach the Holocaust, and to that end, the museum emphasizes 10 methodological guidelines. Although a number of these guidelines were helpful in writing this text, one of them in fact inspired it: avoid simple answers to complex questions.

When teaching about the Holocaust, educators need to be aware that it was an incredibly complex event without easy answers. Thus, while we as teachers so often like to speak in generalities, the real memory of the Holocaust, and the real life-changing lessons of the Holocaust truly begin to surface when we examine the stories of the individuals. Indeed, the Holocaust was a tragedy for millions of Jews, yet it was also a tragedy for millions of Jewish *individuals*. Each of those individuals has a story and an experience that was different from that of his or her neighbor. Those stories need to be told.

Therefore, while at the conference, we were encouraged to investigate further and to ask more questions. I was encouraged to look at the stories. In our last activity together, a man named Glenn Kurtz came to speak with us about a book, *Three Minutes in Poland*, that he had written and an adventure he had embarked upon after finding an old home movie in his grandparents' closet. This movie became the touchstone for a number of fascinating experiences. He discovered the location of the movie: a small town in Poland. He began to unearth the history of the town, learning that it had been completely destroyed by the Nazis. And most astonishingly, he met a man who had lived in that town, had survived the Holocaust, and who began to identify people in the film.

I was awed by his story of discovery.

I am not sure when I first heard about Christadelphians and the Kindertransport, but it was on that day—the last day of the Belfer Conference—that I knew I should know more. This became my first step in writing this book.

A few months passed, and I received an e-mail from Jen Goss, one of my instructors from the Belfer Conference. We had been corresponding about various Holocaust-related topics when I received a note from her, mentioning that the Echoes and Reflections training program, a course born out of the partnership between the Anti-Defamation League, the USC Shoah Foundation, and Yad Vashem, was looking for middle school or high school teachers to pilot its new online training module. I signed up.

This book is a direct result of that training.

Echoes and Reflections is another course for teachers about teaching the Holocaust—and one of the unique things about it is the use of visual history. With the assistance of the USC Shoah Foundation, a number of survivor testimonies—videos of survivors telling their stories—are integrated into the curriculum. Survivors' individual experiences are brought together to make an impression on the students.

Once again, there was an emphasis on the individual.

At the end of this program, trainees had to create a final project, a lesson they would present to their students. This assignment served as the final push I needed to begin conducting my research, and to build a unit on Christadelphians and the Holocaust. I had known that Christadelphians helped the Jews during WWII—but I had never known to what extent. The Belfer Conference inspired me to search this out further and to carry out my own research. Echoes and Reflections gave me a deadline by which I needed to begin.

Thus, the seeds of this project were planted in the research that would become my final project.

Since then, this book has had its own story. As with Glenn Kurtz, who began by unearthing history, making connections, and reuniting individuals, I too have had my own share of simply astonishing experiences. In one instance, a refugee had never learned what had happened to her father—only that he had been sent "to the East." This research uncovered her father's fate and answered a question over which she had agonized for 70 years.

In another instance, I was privileged to interview a survivor now living in Australia. Just two days after that interview, I received an e-mail from a Christadelphian in London stating that he had recently digitized his father's home movies and that, while going through one such movie, he spotted two

Jewish refugees but was uncertain who they were. It turned out that one was the man I had just interviewed the previous Thursday and that I was able to identify him: we had just discovered a home movie of him and his sister that neither of them had ever seen.

Research can yield incredible results, but the human connections, the people you meet, and the friends that you make through it are precious, too.

Thus, although this book discusses the Holocaust in some generalities—it is, after all, a book about what the Christadelphians in general did to save Jews during the Holocaust—the book mainly tells the story of individuals involved. Where it has been possible, I have attempted to find and tell the experiences of Jewish men and women who, when children, were rescued from the Nazis and housed and supported by Christadelphians.

As a Christadelphian, I inevitably bring certain biases to my research. In writing this book, I have attempted to put those biases aside and simply tell the stories. I have contacted refugees whose experiences with Christadelphians were entirely positive, and a very few whose experiences were tarnished with grief and frustration—not only because they were in a new country with a new culture and a new language but also because of their Christadelphian foster families. Nevertheless, every refugee I spoke with expressed gratitude to those Christadelphian families who had been willing to open their homes to complete strangers to preserve their lives from the flames of the Nazi horror. In other words, I did attempt to check my biases—but the feelings I encountered through my discussions with Jewish refugees were, while occasionally marked by tales of frustration or bitterness with Christadelphians (both personally and communally), overwhelmingly positive.

Prior to the book's publishing, each refugee's story was read by the refugees themselves and/or their family members and, in many cases, by the Christadelphian families that housed the refugees. I sought approval, and received it, for each individual story. I took these actions with the hope of ensuring that the record presented in these pages is as close to historical truth and as bias-free as possible.

In telling these stories, the first portion of this book examines the general Christadelphian response to the Holocaust. The second portion conveys those experiences of the individual refugees—in an attempt to show that ultimately, history cannot simply be remembered in batches of statistics and generalities but rather should be seen and understood through the lens of the individuals who genuinely lived this history. Indeed, this book is their story.

# Part I

Christadelphians and the Jews

# CHRISTADELPHIANS AND THE JEWS

On this occasion we remember Christ specially as the Saviour of Israel. We are to have a special collection for the Jewish Refugee Relief Fund, and well we may; for 'Salvation is of the Jews' . . . This is not the first time we have had such a special Jewish Relief Collection. Fifty-seven years ago, in 1882, on the occasion of the Russian persecutions, we had such a collection, and the late brother Roberts in the Sunday morning exhortation (Christadelphian, April, 1882), made our indebtedness to Israel, and our acceptance of 'the hope of Israel,' the basis of his appeal.

Again, thirty-six years ago, in 1903, on the occasion of the atrocious Kischeneff massacres, we had another, which was briefly referred to by the present writer (Christadelphian, 1903, p. 319), in a note on 'Jacob's Trouble.' Many of us then said, It is written, 'Cursed is he that curseth thee' O Israel. Russia will suffer for this. And truly it was so in the Russo-Japanese war. The destruction of the 'Russian Armada' was an event unparalleled in naval history.[1]

The excerpt above is a transcription of an address given at a Sunday morning Christadelphian meeting by C. C. Walker, the former editor of *The Christadelphian* magazine, the leading magazine and mouthpiece of the community. It was published on March 1, 1939. The talk was likely given on a Sunday morning in February 1939. By that time, Germany's hatred against the Jews had been official policy for six years. *Kristallnacht* had occurred in the previous November, and the

3

*C. C. Walker, editor of* The Christadelphian *magazine from 1898 to 1937.*

nations of the world had watched as Adolf Hitler marched his troops into the *Sudetenland* of Czechoslovakia.

At the same time, this was also when, as will be seen, many Christadelphians had opened up their homes and their families, taking in Jewish refugee children. And in fact, in the very same issue of the magazine, a letter was printed, which is also dated at the beginning of February 1939:

> The Rt. Hon. the Earl Baldwin,
> c/o *The Times*,
> Printing House Square,
> London, E.C.4.
>
> *Feb. 4th*, 1939.

My Lord,

I have pleasure in sending a cheque for £1,000 (One thousand pounds) which sum has been contributed by Christadelphian Ecclesias, largely in the British Isles, and other readers of *The Christadelphian*, to the Fund which bears your name, for the Relief of Jewish Refugees.

Will you be good enough to earmark this sum in equal proportions for the relief of German Jewry and Jewish Refugee Children.

Please acknowledge this remittance as from 'Christadelphian Ecclesias and readers of *The Christadelphian*.'

I have the honour to be, My Lord,
Your obedient servant,
John Carter.
69, Eaton Square, S.W.[2]

This rather large sum, particularly in 1939,[3] was the culmination of donations from approximately 140 Christadelphian churches and a number of Christadelphian individuals.[4] A second contribution of £250, also gleaned from Christadelphian churches and readers of *The Christadelphian* magazine was given to Lord Baldwin in May of the same year.[5] These two collections demonstrate that the aid that was given by Christadelphians to the Jews throughout the Holocaust was part of a community-wide movement. It was not simply the work of one man or a small group. It was an effort made by the Christadelphian body as a whole.

Perhaps that is what really makes this rescue effort unique. Although the Quakers are indeed a similar story, and though they too worked for the sake of Jewish refugees in the 1930s and 1940s, there are not many entire Christian communities that can claim the same. With so many other Christian groups, there were individuals who saved Jews, and some, now recognized as "righteous among the nations," risked their lives in doing so. But at the same time, within that same denomination, there were those who were condemning the Jews and turning a blind eye, or even taking part in the persecution themselves.[6] Perhaps some of the most frightening language came from the Catholic Church. Father Charles Coughlin, an extremely famous Catholic radio priest in the United States,[7] made a chilling statement in 1938—after boycotts of Jewish businesses, individual attacks on the Jews, and numerous restrictions had already been placed on the Jewish people in Germany: "When we get through with the Jews in America, they'll think the treatment they received in Germany was nothing."[8]

After the events of *Kristallnacht*, that same year, Coughlin attempted to defend the massive pogrom.[9] He was not the only Catholic prelate to use this type of rhetoric at such an inopportune time. In 1944, after millions of Jews had been deported to inhumane conditions in ghettos or concentration camps (and millions had been murdered, although that was largely unknown at the time), Gyula Czapik, the archbishop of Eger in Hungary, said the following: "What is happening to the Jews at the present time is nothing but appropriate punishment for their misdeeds in the past."[10]

Though there were a number of Catholic prelates and individuals who risked their lives to save the Jews, there were also those who did not feel that the Jews were worth saving. The Jasenovac concentration camp, along with other concentration camps in Croatia, is another case in point, as it was run by Catholic priests.[11]

Moreover, this type of rhetoric was not confined to the Catholic Church. Going back a few centuries, but decidedly pertinent to the period, Martin Luther was notoriously antisemitic, claiming that the synagogues should be burned and that the Jews should be compelled to work as slaves.[12] It is thought by some that it was no coincidence that Luther was a German, that Hitler wrote of his admiration for Luther in *Mein Kampf*,[13] and that his advice was essentially followed on *Kristallnacht*, when nearly 200 synagogues were burned, Jewish houses were destroyed, and over 30,000 Jewish men were taken to camps like Dachau and Buchenwald to serve as slaves. These connections, along with one other—that *Kristallnacht* happened to take place on Luther's birthday— were noted and lauded by a Lutheran bishop at the time. James Carroll in his history of the relationship between Christianity and the Jews explained:

> The Lutheran bishop of Thuringia, Martin Sasse, exulted, 'On November 10, 1938, on Luther's birthday, the synagogues are burning in Germany.' The bishop was referring, of course, to Kristallnacht. His joy was expressed in the foreword to his collection of Luther's anti-Jewish writings, which the bishop was publishing in the hope that the German people would take to heart the words, as he put it, 'of the greatest anti-Semite of his time, the warner of his people against the Jews.'[14]

When studying the history of the Protestant and Catholic churches, one finds a clear trend: many Christians despised the Jews. Nevertheless, despite the feelings that permeated the community, a number of Christians, though certainly not the majority, chose to act and save Jews during the Holocaust— sometimes in spite of their own antisemitism.

The Christadelphian community, however, was quite different. Though its rhetoric toward the Jews occasionally reached the point of referring to them as "blind" or "stubborn," though it did believe that a "time of trouble" would come upon the Jewish people (Jeremiah 30:7; Daniel 12:1), and though they did attempt to preach to the Jews (as will be noted later), there was never open hostility, and the Christadelphians were determined not to be a part of bringing that time of trouble upon the Jews. Conversely, Christadelphians often expressed a love for the Jewish people. This love was exhibited not only in their words but also in their actions. Time and again, Christadelphians donated money to the Jewish cause, and during the dark years of the Holocaust, a terrible time of trouble, they, as a community, physically contributed to the relief of the Jews by saving Jewish children.

For some reason, something made this small group of Christians different. At a time when many Christians were condemning the Jews, Christadelphians came together to collect money for them, to provide aid, and even to admit them into Christadelphian houses. The Christadelphians did this as a community.

And, according to the Walker excerpt above, this was not the first time they had contributed to Jewish relief.

Why?

What made this small band of Christians so different? What made them so concerned about the fate of European Jewry? What made them so willing to give of their own substance—as a community, and not just individuals—to aid Jewish relief?

This book seeks to answer those questions.

In that attempt, this book will first focus on the history of the Christadelphian movement and its beliefs. From there it will note its interactions with the Jews from the time of its inception, and it will propose a theory regarding the Christadelphian community's intriguing history with the Jewish community.

**Who Are Christadelphians?**

Christadelphians might define themselves as a worldwide family, bound together by a common love of the Bible, both the Hebrew and Christian portions (known as the Old and New Testaments by Christians), as well as a common set of beliefs about God, Jesus, and the Kingdom of God. This unique set of beliefs sets Christadelphians apart from the majority of Christianity, yet brings them closer together, as tightly knit as a family, with bonds of trust and hospitality overriding countries, cultures, and even familiarity. It is not uncommon for a Christadelphian to open up his or her home to another Christadelphian, even to one who is a complete stranger.

Placing a date on the inception of the Christadelphian community is a bit of a challenge. Christadelphians are a lay community, meaning that they do not have paid ministers or pastors, and the work is shared among community members termed "brothers" and "sisters." There is no official leader of Christadelphians, nor is there any official structure in which the community is organized. Groups of believers organize together into "ecclesias" (a transliteration of the Greek word for "assembly" or "congregation") based on geographic location. These groups meet at least once a week, breaking bread and drinking wine in remembrance of Jesus Christ, following the example that he set in the gospels (Matthew 26:26–28). The Christadelphian community is a collection of these ecclesias, all of which share a common set of beliefs known to the community as "first principles."

Therefore, Because of its decentralized nature, it is difficult to know precisely where to begin with the history of the Christadelphian community. Many Christadelphians would likely place the beginnings around the year 1849—the year a man named John Thomas, the son of a Christian minister, wrote a book titled *Elpis Israel*, meaning, "The Hope of Israel." This book was the culmination of over 15 years of Mr. Thomas's studies, which led to a separation between him and the Campbellite churches in which he had been lecturing and teaching.

*John Thomas, author of* Elpis Israel.

The Christadelphians were largely the group that was formed by those who read John Thomas's book (or heard his lectures) and agreed with its tenets. As the years passed, increasing numbers came to agree with Mr. Thomas's conclusions and were baptized into this community. Nevertheless, owing to its decentralized nature, the group did not in fact have a name until nearly 20 years after the book *Elpis Israel* had been published.

The name came into being during the United States Civil War because those who agreed with Mr. Thomas's teaching were conscientious objectors from military service, and to be recognized by the U.S. government as conscientious objectors, religious organizations required a name. The name chosen was "Christadelphians," a combination of the Greek words *Christ* and *adelphos*, which translates to "Brethren in Christ."

Worldwide, there are approximately 50,000 Christadelphians, found in 120 countries.[15]

**Beliefs**

More than anything else, it is the beliefs, the first principles, of the Christadelphian community that have held the members together. Their beliefs are unique, and agreement with them is a requirement for joining the community.

Far and above, the belief that permeates all of the community's teaching is that the Bible, both the Jewish and Christian portions, without the books of the Apocrypha, is wholly inspired by God and is unerring, except in matters of translation or transcription. This tenet is what motivates many Christadelphians to read the Bible daily—typically following a standardized reading plan, known to many Christadelphians as the "daily readings" that leads them through the entire Bible in one year. Moreover, Christadelphians encourage their

# ELPIS ISRAEL;

A BOOK FOR THE TIMES:

BEING

## AN EXPOSITION

OF THE

# KINGDOM OF GOD,

WITH REFERENCE TO

## "THE TIME OF THE END,"

AND

## "THE AGE TO COME."

BY

## JOHN THOMAS, M.D.,

RICHMOND, VIRGINIA, UNITED STATES.

"For the Hope of Israel I am bound with this chain."—*Paul.*

## LONDON:

PUBLISHED BY THE AUTHOR;

AND MAY BE OBTAINED AT 3, BRUDENELL PLACE, NEW NORTH ROAD, HOXTON.

1849.

members to engage in personal Bible study, which is then presented by the community members at various functions.

This emphasis on the Bible and Bible reading is what led Christadelphians to develop a number of other beliefs—beliefs that have set them at odds with the majority of Christians. One notable belief concerns the Christadelphian stance toward Jesus. Rather than teaching that Jesus is the second person of the Trinity and is God Himself, as is propounded by many Christian churches, Christadelphians teach that Jesus is the Son of God, and a representative of his Father, rather than God in the flesh.

Another doctrine unique to Christadelphians is the resurrection, with its connection to the promises to Abraham. Abraham, the Hebrew patriarch, was given a set of promises by the Almighty. One of these promises was that he would be given the land of Israel (along with quite a bit of adjoining territory; Genesis 13:15–18, Genesis 15:18). Nevertheless, according to the Biblical record, that promise was never fulfilled. Abraham only received a small plot of land near the city of Hebron (Genesis 23:17–20). Stemming from this, it is believed that someday, Abraham must live again—in order that the promise made to him might be fulfilled. They believe that the overwhelming teaching of the Hebrew Bible is that when one is dead, he or she is unconscious, having returned to dust (Genesis 3:19, Psalm 6:5, Ecclesiastes 9:4–5, Isaiah 38:18).

Christadelphians therefore believe that Abraham, and all of those of faith, will one day be resurrected. At the present time, they are in the ground, turned back to dust, waiting for when the Messiah, whom the Christadelphians believe to be Jesus, will come to fulfill those promises made to Abraham. The land will be given to Abraham. The whole world will be blessed in him. An era of peace and righteousness and love will overcome all the trouble and pain currently upon the world (Malachi 4:3–4).

This is the Christadelphian hope—a hope that they believe is the hope taught in the Bible. The Jewish Messiah will come, will rule over the world, and all the nations will recognize his goodness and his righteousness. The true hope, according to Christadelphians, is not eternal life in heaven, nor is the true consequence of disobedience eternal torture in hell. Instead, the hope is an earthly kingdom in which the promises made to Abraham are realized and the promise made to David—that one of his descendants would rule upon his throne forever—is fulfilled in an era of joy and peace. The consequence of disobedience, for those who are unfamiliar with the gospel, is simply returning to the dust at death.

Of further note, Christadelphians treat baptism differently from some other Christian groups. The community does not baptize infants, believing that baptism is something that should occur after a man or woman has understood the gospel and has decided to commit to it. Any of the Jewish children who were eventually baptized as Christadelphians (there were a handful) were likely encouraged by their host families but were also deemed old enough to make their own choices (generally in their late teens or early 20s). When the individual decided that he or she wanted to join the community through baptism, they likely wrote a letter to the local ecclesia requesting an interview. In the interview, they underwent rigorous questioning, and if it was agreed by the interviewers that they understood the gospel and indeed wanted to give their lives to it, a baptism, by full immersion in water, was arranged.

Many of these beliefs tend to distance Christadelphians from the majority of the Christian world. For many Christians, a belief in the Trinity and the divinity of Jesus is essential to being a Christian—those who do not hold to this belief are often excluded from the Christian community. The belief in a resurrection and a Kingdom of God, rather than in the immortality of the soul and an afterlife in heaven or hell, also distances Christadelphians from other Christian groups.

This distancing is not just the result of other Christians however. Christadelphians themselves feel as though their beliefs are something special and think these beliefs set them apart from the majority of the Christian world. This separateness contributes to the feeling of a worldwide family—because throughout the world, one Christadelphian can be confident that any other Christadelphian holds to the same set of first principles, is likely reading the same set of Bible passages each day, and has a similar set of values.

## Christadelphians and Jews throughout History

Though Christadelphians, through their more than 160 years of existence have felt at odds with other Christian communities, they have very much felt an affinity for the Jews. Even the first Christadelphian publication, as noted earlier, was called *Elpis Israel*.

Within that book are words that, unlike the historic replacement theology of many Christian denominations, are extremely favorable to the Jewish people. These words were written before the advent of modern Zionism and nearly 100 years before the state of Israel came into existence:

> The restoration of Israel is a most important feature in the divine economy. It is indispensable to the setting up of the kingdom of God; for they are the kingdom, having been constituted such by the covenant of Sinai, as it is written, 'Ye shall be unto Me a kingdom of priests, and a holy nation.'[16]

In the mid-1800s, Christadelphians, as part of their faith, saw the Jews as a special people and expected their return to the land of Israel. Just a few years after *Elpis Israel* was published, a congregation of believers—though they did not yet call themselves Christadelphians, was reported in John Thomas's magazine, *Herald of the Kingdom and Age to Come*, as contributing a small sum toward the relief of the poor Jews in Palestine. The letter was written to the chief rabbi in London and was dated June 12, 1854, written from Edinburgh:

> Dear Sir:—I take the liberty of writing to you, to inquire if you would be willing to take charge of, and transmit, a small contribution to assist in relieving the wants of the destitute Jews in Palestine. The contribution is from a congregation of between thirty and forty members, whose attention has been directed to the subject by several communications in the newspapers.[17]

The chief rabbi, along with a man named Moses Montefiore, responded, via one of his staff, with a letter "to acknowledge with grateful thanks . . . the amount of your generous collection towards the fund now being raised for the poor Jews of Palestine."[18]

Moses Montefiore was a British Jewish banker who donated large sums of money to the Jewish communities in Palestine and who, via the Montefiore Testimonial Fund, helped channel donations from philanthropists and charity groups to the Jews there. His name appeared in connection with the Christadelphians again when another congregation contacted him to give its small donation to him that it might be passed on to the Jews in Palestine. The letter, which also appeared in *Herald of the Kingdom and Age to Come*, is from Halifax, Nova Scotia, and is dated August 30, 1854:

Dear and Respected Sir,—Deeply sympathizing with the poor Jews who are suffering for want of food in the Holy Land, and perceiving that they have appealed to you to procure for them relief; and knowing that you will gladly receive any sums of money, however small, which may be forwarded to you to be disposed of in the way that will aid them most, I beg to enclose you £30 sterling, in a Bank Bill on London, at sixty days.[19]

A very kind response was received from Mr. Montefiore himself, including a prayer: "I fervently pray that our Almighty Father may bless with thousand fold the store of those whose hearts yearn towards the Land whence the Holy Word went forth."[20]

But these were just the contributions of individual Christadelphian ecclesias. The whole community in fact supported this type of involvement. Twenty years later, Mr. Montefiore was still involved in the colonization of Palestine, and by that time, it was not just individual ecclesias that were contributing to his colonization scheme but the entire Christadelphian body.

In August 1875, The Christadelphian magazine reported that the Christadelphian community in total had contributed £130 to advance Montefiore's work.[21] At the time, the average yearly wage in Scotland was, by a high estimate, approximately £2 a week, or £104 per annum.[22] In 1870, miners in Northumberland and Durham received, on average, 27s per week, or £70 4s per annum; agricultural workers in Dorsetshire received a meager 7s or 8s per week, or £18 4s or £20 16s per annum.[23] Indeed, the contribution from the Christadelphian community, also considering that it was taking collections for other causes, namely for members of its own community, is quite an impressive sum.

Perhaps in a more striking instance, the community collected still additional funds for the Jewish people, and those funds were used to make a lasting impression upon the land of Israel. In March 1882, the magazine published an article about the "Jewish Emigration Fund," urging its subscribers to contribute to the Jewish cause:

> The fund . . . has been instituted to assist the maltreated sons of Israel. . . . We could not expect to add much to the fund, which is attracting such large contributions from wealthy Jews and Gentiles. But that is no reason why we should not add our mite. Each ecclesia might fix a Sunday suitable to its circumstances for a free-will gathering.[24]

As such, the Christadelphian brotherhood once again brought its resources together for the sake of "the maltreated sons of Israel." By May of 1882, just two months after the proposed communal contribution, many of the donations had been collected and came to a sum of over £150. At that time, it was proposed that these resources be earmarked for a certain Laurence Oliphant, specifically to be spent in connection with the colonization of Palestine.[25]

Laurence Oliphant was a well-known Englishman, who was a former member of Parliament, an author and journalist, and a gentile philanthropist. Moved by the fervor of the Eastern European Jews to return to their homeland, Oliphant toured Palestine and created a plan for the Jewish settlement of the area. In 1882, he bought a house in Haifa and moved to Palestine.[26]

Through the financial backing of the Christadelphians, which began with the contribution in 1882, he was able to settle Jews in the land. One of the major achievements accomplished with

Christadelphian money was the settlement of a portion of the community of Rosh Pina, which remains in Israel today. Below is an excerpt of a letter, written by Lawrence Oliphant in 1883 to Robert Roberts, the editor of *The Christadelphian* at that time:

> Haifa, 2nd June, 1883
>
> My Dear Sir . . . The present application of the money was most providential. . . . This land, although it belongs to your subscribers, will be part of the colony of Janna, or, as it is called by the colonists, Rosh Pina, —'the Head of the corner,' an expression used in the verse, 'The stone which the builders rejected, the same is become the head of the corner . . .'
>
> Yours truly,
> L. Oliphant[27]

The money given by the subscribers of *The Christadelphian* magazine was used to purchase land for the colony of Rosh Pina and, as Oliphant went on to say in his letter, not only had the subscribers sent money, but they also had sent boxes of clothes to the colonists.

Rosh Pina is one of the oldest *moshavot* (an agricultural community in which the land is privately owned rather than communally, as it is on a kibbutz) in Israel.[28] As of 2009, Rosh Pina had a population of approximately 2,700.[29]

In January 1884, the Christadelphian ecclesias resolved that they would make an annual contribution to Mr. Oliphant's work with the Jewish settlers.[30] After this, from 1884 to 1888, the year that Mr. Oliphant died, the pages of *The Christadelphian* magazine were filled with stories about how the donated money was being used, the value of the boxes of

19

*Top: Laurence Oliphant*
*Bottom: Robert Roberts, editor of* The Christadelphian *from 1864 to 1898.*

clothing that the brethren sent to the Jews in Israel, and the interaction between the Christadelphians and Mr. Oliphant.[31] In 1892, the Christadelphian community began working with the Jews in Israel via Alice Davis, known as "Mrs. Davis" in the magazine, an American woman who had moved to Jerusalem and established herself there in 1881.[32] Eventually, from letters that she wrote to the magazine, it seems as though she came to appreciate Christadelphian literature, as well as some of the unique Christadelphian doctrines,[33] and distanced herself from other Christian churches.[34] Because of this, over the 12 years in which the Christadelphian body funneled donations to the Jews through her, there was a sense in which the Christadelphian community had one of its own on the ground, both distributing the funds, and sharing *The Christadelphian* magazine with those who would care to read it or have it read to them. Some pertinent excerpts from her letters—specifically in relation to the distribution of the funds, are below:

On June 12, 1893, she wrote:

> You have done a good work for Jerusalem. . . . I am caring for several poor widows with children. You need not send more until the cold weather comes, when they will need it so much more for food and bedding. There is sure to be great distress soon.[35]

On July 17, 1895, she wrote:

> Your kind letter with cheque came safely. I have no words to express my gratitude. I went at once to Dr. D. Arbela and took more than half the money to him and asked what was the wisest plan to do the most good with our small means? He said at once: 'One of our poor hard-working Persian Jews has built a small room for his family, and they have lived in it for more than a year without a roof; to help this poor man to cover his

21

room is the best thing to do.' Then there will be enough to pay other rents and buy water for those who have none.[36]

The consistent donations to Alice Davis's work continued, and on June 8, 1903, she wrote:

> Beloved Friends,—Your kind gift for our poor persecuted people came safely to me. I was so grateful for such a kindness at this time, when there is so much misery among our poor people. Many of those poor Jews have arrived here from Russia, and the tale they tell of their sufferings is too awful to hear. People who were comparatively rich stripped of all they possessed and obliged to flee like wild beasts. Little wonder they have such a horror of Christianity.[37]

On January 3, 1904, just a few months before her last letter, she described a heart-wrenching scene:

> I must try and tell you about a Jewish family that I have been caring for for several months. I went to see them and found them living in a room not more than eight feet square. It was a room built of old boxes and old tin cans, the floor was cold earth, and in this miserable place lived five people. The husband has been gradually growing blind, the wife and mother goes out daily to wash and scrub or anything she can get to do to support the family. It was impossible to think how these poor people could sleep, as I saw no beds—only a few old quilts piled up in one corner. I was heartsore at the sight; but thank God, and the dear friends, I had the means to make the poor souls comfortable with straw matting for the ground floor, and some bedding and warm clothing. I have no words to tell you of the gratitude of these poor people. They tried to kiss my

feet. I told them it was all from God. It does seem awful to know that God's people, Christ's brethren, should live in such a horrid state, and there are so many in the same condition. How I do wish I could help all these poor people. I can only pray, 'Thy Kingdom Come.'[38]

The last letter appears to have been written on June 6, 1904. After that, Alice Davis, a dedicated worker for the Jewish people in Israel, disappears from the archives of *The Christadelphian* magazine. At that point, she was 78 years old.[39]

Nevertheless, the Christadelphian donations to the Jewish people continued. In 1905, there was a major pogrom in Russia. At the news of this, a special collection was taken, and the Christadelphian community donated £50.[40] That same year, the community also gave £20 to the Jewish Colonial Trust, the financial institution of the Zionist movement.[41] In 1912, the community donated money to endow a bed in the L.J.S. Hospital in Jerusalem—naming it the "Elpis Israel" (Hope of Israel) bed.[42] In 1916, in the midst of World War I, it made multiple donations, all to the Jewish Colonial Trust,[43] for a total of £240 that year. The next year, the community gave £110, once again for "the relief of European and Palestinian Jewish Refugees."[44] In 1918, the community made three donations to the Jewish Colonial Trust, totaling £400 for the year.[45] For perspective, in 1916, £31 4s to £39 per annum was an average wage in agricultural work for women.[46] That same year, a constable who had served in the "City and Metropolitan Police" for 20 years, a well-respected position, received 52s per week, or £135 4s per annum.[47] Moreover, according to the records of the debates of Parliament, the inflation of the cost of living during the war was quite significant: "Food, clothing, etc. . . . during the War increased by at least 50 per cent."[48]

Every year, from 1919 to 1941, the archives of *The Christadelphian* bear witness to the donations that this Christian community gave to the Jewish refugees. As noted at the start of this chapter, some of these donations were quite large, surpassing £1,000.

Yet, throughout the latter portion of that period, the community did much more than simply donate money. As the Christadelphians throughout the world discovered what was occurring in Germany beginning in 1933 via copies of *The Christadelphian*, any other Christadelphian periodical, or simply the newspaper, they found themselves appalled and stirred to action.

**What They Knew**

Much of what was printed in the Christadelphian magazines was simply taken straight from various papers—the Christadelphians at this time were fairly well-informed of what began taking place in Germany and its surrounding nations, after Hitler became chancellor in 1933. What follows are some excerpts of articles printed in a number of Christadelphian magazines from 1933 to 1938.

In April 1933, *The Christadelphian* magazine reported, "There has been enough of murder to make the 600,000 Jews of Germany go in terror of their lives. Many are in flight and homeless."[49]

That same month, *The Testimony*, another Christadelphian magazine based in Britain explained:

> German Jewry was famed the world over for its industry and integrity. Hitler brought it to ruins in less than a month. Intimidation was followed by indignities on the Jews; then came systematic persecution and

hounding from office and shop; finally there was the Haman-like decree to boycott all Jews and their businesses. . . . There is little doubt that these things have been accompanied by floggings, torture and death. . . . This is a settled, deliberate policy of the Hitler Government, not a sudden outbreak of fanaticism, or of repression, born of panic. Hitler's twenty-five points were drawn up in 1920 and were declared to be unalterable—another reminder of a Bible parallel, for Haman hoped the same for his decree.[50]

One month later, in May 1933, *The Fraternal Visitor* reported on the restrictions that Germany had imposed on the Jews, along with the effects:

Germany's drive to remove from official positions, all Jewish judges, lawyers, teachers, doctors, and Civil servants, was carried out with thoroughness. Nuremberg Christian city officials, and employees married to Jewesses, have been advised to secure divorces. Some of the Jews have been driven to commit suicide. All sports federations are to be cleansed also. Special hours are fixed for Jews to use the public bathing establishments. The entry of Jewish students into the universities is stopped, pending the announcement of the quota allowed by the Government. Schools are limiting the number of Jewish children, and discharging those over the quota permitted. A clergyman at a national convention in Berlin of the 'German Christian Movement' said that 'St. Paul's reference to the equality of Jew and Greek in the Epistle to the Romans, applied to things spiritual and the world beyond, but not to this world, where race purity was ordained by God.'[51]

As early as August 1934, the same Christadelphian magazine, *The Fraternal Visitor*, made a chilling report: "Even to-day Hitler under his own name in print is circulating his recommendation of poison gas for Hebrews."[52]

In May 1935, *The Berean Christadelphian* explained to its readers what *The Times* believed to be Hitler's policy at that point:

> At the same time, the position of the Jews in almost all countries continues to worsen. More and more restrictions are imposed in Germany, apparently with the deliberate object, says *The Times*, of forcing them to emigrate: 'The facts force one to the conclusion that the Government is now trying to drive all the Jews out of the country'[53]

In January 1936, *The Christadelphian* quoted for its readers what had been written in *The Jewish Chronicle* about attacks in Poland. The news was frightening:

> From Poland the news is heartbreaking. A correspondent of the Jewish Chronicle, writing from Warsaw, says:—
>
> > Following the fierce propaganda campaign carried on by the anti-Semites a new wave of attacks on Jews has swept the country. In no less than fourteen Polish towns and cities Jews have been assaulted during the last few days. In Warsaw, serious anti-Jewish riots were organised at the University, and the example was followed in Vilna and Lemberg. In Lemberg a regular anti-Jewish manhunt was staged, not even girl students being spared. A later report states that one Lemberg Jewish student, Samuel Rosenberg, has since died

of his injuries. At Cracow University in the course of anti-Jewish demonstrations, one Jewish student was seriously wounded. Warsaw University and the Agricultural High School have now been closed down indefinitely.

Even more grave were the attacks on Jews in the smaller towns. In the township of Pogon, near Sosnowiec, where a bomb was exploded near the Synagogue, one of the victims of the explosion, a fourteen-year-old boy, Abraham Rosenblum, has died of his injuries.'[54]

Hundreds of Jewish shops have been wrecked and looted in Lemberg (Poland). The Synagogue was attacked and worshippers, including the Rabbi, wounded. Jewish cemeteries have been desecrated and tombstones overthrown in other parts of Poland.[55]

The Testimony magazine, in September 1936, revealed to Christadelphians some of the vitriolic rhetoric coming out of Germany:

Some idea of the nature of the campaign carried on against the Jews in Germany can be culled from the following extracts:—

Dr. Goebbels writes:—

'A Jew is for me an object of physical disgust. Christ cannot possibly have been a Jew. I don't have to prove that scientifically. It is a fact. I treasure an ordinary prostitute above a married Jewess.'

From the official newspaper 'Judenkenner.'

> 'German national comrade, do you know that the Jew:
> Violates Your Child. Mocks Your Honour. Sullies Your Wife. Scorns Your Morals. Destroys Your Church. Murders Your Parents. Rots Your Culture. Steals Your Property. Infects Your Race.'[56]

Slightly more than one year later, in December 1937, *The Fraternal Visitor* reported on the state of the Jews in Poland. They too were persecuted by their government:

> For over two years, Jews living in Poland are reported to have been suffering intense persecution in every phase of their daily lives. The Polish Government has agreed to a policy of economic pressure which take the form of private and official boycott of Jewish trade and industry, purging the Jews from the professions and crushing them with exceptional taxation. It is the policy of the Polish anti-Semites to enforce Jewish emigration from Poland, a policy which threatens the security of the three and a half million Jews living there. It is obvious that the Jews have nowhere to go, and the clamour for their expulsion is one of the inhuman results of the extreme 'Nationalist' creed.[57]

One month after the *Anschluss*—the occupation of Austria by Germany in March 1938, The Christadelphian described the unfortunate state of the Jews in Austria. The evils that had been inflicted upon the Jews in Germany were now inflicted upon them:

> There are 180,000 Jews in Austria. They are said to be 'in a state of panic and hopelessness.' Prayers are being offered in the Synagogues for the safety of Austrian

Jewry and refugees are already flowing in streams toward the frontiers. It is sad to read that some of these have been refused permission to land in England and have been sent back to France. One of these unfortunates took poison but was treated promptly by a doctor and his life was saved. He might have said with bitter truth that Austria would not let him live and England would not let him die.

Raiding of Jewish houses has begun, carried out by 'storm troopers,' and all money confiscated. Among the raided places are the offices of the Jewish National Fund, the Austrian Zionist Federation, the Palestine office, the Keren Hayesod, and the editorial office of the Zionist paper, Stimme. A list of prominent Jews is given who are under arrest, and cries of 'Perish Judah' are heard in the streets of Vienna. The Times publishes reports of shop-looting in the same city.

All Jewish officials have been dismissed, Judges and State Attorneys among them. The legal profession is declared closed to Jews, and Jewish doctors are disqualified from certain services. On cafés appear notices, 'No Jews served here.'[58]

Then, on November 9 to 10, 1938, came *Kristallnacht*, a massive pogrom unleashed against the Jewish population of Germany, Austria, and parts of Czechoslovakia. In December of 1938, *The Christadelphian* magazine reported:

The death of Herr Vom Rath, Third Secretary at the German Embassy in Paris, some days after he had been shot by a 17-year-old Polish Jew, has intensified the persecution of the Jews in Germany.

Put into the cold terms of a catalogue the rioters have burned scores of Synagogues in cities and towns from Berlin in the north to Cologne in the West, and Vienna in the east.

They have wrecked and plundered thousands of Jewish shops and restaurants; assaulted men, women and children in the streets and in their homes; arrested many thousands of people (10,000 in Vienna); drove between 25 and 30 Jews to suicide; and attacked a Jewish kindergarten.[59]

That same month, December 1938, *The Fraternal Visitor* also described the horrors of *Kristallnacht*. Readers of these publications, as well as readers of many newspapers throughout the world, saw the violent state into which Germany had fallen:

GERMANY'S vengeance for the murder of Herr von Rath by a Polish Jew in Paris has been terrible indeed. On Thursday morning, November 10th, by a plan which must have been concerted, thousands of Jews were beaten up, their shops were wrecked and looted, and nearly all their synagogues were burned to the ground. Government action then began by the arrest and consignment to the concentration camps of thousands of innocent people. Everywhere the Jews went in fear of their lives, leaving their homes and seeking shelter from their persecutors. A collective fine of about £80,000,000 has been imposed upon the Jews in Germany and they have been compelled to make good the damage done to their property by Nazi mobs. Henceforth they will be excluded from all economic activity in Germany, and new restrictive laws are imposed daily which make it more and more difficult for the Jew to stave off pauperisation and starvation.

Seldom has the common instinct of the civilized world been so deeply aroused as by Germany's treatment of the Jews.[60]

Commenting on *Kristallnacht*, *The Testimony magazine* declared that this was the beginning of the end:

Let us not mistake the horrific nature of what happened in Germany. The diabolical action against the Jews was no spontaneous outbreak of anger because Herr vom Rath of the German embassy died at the hands of a Polish Jew in Paris. Certain suspicions and allegations were brought to a focus in the House of Commons in a striking speech by Mr. Noel-Baker, who told his fellow members that in a concentration camp near Weimar 70 Jews were killed during the night of November 8th–9th—*before it was known vom Rath was dead!* The Jewish home for consumptives was destroyed and the patients driven away with only their night attire. The patients in the Jewish Hospital at Nuremberg were lined up on parade, and one dropped dead. . . . Children in a boarding-school were driven away at 2 a.m. without adult help or protection into the night. A new offensive on the Jews was being considered before the shooting incident in Paris, and *The Times* declared: 'All indications point to centralised direction.' It also said: 'Either the German authorities were a party to this outbreak or their powers over public order and a hooligan minority are not what they are proudly claimed to be'. That appeared on November 11th. It is now clear that it was part of deliberate policy. The shooting in Paris came as a timely excuse for setting it in motion. The Jews are to be hunted out of Central Europe.[61]

Reading through these quotations, it is simply astonishing to see what was actually known about the persecution of the Jews at that time. The Christadelphian community, informed by both the newspapers and its own magazines, recognized what was happening to the Jews. And thus, when Great Britain chose to open up its doors via the Kindertransport, the Christadelphians, who had been watching the events in Germany, Poland, and Austria with horror, began to act. This time, they were not simply confined to donations for Jewish refugees in other countries—although those continued. Now, the Jewish refugees were brought to their doorstep.

**What They Did**

To provide relief to the Jewish people after *Kristallnacht*, the Christadelphians took two major steps. Aside from giving donations, they created two hostels and took hundreds of refugees into their homes.

The hostels were created in response to a growing need for a place for young men to live. Often, when families requested a child, they wanted a girl or a young boy. Thus, many of the teenage boys could not find a place to live.[62] The hostels provided that place. The two hostels founded by Christadelphians were called Elpis Lodge and Little Thorn, with the former being located in Birmingham and the latter in Rugby. Barry Turner, in his book about the Kindertransport, . . . *And the Policeman Smiled*, summarized the work the Christadelphians did with the hostels:

> Among the non-Jewish organisations responsible for hostels, the Christadelphians were to the fore. With their faith rooted in Jewish law, the Christadelphians had a long-standing interest in cooperative ventures, contributing generously to attempts to reestablish the Jewish people in Palestine. When the exodus of

children from Germany and Austria began, they were among the first to respond.

A refugee mother and her two teenage sons were the founder residents of one of the earliest Christadelphian hostels—Little Thorn, on the Hilton Road in Rugby. Here a small group of Jewish boys were given a home and were trained for careers in leather manufacture, cabinet-making, and engineering. The hostel also became a focal point for refugees to gather and socialise at week ends.

Also in the Midlands, Elpis Lodge ('Abode of Hope') opened in April 1940 at 117 Gough Road, Edgbaston. Managed by Birmingham Jewry, the running of the hostel was funded by the Birmingham and Coventry Christadelphian Ecclesias. Dr Hirsch, previously headmaster of a school in Frankfurt, and his wife were wardens of the hostel, which accommodated twenty teenaged boys.[63]

These two hostels, both funded by Christadelphians, were run very differently. Little Thorn was owned and operated by Christadelphians, whereas Elpis Lodge was managed by Dr. Hirsch and run on Orthodox lines. As such, it was a bit of a joint venture between the Jews and the Christadelphians of Birmingham.

Some of the refugees whose stories are told later in this book, and subsequent books in this series, are refugees who lived at either Little Thorn or Elpis Lodge, and the environment in those two homes are elaborated on there. For now, suffice it to say that the two homes were supported by Christadelphians yet run very differently.

These actions taken together highlight that since their inception, the Christadelphians have financially contributed to Jewish relief. Then, in reading of the Jewish treatment in Germany and the surrounding nations throughout the 1930s, they were moved to respond when Parliament agreed to accept Jewish children into the country on a temporary basis. When it was recognized that a number of teenage boys needed a place to stay, the Christadelphians opened up two hostels.

Yet perhaps the greatest question prompted by this history is: why? Why was it that this Christian group—a group that was not Jewish, nor did its inception have any connections to Jews—had such affinity for the Jewish people?

## Christadelphians and Preaching

The answer cannot simply be that the Christadelphians were a humanitarian group. Indeed many were moved to act out of a care for mankind, but the Christadelphians do not have this same type of record with any other group of people—there is no other group to whom the Christadelphians have given such consistent aid and for its sake, been willing to endure such hardship—only the Jews. Thus, although humanitarian reasons explain part of the answer, they do not explain this specific affection for the Jews.

Perhaps, just as it was for much of Christianity in its interactions with the Jews, the Christadelphians sought to convert them. Evidence for this can indeed be found in aforementioned donations. Though the Christadelphians gave to the Jewish people, their gifts were sometimes accompanied by a letter—and this letter explained the Christadelphian position toward the Jewish faith.

As part of the letter that was sent introducing the donation to the chief rabbi of London from the Christadelphian congregation at Edinburgh in 1954, the treasurer of the congregation, on behalf of the assembly, wrote:

> While rejoicing in so much unity of sentiment with the Jews in reference to their faith and hope, it must of necessity be a matter of regret that there should be any important difference of opinion between us. As it would, however, be mere affectation in us to conceal the main point on which we differ from you, we trust you will forgive a plain allusion to it. We believe that Jesus of Nazareth shall sit on the throne of David, when the kingdom is restored to Israel.[64]

The writer then proceeded to share a number of passages from the Hebrew Bible, which passages affirmed to him and the congregation that the Jewish Messiah was to be killed and resurrected. He then continued:

> These testimonies convince us that the Messiah was to die and be buried; that he was to have an early resurrection from the grave; and that he was to ascend to the right hand of God, whence to come in power and glory, 'to raise up the tribes of Israel,' and also to be for a 'light to the Gentiles, and the salvation of God unto the end of the earth.'

> We trust that should any apology be necessary for intruding at such length on your attention on the present occasion, it will suffice to state, that we felt anxious to inform you that, although Gentiles, and differing from you on a very important point, we have no sympathy with the purely Gentile idea of a Messiah coming for no other purpose than to burn up the earth, convey his friends to some ethereal paradise, and consign his enemies to everlasting torment in the flames.[65]

Though Christadelphians did give generously, their conscience would not simply allow them to give without reservation—their giving was always accompanied by a few words of doctrine and perhaps reproof. In this case, the exposition was given extremely cautiously, perhaps because it was written to a rabbi, but it was given nonetheless. The response of the chief rabbi, however, was very clear:

> I am requested by the Chief Rabbi to acknowledge your kind favor, and while thanking you for the sympathy you express for his suffering co-religionists in the Holy Land, most respectfully declines entering on any religious discussion.[66]

Though the letter from the congregation had ended with a request to continue discussions, the representative of the chief rabbi gently refused.

In the second instance documented in this chapter, with the donation from Nova Scotia, another doctrinal treatise accompanied the donation:

> [We] worship the God of your fathers, and believe that Jesus, who was rejected and delivered by Judah into the hands of the Romans, is the Messiah; that his soul was not left in hell, nor did he see corruption, but was raised by God on the third day, and was exalted to the right hand of the Divine Majesty of the heavens. We are a poor people, very poor for the most part, but we are rich in faith, believing all that the prophets have spoken, so far as we can understand. We belong to no denomination, and have no creed but the Bible. We are Christians, firmly believing that Jesus is the Christ, the Son of God, begotten by the Holy Spirit in the womb of a Virgin of the house and lineage of King David; and

hence that he is the seed promised to Eve, to Abraham, and to David, that he is the heir of all things which God hath promised to Messiah,—the throne and kingdom of David, the world and all that is therein. Our hope is identical with the hope of Abraham, Moses, David, and all the faithful of Israel; we look and 'pray for the peace of Jerusalem,' for the restoration of the land and nation of Israel . . . But I must draw to a close, lest I weary you with a recital of those things with which you are doubtless familiar . . .

After expressing his excitement about the future Kingdom, the brother then expressed the fact that the community saw both Jews and Christians to be in error:

O that the veil were taken away from the minds of Jew and Gentile, that they might believe all that the prophets have spoken, and be saved eternally. But, alas! there is no hope of that until the great Enlightener appears. Individuals will be turned from darkness unto light, but nothing great can be expected until the Lord comes. 'The Redeemer shall come to Zion and turn away ungodliness from Jacob;' till then, 'darkness must cover the earth and gross darkness the people.' . . . We hope to rejoice with Israel when the time comes.[67]

Although men of these times certainly did not mince words, and though it is unlikely that Christadelphians would write so bluntly to Jews like this today, the same beliefs still hold. Christadelphians believe that Jesus is the Messiah. Moreover, they believe the words of the Hebrew prophets, many of whom speak of a revival of faith that will take place among the Jewish people in the last days.

Nevertheless, perhaps unlike other Christian groups, although the Christadelphians see the Jews as being in error, there is clearly a difference between how Christadelphians have acted on these feelings.

As shown above, following the same pattern set down by most of Christianity, Christadelphians have long sought to preach to the Jews. However, one of the major differences is the way in which this preaching was done. Here it was carried out in very cautious terms, and when the chief rabbi stated that he would no longer like to discuss the matter, the discussion was closed. There was no persecution. There was no hatred. There was no withdrawal of the donation.

That is a critical difference.

If, indeed, the purpose of Christadelphians giving relief to the Jews had been conversion, the Christadelphians would have ceased doing so many decades ago, as conversion simply did not happen.

Adding to that, this focus on preaching is not one solely directed to Jews. A Christadelphian would preach to anyone: Jew, Protestant, Catholic, Hindu, Muslim, Buddhist, any religion and at any time, simply because Christadelphians feel that their understanding of Scripture is unique and that this specific understanding is indeed what is termed "the gospel" and what is essential for salvation.

Nevertheless, regarding Jewish refugees, it is essential to note that *the purpose* of aiding them was not conversion. Dr. Chana Revell Kotzin, in her doctoral thesis "Christian Responses in Britain to Jewish Refugees in Europe: 1933–1939," described and quoted Alan Overton, one of the chief organizers of the Christadelphian aid for Jewish refugees:

> Overton displayed measured enthusiasm and caution
> when informed that a refugee mother of a child had

expressed interest in Christadelphianism 'I am interested to hear that the mother of a child has shown interest in the Truth and although I do not believe it is wise to try and force this upon the refugees, it is very pleasing to hear of such a case where the refugee of their own volition take that interest.'[68]

Conversions were clearly something that Christadelphians saw as positive, but they were not the purpose of aiding refugees. The same was the case in relation to refugee children.

One example of this can be seen in Elpis Lodge—the Birmingham hostel funded by the Christadelphians. Although it was supported by Christadelphian donations, it did not function on Christadelphian standards but rather Jewish Orthodox standards. The warden was Jewish, and the hostel was organized according to his specifications.

Moreover, to further support this claim, one of the questions for my interviews of the former refugees has been, "Did you ever feel any pressure to become a Christadelphian?"

To date, nearly every response received has been in the negative—he or she did not feel pressure to become a Christadelphian. One interviewee repeatedly stated that she chose to join the Christadelphian community and was not "coerced," wanting to clearly emphasize this point. Another former refugee stated that there was never a question that he was Jewish. His older brothers, who also were living in England, made it extremely clear to the Christadelphian family with whom he lived that he was a Jew and was not to become a Christadelphian. And he did not.

Instead of stating that they felt pressure, many expressed their extreme appreciation for Christadelphians and for the warm acceptance they, as refugees, felt from this community. Indeed, they affirmed that they did attend Sunday school and stated that they likely did not have a choice in the matter, but that was merely what the family did, and they were part of the family. They were not, at their young ages, simply going to be left at home alone while the rest of the family went to church on Sunday. As noted in their stories that follow, many also expressed that they enjoyed this time at Sunday school. Herbert Holden, a former Jewish refugee from Czechoslovakia, wrote a brief memoir in the book *I Came Alone*. There, he expressed his feelings about the Christadelphian Sunday school:

> We went to church regularly (the family were Christadelphian) and I looked forward to this as someone would invariably give me sixpence or even a shilling. Once, in fact I was given half a crown – I couldn't wait to meet that particular lady again.[69]

This was the experience for many of the children. They learned about the Old Testament stories—stories with which a number of them were familiar because they were the history of the Jewish people—and the children were treated with kindness.

Instead of feeling as though the Christadelphians were trying to take them from their family roots, some children expressed that the Christadelphians actually sought out Jewish organizations in an attempt to connect the children with their history, culture, and religion.

What will be seen in a number of the stories is that these refugees' lives were greatly touched by the respect and care shown, even though they did have to attend Sunday school and even though the values of the Christadelphian family became the values expected of these children. In living with a Christadelphian family, they found themselves surrounded by people who cared for them, and though the families believed the teachings of the New Testament, they saw the children as part of a special group of people and treated them with the utmost love.

Summarizing the work that Christadelphians did, Dr. Nicholas Burkitt, in his study on "British Society and the Jews," wrote:

> The Christadelphians, like the Society of Friends, the Plymouth Brethren, Methodists and Unitarian Church, fully accepted the Jews for what they were and therefore respected the Jewish faith. The same could not be said of the Christian Jewish Alliance, nor the Barbican Mission to the Jews, whose aim was to convert Jews to Christianity.[70]

Indeed, that was the difference. Although some Jewish children did convert to become Christadelphians, that was not the "aim" of the Christadelphian relief to the Jews. It was not conversion. Instead, something else moved the community to action, both then and year after year as they contributed hundreds of pounds to Jewish relief funds.

The community was roused, not simply by humanitarian motives, and not by a desire for conversions, but by a fervent belief.

## Why?

In 1854, when the congregation in Scotland made its contribution to the Jews of Palestine, it made its reasoning very clear: it was because the congregation believed in the promises made to Abraham and David. The congregation's members expressed these beliefs in their letter:

> The members of this congregation have been led to take a more than ordinary interest in the people of

Israel, from the fact that they believe, in their obvious sense, the promises made to Abraham, Isaac, and Jacob, as recorded in the books of Moses; and are confidently expecting their fulfilment, and the consequent blessedness of the nations of the earth. They are looking for, among other things, the restoration of the kingdom and throne of David in the Holy Land, when both the houses of Israel shall be united in one nation. . . . Clearly understanding these things as coming events which are even now casting their shadows before, and deeply feeling their importance in connection with the realization of the world's blessedness as promised to Abraham, it would ill become us to look with indifference either on the sufferings of the Jewish people in past times, or on those now more especially pressing on them in their own country.[71]

There is one main reason expressed within this selection: that they believe in the promises made to Abraham and his descendants. This reason branched out in two primary directions: first, that eventually the promises will be fulfilled and the earth will be blessed with the establishment of God's kingdom, and second, that the suffering of the Jewish people at that time, as the descendants of Abraham, should not be ignored.

In other words, the Christadelphians felt that they needed to support the Jews to help further the fulfillment of the promises and because the Jews were the offspring of Abraham, the one to whom the promises were made. As such, they were a special people.

These same two ideas appear constantly in relation to the donations Christadelphians made to the Jewish relief funds.

Explaining the Christadelphian community's feelings and the reasons for the donations to the Montefiore Testimony Fund, Robert Roberts, the editor of *The Christadelphian* at the time, made a brief statement and then included quotes from some of the letters that individual Christadelphians or their ecclesias had sent with their donations to the Montefiore fund. These letters, along with Robert Robert's statement, continue to echo the same themes: a desire to further the fulfillment of prophecy and to help the Jews because of their special heritage. The article below was published in 1875:

> Admiration for Sir Moses is not a sufficient attraction to their subscriptions, but the work which Sir Moses proposes to be done is powerful to evoke their very highest interests; for in the doing of the work, they behold the beginning of the kingdom of God— certainly in a very mustard-seed form, but still in that phase which is the first to be witnessed. When Christ comes, a natural beginning has been made in the restoration of Israel and reclaiming the land from desolation. This is evident from Ezek. 38:1–16.; and other parts. It corresponds to the revived work of the truth which Christ also finds at his coming during the sixth vial. This view of the case explains the phraseology of the letters in which contributions have been forwarded, and of which the following are specimens. . . .

> 'I send you 10s. towards the proposed work in the Holy Land. I rejoice exceedingly in the prospect of returning favour to Zion so long foretold by all the prophets of Israel, and so long looked forward to by all the servants of God who wait on His word and run in the way of His commandments. I think it a great honour to cast my mite into the treasury of the Lord for such a purpose. I wish it were much more. May the God of

Jacob speed the work and speedily return to 'the many thousands of Israel'...

'Please accept the enclosed P.O.O., on behalf of the Montefiore testimonial, from a brother and three sisters who rejoice at the opportunity thus presented them of adding their mite in aid of a scheme which has for its object the rebuilding of the tabernacle of David from the desolation of many generations, and who rejoice to know that the time to favor Zion has at last arrived, which brings in that new and much longed-for era when all nations shall be blessed in Abraham and his seed.'

'I also send from a brother by way of subscription for the Jewish Colonization of Palestine. May God prosper the cause and hasten His great purpose in the earth.'

'I am amongst those who long for the prosperity of Zion, and therefore send what I can to increase the fund for the Jewish colonization of Palestine, hoping that others will do the same.'

'In aid of the Montefiore Colonization Scheme, which I trust will be a successful one. The object is so very grand, I feel so sorry I can contribute so poorly.'

'I wish to add my mite to the blessing of Israel.'

'In aid of the Montefiore Holy Land Colonization Scheme; with a hope that it will not be long before the beloved city will become the joy of the whole earth.'

'The other 8s.6500. to the Palestine Colonization Scheme; if too late for the general collection, you can send it to some other agent, so as to reach the right end, in the name of one who longs for Zion's good.'

10s.6500.:—'I wish it were in my power to forward this amount tenfold, but with me, this is the day of small things.'

'Hoping that the time may soon come when Israel's sons shall rest peacefully in the land promised to their fathers.'

'We have much pleasure in forwarding the enclosed in [sic] behalf of our beloved country.'

'Trusting the time is near at hand when Israel will be established in their own land.'

'I forward the enclosed towards the Palestine testimony, and would like to do more. Consider it the 'widow's mite.' My heart is with it, and, by all means, we ought to care for the land promised to Abraham's faithful ones. Under any circumstances, our hope and joy is that our Master will soon come to take charge of it himself personally.'

'For the relief of the poor Jews, hoping the time is fast approaching when the question shall be answered in its fulfilment, so long asked in bitter anguish, 'How long O, Lord! holy and true; wilt thou not avenge us on our adversaries?[72]

The Christadelphians who gave to the Montefiore Testimonial Fund did not do so out of any specific admiration for Montefiore, but specifically because they were excited by the proposition of prophecy being fulfilled, and because they wanted to do what they could for "the poor Jews." Thirty years later, when the Christadelphian community donated to support the Jews after the Russian pogrom in 1905, they expressed the same sympathies, once again recorded in *The Christadelphian* magazine:

> The money is mostly subscribed by local lovers of Israel, who believe all things that are written in the law and the prophets, and are therefore looking for the deliverance therein promised.[73]

They did this because they loved Israel and believed that, according to the "law and the prophets," the Jews were a chosen people through whom, as the promises to Abraham expressed, the world would be blessed.

Again, when the money was donated to the L.J.S. Hospital for the "Elpis Israel" bed, an explanation for the name was given in the donation letter. Reported in *The Christadelphian* in October 1912:

> They would like it to be called the Elpis Israel bed, expressive of their appreciation of the Hope of Israel, and of that good time to come when 'the inhabitant shall not say, I am sick' (Isa. 33:24.).[74]

This was not just the Christadelphian hope; it was the "Hope of Israel," that hope for which the Christadelphian body had been founded in 1849. It was the book, *Elpis Israel*, or the Hope of Israel, that had led to the creation of the Christadelphians. Contained in this book was an exposition of the way in which the hope of the Bible believer was intimately connected to the promises that had been made to Abraham, the patriarch of Israel.

Over and over, the reasons were the same. The *beliefs* of the Christadelphians compelled them to take action.

Progressing into the 1930s, the same two reasons are demonstrated in a request for prayer for the Jewish people. In December 1938, *The Testimony* magazine entreated its readers:

> Readers of 'The Testimony' are earnestly asked to join their prayers and petitions that our Heavenly Father in His mercy may bring a speedy end to the sufferings of His people, Israel after the flesh, and hasten the time when they shall be gathered to their Land of Promise.[75]

Yet, when it came to the specific relief the Christadelphians offered to the Jews in the late 1930s and early 1940s, a part of this reasoning, by necessity, must have been different, as the donations that Christadelphians made for Jewish refugee children, the establishment of the hostels, and the opening up of their own homes in England did not specifically further the fulfillment of the promises to Abraham. These relief efforts did not directly encourage and promote the colonization of Palestine.

Therefore, perhaps *the main reason* that the Christadelphians opened their houses to these children was simply because the refugee children were Jews.

The Christadelphians believed the promises that were made to Abraham and his children throughout the book of Genesis. And they believed that because of God's love for Abraham, and because the Jews were a special, covenant people to God, they should be given aid.

In an interview conducted for this series of books, Inge Beecham, a Kindertransport survivor who lived with Christadelphians, explained that it was these feelings about the Jews that caused the Christadelphians to act. In her interview, the interviewer stated, "Christadelphians have a role for Israel that's very distinctive," to which Inge replied, "That was the reason they took children in, in the first place."[76]

Susanne Woodin, who came to live with the Hanslips when she was 8 years old, described the ideas that Mrs. Hanslip, a Christadelphian, shared with her about Jews and Christians:

> True Christians do not hate Jews. Jesus was a Jew. . . . In fact true Christians love Jews and try to help them. That was why she had wanted to give a home to a Jewish child.[77]

Ernst Huehns, a Kindertransport survivor who lived with Mr. and Mrs. Clamp, again Christadelphians, wrote in his autobiography:

> Mr and Mrs Clamp were very religious, being Christadelphians, and they believed that the Jews were God's chosen people. It was for this reason that this small sect had decided to help German Jewish children and that was why I went to them.[78]

This was the community's motivation. It was not worldly praise or accolades. It was not overly humanitarian interests. The motivation that compelled this community to act was its beliefs, and this is summarized aptly in an article that appeared in *The Christadelphian* in January 1939:

> It is true that Israel's 'branches' were broken off the Olive Tree because of unbelief. But we Gentiles have been grafted in, and are partaking of the 'root and fatness' of the Olive Tree. We are of 'the commonwealth of Israel' by our union with Jesus Christ, and sympathy with the 'Jew natural' has always been a characteristic of 'Israel after the spirit.' To use Paul's words, 'We Gentiles have been made partakers

of their spiritual things,' and although written of Jewish saints, we may apply what he says is our reciprocal duty, 'to minister unto them in carnal things.[79]

The Jews are "beloved for the fathers' sakes" (Romans 11:28). They are a special people. And, while some of the other motivations discussed were certainly part of why the Christadelphians acted on behalf of the Jews in the 1930s and 1940s, the Christadelphians' overriding and greatest impetus was their beliefs in the promises to Abraham and the Hope of Israel.

Perhaps in a world where the importance of beliefs is at times negated or minimized, it is good to remember that doctrines do indeed influence actions.

## Conclusion

Many books have been written on the Kindertransport. A handful of these mention the role of the Christadelphians in housing some of the refugee children. Walter Lacquer, in his book *Generation Exodus*, wrote:

> An organization had been established in Britain to find foster homes for the children. But not all of these arrangements worked out and for many, particularly for the older children, other provisions had to be made, concentrating them in temporary shelters, frequently holiday camps such as Dovercourt Bay. Particularly helpful in the process of refugee absorption were some of the nonconformist churches such as the Quakers, the Christadelphians, and the Plymouth Brethren.[80]

Mark Harris and Deborah Oppenheimer also mentioned the Christadelphians in the book *Into the Arms of Strangers*:

The Christadelphians, a Christian group, worked in complete harmony with the Jewish community and ran several hostels in the Midlands.[81]

Yet no thorough study of the stories of the refugees who lived with the Christadelphians has been undertaken. Sometimes individual stories get lost in the facts and the figures. Therefore, this book, along with the subsequent books published in this same series, is an attempt to tell those stories.

---

[1] C. C. Walker, "Joseph," *The Christadelphian,* March 1939, 100.

[2] John Carter, "Jewish Refugee Fund," *The Christadelphian,* March 1939, 132.

[3] The average annual wage of a clerical officer in September 1939 was £350 per annum. "National Average Wages," *Hansard, 29 November 1960,* accessed April 25, 2016, http://hansard.millbanksystems.com/written_answers/1960/nov/29/national-average-wages.

The Hansard records in 1939 describe a case of a miner who was employed for £2 13s per week, or £137 16s per annum. "Debate on the Address," *Hansard, 29 November 1939,* accessed April 15, 2016, http://hansard.millbanksystems.com/commons/1939/nov/29/debate-on-the-address#S5CV0355P0_19391129_HOC_55.

[4] John Carter, "Jewish Refugee Fund," *The Christadelphian*, March 1939, 132.

[5] John Carter, "Jewish Refugee Fund," *The Christadelphian,* June 1939, 277.

[6] Susan Zucotti, *Under His Very Windows: The Vatican and the Holocaust in Italy* (New Haven: Yale University Press, 2000).

Michael Phayer, *The Catholic Church and the Holocaust: 1930-1965* (Bloomington: Indiana University Press, 2000).

[7] "No American Catholic had ever before achieved such commanding attention and approval in the United States. A Roseford, Illinois, priest voiced an opinion undoubtedly shared by millions of others: 'If Father Coughlin be not the most useful citizen in America, he is among the first in that distinguished category,' In December 1938, 45 radio stations carried his weekly address that 3.5 million Americans listened to regularly; another 15 million had head him at least once. Two-thirds of his loyal followers and more than half of those who tuned in occasionally subscribed to his views while polls showed that the lower the economic class, the larger the percentage of people who approved the radio priest's views. . . . His office received approximately 80,000 letters a week, 70 percent of which came from Protestants, and it took 105 staff members to read them." Leonard Dinnerstein, *Anti-Semitism in America* (New York: Oxford University Press, 1994), 118.

[8] Father Charles Coughlin, (Speech given at a rally in New York, 1938), quoted in James Rudin, *Christians & Jews Faith to Faith* (Woodstock: Jewish Lights Publishing, 2011), 88.

[9] Bill Kovarik, *Revolutions in Communication: Media History from Gutenberg to the Digital Age* (New York: Continuum, 2011), 225.

[10] Gyula Czapik, Archbishop of Eger, (1944), quoted from Michael Phayer, *The Catholic Church and the Holocaust: 1930-1965* (Bloomington: Indiana University Press, 2000), 106.

[11] David Cymet, *History vs. Apologetics: The Holocaust, the Third Reich, and the Catholic Church* (Lanham: Lexington Books, 2012), 337.

[12] Martin Luther, "The Jews and Their Lies," Jewish Virtual Library, accessed March 21, 2014, http://www.jewishvirtuallibrary.org/jsource/anti-semitism/Luther_on_Jews.html.

[13] Adolf Hitler, *Mein Kampf* (Boston: Houghton Mifflin, 1971), 213.

[14] James Carroll, *Constantine's Sword* (New York: First Mariner Books, 2002), 428.

[15] "Christadelphians," *BBC.co.uk,* last modified June 25, 2009, http://www.bbc.co.uk/religion/religions/christianity/subdivisions/christadelphians_1.shtml

[16] John Thomas, *Elpis Israel: Being an Exposition of the Kingdom of God ; with Reference to the Time of the End, and the Age to Come* (Findon: Logos Publications, 2000), 452.

[17] James Cameron, "Letter from certain Friends of Judah to the Chief Rabbi in London," *Herald of the Kingdom and Age to Come*, September 1854, 205.

[18] Aaron Levy Green, "Letter from certain Friends of Judah to the Chief Rabbi in London," *Herald of the Kingdom and Age to Come*, September 1854, 206.

[19] Anonymous, "Copy of Letter Addressed to Sir Moses Montefiore," *Herald of the Kingdom and Age to Come*, March 1855, 63.

[20] Moses Montefiore, "Letters Received in Reply to the Foregoing," *Herald of the Kingdom and Age to Come,* March 1855, 64.

[21] Robert Roberts, "Editorial," *The Christadelphian*, August 1875, 134.

[22] "From 20s. to 25s. a-week was the ordinary average wages of working men in Scotland at that time. . . . But, Sir, things have changed very much since that period, and the average wages of working men have nearly doubled" "[BILL 7.] SECOND READING," *Hansard, 17 March 1875,* accessed April 15, 2016, http://hansard.millbanksystems.com/commons/1875/mar/17/bill-7-second-reading #S3V0222P0_18750317_HOC_8.

[23] "Second Reading," *Hansard, 21 February 1870,* accessed April 15, 2016, http://hansard.millbanksystems.com/commons/1870/feb/21/second-reading#S3V0 199P0_18700221_HOC_48.

[24] J. J. Andrew, "Editorial," *The Christadelphian*, March 1882, 131.

[25] Robert Roberts, "Editorial," *The Christadelphian,* May 1882, 228.

[26] Thomas Amit, "Laurence Oliphant: Financial Sources for His Activities in Palestine in the 1880s," *Palestine Exploration Quarterly* 139, no. 3 (2007): 205-212, accessed April 22, 2016, doi:10.1179/003103207x227328.

[27] L. Oliphant, "The Christadelphian Contribution to Palestine Colonization," *The Christadelphian*, August 1883, 340.

[28] "Rosh-Pina," *Goisrael.com,* accessed April 15, 2016, http://www.goisrael.com/Tourism_Eng/Tourist Information/Discover Israel/Cities/Pages/Rosh-pina.aspx.

[29] "Table 3. - Population(1) of Localities Numbering Above 2,000 Residents," *Cbs.gov.il,* accessed April 15, 2016, http://www.cbs.gov.il/population/new_2010/table3.pdf.

[30] Robert Roberts, "Editorial," *The Christadelphian*, January 1884, 33.

[31] The following are just a few of the many examples of the cooperation between the Christadelphians and Mr. Oliphant: Robert Roberts, "Editorial," *The Christadelphian*, March 1884, 132.
Robert Roberts, "The Jewish Contribution," *The Christadelphian*, February 1885, 49.
Robert Roberts, "Interviews with Mr. Oliphant," *The Christadelphian*, January 1887, 35.

[32] Emerson Sterns, "Dr. D'Arbela and Mrs. Davis, of Jerusalem: Who They Are," *The Christadelphian*, February 1893, 69.

[33] In her letters, Mrs. Davis consistently thanked Robert Roberts, and later C. C. Walker, for sending her copies of The Christadelphian magazine, which she claimed to read regularly. In months when it did not arrive, she asked what had caused the delay. Adding to that, She occasionally wrote that she was hoping for the coming kingdom—something which is central to the Christadelphian beliefs. Even more, she stated that it was via this magazine that she was able to hear "the truth," which is a phrase repeated used by Christadelphians to describe what they understand to be "the gospel," and used very much used it in the same sense that it would be used by Christadelphians.

August 8, 1900 - "Many thanks for the Christadelphian. Many people come to get me to read it to them, and I assure you that they manifest peculiar interest in its contents. . . . My love to all the dear ecclesia. In trial and hope of the coming kingdom of peace." A. E. Davis, "Letter from Jerusalem," *The Christadelphian,* October 1900, 430.

July 24, 1900 - "The Christadelphian was duly received, thanks. We enjoy reading every word of it, and it is our only means of hearing the truth." A. E. Davis, "Letter from Jerusalem," *The Christadelphian,* September 1900, 383.

November 2, 1903 - "I think you understand I have not one friend here who sympathises with me in the truths which the Lord has been pleased to open to us. . . . Thank God for all His blessings. I believe you, dear friend, will live to see righteousness and peace, and the kingdom of Israel set up on this earth." A. E. Davis, "Letters from Jerusalem," *The Christadelphian,* January 1904, 36.

She also received a copy of Nazareth Revisited and another Christadelphian book, of which she spoke very positively:

January 18, 1893 - "Dr. Merrill, our Consul, brought to me the two beautiful books which you so kindly sent. They came safely. Nazareth Revisited is a charming book. I have read it with delight, and have also read portions of the chapters to my friends who visit me, all of whom pronounce it 'charming'. . . . I have read and re-read chapter 19. It is so beautiful." A. E. Davis, "Affairs in Jerusalem," *The Christadelphian,* April 1893, 147.

[34] Her expositions of the Bible that can be found in her letters align with the beliefs that Christadelphians hold. She also distanced herself from other Christian groups, referring to them referring to them as "Mystery of Babylon," a phrase from the Book of Revelation, which Christadelphians have been apt to use in their description of other Christian denominations. While distancing herself from them, she aligned herself with the Christadelphians by stating that she wished that she could be with them to meet together on Sundays.

November 30, 1903 - "I hope our dear friends in Birmingham are all well. I think of them often, and wish it were possible to be with them on Sundays. It seems to me that every religious person here is a fanatic. I have no part with them. Love to all." A. E. Davis, "Letters from Jerusalem," *The Christadelphian*, January 1904, 36.

April 4, 1904 - "An American Chapel was dedicated yesterday, the first ever built here. I am sorry to say that the people are all fanatics, and, of course, I can take no part with them, but at least they do something towards the building of Jerusalem. I think the Lord has a use for fanatics, or they would not exist. It is all 'Mystery of Babylon.' They sit in judgment upon their friends and enemies, and send their friends to heaven and their enemies to hell. We certainly do need a reformed religion." A. E. Davis, "Letters from Jerusalem," *The Christadelphian*, July 1904, 326.

[35] A. E. Davis, "From Jerusalem," *The Christadelphian*, August 1893, 309.

[36] A. E. Davis, "Letter from Jerusalem," *The Christadelphian*, October 1895, 389.

[37] A. E. Davis, "Letters from the Holy Land," *The Christadelphian*, July 1903, 324.

[38] A. E. Davis, "Letter from Jerusalem," *The Christadelphian*, February 1904, 85.

[39] In this letter, Mrs. Davis stated that she was 77 years old. A. E. Davis, "Letters from the Holy Land," *The Christadelphian*, July 1903, 324.

[40] Written on November 29, 1905 - "Dear Sir, —I beg to enclose cheque £50, and to ask that you will kindly add it to any fund you may have for the relief of the survivors of the latest Russian atrocities." C. C. Walker, "Birmingham Miscellanies," *The Christadelphian*, January 1906, 36.

[41] "Thanks for newsclip with letter of Jewish Colonial Trust. We sent £20 to them from the Jewish Relief Fund, and are making a special local collection in Birmingham in aid of the Russian victims." No Author, "Notes," *The Christadelphian*, December 1905, 572.

[42] C. C. Walker, "The 'Elpis Israel' Bed," *The Christadelphian*, October 1912, 466.

[43] C. C. Walker, "Jewish Relief Fund," *The Christadelphian*, May 1916, 228.
C. C. Walker, "Jewish Relief Fund," *The Christadelphian*, July 1916, 325.
C. C. Walker, "Jewish Relief Fund," *The Christadelphian*, September 1916, 420.

[44] C. C. Walker, "The Jewish Refugees," *The Christadelphian*, July 1917, 324.

[45] C. C. Walker, "Jewish Relief Fund," *The Christadelphian*, April 1918, 181.
C. C. Walker, "The Jewish Relief Fund," *The Christadelphian*, June 1918, 278.
C. C. Walker, "The Jewish Relief Fund," *The Christadelphian*, August 1918, 374.

[46] "War Service for Women," *Hansard, 11 May 1916*, accessed April 15, 2016, http://hansard.millbanksystems.com/commons/1916/may/11/war-service-for-women#S5CV0082P0_19160511_HOC_226.

[47] "City and Metropolitan Police." *Hansard, 31 May 1916*, accessed April 15, 2016, http://hansard.millbanksystems.com/written_answers/1916/may/31/city-and-metropolitan-police#S5CV0082P0_19160531_CWA_59.

[48] Ibid.

[49] C. A. Ladson, "The Jews and Zionism," *The Christadelphian*, April 1933, 176.

[50] Edgar Taylor, "In the Footsteps of Haman," *The Testimony*, April 1933, 101.

[51] T. L. Davies, "Events of the Month," *The Fraternal Visitor*, May 1933, 132.

[52] T. L. Davies, "Events of the Month," *The Fraternal Visitor*, August 1934, 218.

[53] W. J. White, "Signs of the Times," *The Berean*, May 1935, 192.

[54] C. A. Ladson, "The Jews and Zionism," *The Christadelphian*, January 1936, 36.

[55] C. A. Ladson, "The Jews and Zionism," *The Christadelphian*, June 1936, 271.

[56] Edgar Taylor, "Ye Shall Be an Execration," *The Testimony*, September 1936, 350.

[57] R. T. W. S., "Current Events," *The Fraternal Visitor*, December 1937, 326.

[58] C. A. Ladson, "The Jews and Zionism," *The Christadelphian*, April 1938, 176.

[59] C. A. Ladson, "The Jews and Zionism," *The Christadelphian*, December 1938, 557.

[60] R. T. W. S., "Events of the Month," *The Fraternal Visitor*, December 1938, 322.

[61] Edgar Taylor, "Back to the Mandate," *The Testimony*, December 1938, 494.

[62] "By and large, potential foster parents preferred younger children to older ones and girls to boys." Judith Tydor Baumel-Schwartz, *Never Look Back: The Jewish Refugee Children in Great Britain, 1938-1945 (Shofar Supplements in Jewish Studies)* (Purdue University Press, 2012, Kindle edition), 63.

[63] Barry Turner, . . . *And the Policeman Smiled* (London: Bloomsbury, 1990), 163-164.

64 James Cameron, "Letter from certain Friends of Judah to the Chief Rabbi in London," *Herald of the Kingdom and Age to Come*, September 1854, 205.

65 Ibid., 206.

66 Aaron Levy Green, "Letter from certain Friends of Judah to the Chief Rabbi in London," *Herald of the Kingdom and Age to Come*, September 1854, 206.

67 Anonymous, "Copy of Letter Addressed to Sir Moses Montefiore," *Herald of the Kingdom and Age to Come,* March 1855, 63.

68 Chana Revell Kotzin, "Christian Responses in Britain to Jewish Refugees in Europe: 1933-1939" (doctoral thesis, University of Southampton, 2000), 146-147.

69 Herbert Holden, "Herbert Holden," in *I Came Alone: the Stories of the Kindertransports*, ed. Bertha Leverton and Shmuel Lowensohn (Sussex: The Book Guild Ltd., 1990), 149.

70 Nicholas Burkitt, "British Society and the Jews: A Study into the Impact of the Second World War Era and the Establishment of Israel, 1938-1948" (PhD diss., University of Exeter, 2011), 77.

71 James Cameron, "Letter from certain Friends of Judah to the Chief Rabbi in London," *Herald of the Kingdom and Age to Come*, September 1854, 205.

72 Robert Roberts, "The Jews and Their Affairs," *The Christadelphian,* June 1875, 328.

73 C. C. Walker, "Birmingham Miscellanies," *The Christadelphian,* January 1906, 36.

74 C. C. Walker, "The 'Elpis Israel' Bed" *The Christadelphian,* October 1912, 466.

75 C. H. Arnold, "Prayer Changes Things," *The Testimony,* December 1938, 483.

76 Inge Beecham, interview by Sarah Watts, February 23, 2016.

77 Mrs. Hanslip, quoted in Susanne Woodin, "My Childhood Memories," Typescript, February 2010, 23.

78 Ernst Huehns, *The Luckiest Boy In Germany* (CreateSpace Independent Publishing Platform, 2015), 48.

79 John Carter, "Relief for Jewish Refugees," *The Christadelphian,* January 1939, 33.

80 Walter Laqueur, *Generation Exodus: The Fate of Young Jewish Refugees from Nazi Germany* (Hanover: Brandeis University Press, University Press of New England, 2001), 192.

81 Mark Harris and Deborah Oppenheimer, *Into the Arms of Strangers: Stories of the Kindertransport* (New York: Bloomsbury Pub., 2000), 16.

# Part II

---

## The Children

### Introduction

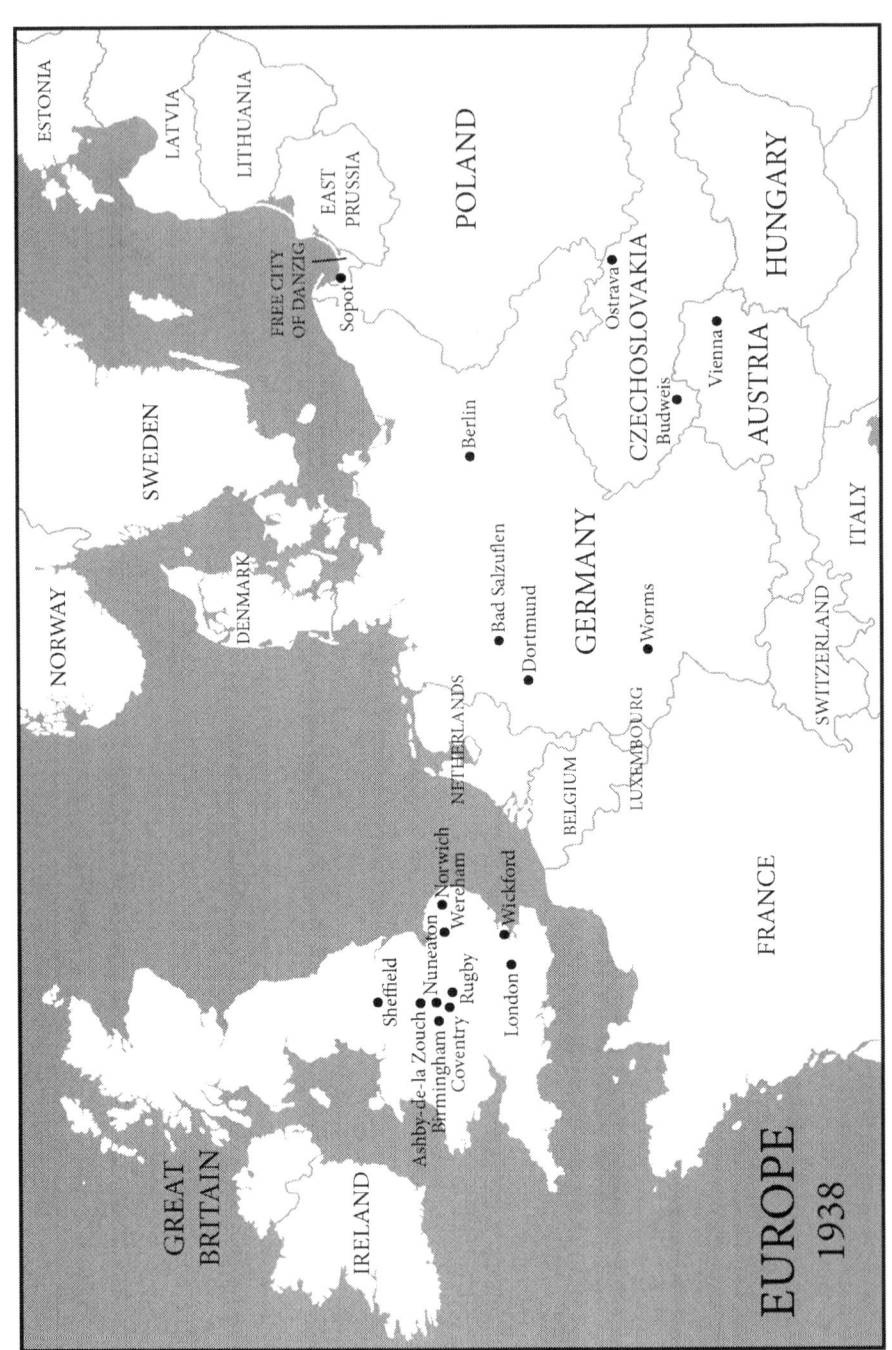

EUROPE
1938

# INTRODUCTION

The morning of November 10, 1938 was the morning after *Kristallnacht*—a massive pogrom launched by Nazi Germany against the Jewish people. The pogrom was supposedly sparked by the murder of a low-ranking German diplomat, Ernst vom Rath, in Paris by Herschel Grynszpan, a 17-year-old Polish Jew.

Grynszpan's parents were just two of the thousands of Jews who had been expelled from Germany on November 7. That day, the Reich had rounded up Jewish Polish citizens living in Germany and dumped them on the border between Germany and Poland, simply because they were Jews. The problem was compounded, however, by the fact that the Polish government also did not want these Jews—just days before it had revoked the Polish citizenship of thousands of Jews living in Germany, leaving them stateless and denying them entry into Poland. Grynszpan's parents had lived in Germany since 1911 and had been Polish citizens all of their lives. Now they were forced into a Polish refugee camp, caught in the middle between two countries that refused to admit them.[1]

Upon hearing of his parents' circumstances, Grynszpan became furious. At the time, he was living in Paris and was not with his family, but he ruminated over what he could do to retaliate against Germany. He purchased a gun and headed toward the German embassy in Paris.

Determined to avenge his parents, Grynszpan found vom Rath. He pulled the trigger, and vom Rath died two days later, on November 9, 1938.

This attack on a German official by a Jew was what was used as a pretext by the Reich as the catalyst to launch the events of *Kristallnacht*. It was just what the German officials wanted. *Kristallnacht* began the night that vom Rath died.

*Kristallnacht* means "Night of Broken Glass" and was so named because hundreds of thousands of windows were broken. That night, over 30,000 Jewish men were rounded up and sent to Dachau, Buchenwald, or another notorious concentration camp. A total of 191 synagogues were burned.[2] *Kristallnacht* occurred throughout Germany and the newly annexed Austria. Many of the following stories include descriptions and experiences of this night.

Though the situation had been bad for the Jews in Germany, it now became desperate. Up until this point, the Jews had been ordered to refrain from performing certain tasks and visiting certain places, had been the victims of nationwide economic restrictions, and had experienced individual acts of antisemitism. But *Kristallnacht* was the first government-sanctioned, all-out assault on German Jewry. This was the turning point for many Jewish families; they realized after *Kristallnacht* that life in Germany was no longer a viable option—but not only was it a turning point for the families, it also was a turning point for the world.

Many nations were simply shocked at what Germany had done. It was difficult to believe that a civilized country would even consider such a thing—what had happened on *Kristallnacht*, with the breaking of the windows and the absolute terror of tearing thousands of fathers away from their children and their spouses, was unfathomable to so many of the world's leaders and their citizens. As recorded in *The Christadelphian* magazine in December 1939, Germany came under condemnation:

The news from Germany of the anti-Jew riots is spread over the front pages of newspapers throughout America under black headlines and is being received with horror and anger."[3]

It was largely due to this international pressure on Germany, the desire of the Nazis to expel all Jews from Germany, and the shock the nations felt at what had happened that the Kindertransport came into existence.

Shortly after *Kristallnacht*, the British government declared that it would accept an unspecified number of Jewish children from the Reich. The number ultimately came to approximately 10,000.[4]

**Lord Baldwin**

The first transports came out of Berlin and Vienna in early December 1938. After the first transport from Berlin, but before the first transport from Vienna, Stanley Baldwin, a former prime minister of Great Britain, made a radio appeal. His appeal was broadcast on December 8, 1938, and he stated:

There are at least 50,000 Jewish children . . . who must be brought out of Germany as soon as the money is available to transport them.

The number who can be admitted into this country must chiefly depend upon the extent to which hospitality can be offered. But the committee which is attending to this part of the work will require very large funds . . .[5]

Before the children could be sent across the channel, the British government required that each child have a guarantor. This guarantor would agree to house and take care of the child.

At the end of February 1939, the British government mandated that all guarantors also act as financial sponsors and pay £50 to cover the child's cost of re-emigration if the child arrived after March 1, 1939.[6] Prior to that, the funds used to guarantee the children's welfare had come from a grant provided by the Lord Baldwin Fund and private donations.

For one month, until April 1, only children who had been financially sponsored by their guarantor families were able to come to England. Beginning in April, however, the Lord Baldwin Fund again offered a large sum of money—agreeing to pay the £50 for any host family that could not afford to do so.[7]

As noted in the previous chapter, the Christadelphian body as a whole contributed over £1,000 to the Lord Baldwin Fund for Refugees.

### The Kindertransport

Bringing the children from Germany, Austria, Czechoslovakia, Poland, and the free city of Danzig was not easy. There was simply an overwhelming number of children whose parents desperately recognized the need to send them to safety.

Committees and individuals worked tirelessly to find homes for the children and to secure clearance from all of the government agencies involved. One of the more well-known individuals involved was Sir Nicholas Winton, who, along with his small team, organized the movement of at least 669 children from Czechoslovakia. Hana Holman and her sister Ruth, as well as Charles Borger and his sister Edit, whose biographies are in the following pages, found refuge in England via Mr. Winton's committee.

It was agreed that the children would travel unaccompanied. Infants were to be cared for by other children on the train. Only a few chaperones were allowed to travel with the children, and it was imperative that they return after the children had been dropped off.[8] If they did not return, it was understood that the transports would cease. Because they could not stay in safety in England, many of the chaperones, as Jews, were murdered in the Holocaust.[9]

The British government agreed that the children would be allowed to enter the country on temporary travel visas, as it was understood that the children would be returned to their families once the situation in Europe improved.[10] At that time, it was not realized that the outbreak of war was so close at hand.

Typically, the children were taken to a train station by their parents. At that point, the children boarded the train and waved goodbye. They traveled by train to Holland, where they then boarded a boat bound for Harwich, England. Generally, after arriving at Harwich, they boarded another train, which took them to Liverpool Street Station in London, where they waited to be collected by their individual foster families.

Approximately 250 Jewish children were taken into Christadelphian homes.

These are some of their stories.

---

[1] "Kristallnacht," *United States Holocaust Memorial Museum,* last modified January 29, 2016, https://www.ushmm.org/wlc/en/article.php?ModuleId=10005201.

[2] Martin Gilbert, The Holocaust: *A History of the Jews of Europe during the Second World War* (New York: Henry Holt and Company, 1985), 69-70.

[3] C. A. Ladson, "The Jews and Zionism," *The Christadelphian,* December 1939, 558.

[4] Barry Turner, . . . *And the Policeman Smiled* (London: Bloomsbury, 1990), 33.

[5] Stanley Baldwin, "An appeal for the Jewish and non-Aryan and Christian refugees," *BBC,* speech, December 8, 1938, https://vimeo.com/117834111.

[6] Judith Tydor Baumel-Schwartz, Never Look Back: The Jewish Refugee Children in Great Britain, 1938-1945 (Shofar Supplements in Jewish Studies) (Purdue University Press, 2012, Kindle edition), 63.

[7] Ibid.

[8] Vera K. Fast, Children's Exodus: A History of the Kindertransport (London: I. B. Tauris & Co. Ltd., 2011), 31.

[9] Ibid.

[10] "Kindertransport, 1938-1940," *United States Holocaust Memorial Museum*, last modified January 29, 2016, https://www.ushmm.org/wlc/en/article.php?ModuleId=10005260.

# CHARLES OHLENBERG

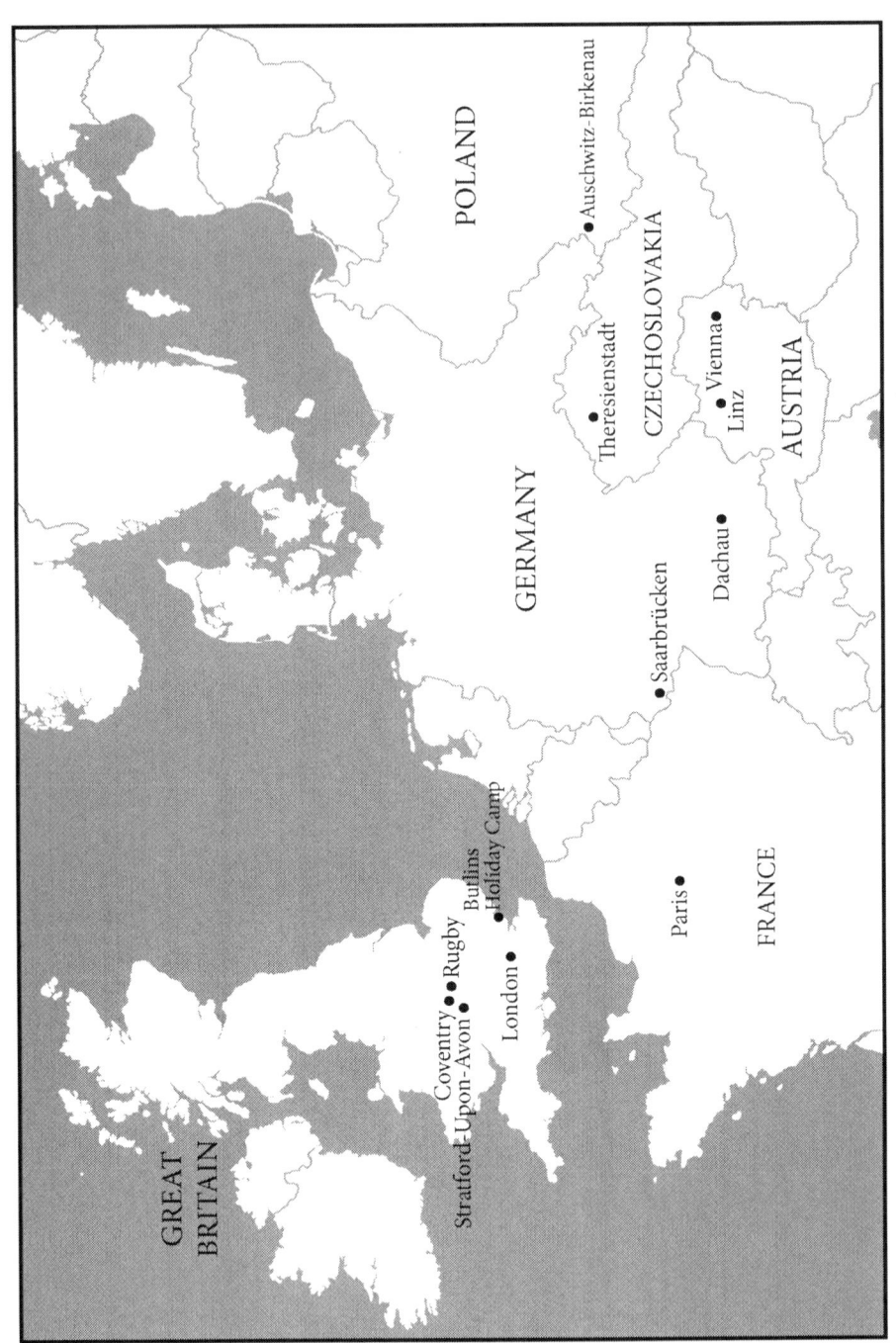

# 1

---

## CHARLES OHLENBERG

Between 1920 and 1923, the currency of the Weimar Republic, the government in Germany following World War I, experienced a period of massive hyperinflation. This drastic decrease in the value of the German mark was largely a byproduct of the Treaty of Versailles. In the treaty, the German government was forced to pay higher reparations than it could raise through taxes. Rather than increasing taxes on a population that was already attempting to recover from war and struggling economically, the German government chose to simply print more money. Unfortunately, inflation is a direct effect of mass-printing additional currency.

This issue came to a head at the beginning of the 1920s, with 1923 being the worst year. In January of that year, there were 1.28 billion notes in circulation. By the end of the year, there were 497 quintillion (18 zeroes at the end)—a difference that was quickly noted in price increases. At its peak, the monthly rate of German inflation was over 3.2 million percent.[1]

This period of outrageous inflation led to events that seem unfathomable: to buy one loaf of bread, women would arrive at a bakery with several wheelbarrows full of money.[2] At one point, waiters had to stand on tables calling out new menu prices every half an hour because prices were rising so quickly. Banknotes became so worthless that they were given to children to use as toys, because they were worth less than actual toys themselves.[3]

These same types of issues also plagued Austria, as the two countries both lacked the gold standard, and both were members of the losing alliance in World War I. After the Great War, Austria found itself with drastically smaller borders than it had possessed before the war had begun—borders that removed it from much of its food supply. As such, the Austrian government spent large amounts of money purchasing food for its people, which when added to its reparations, put it in even greater debt. Just as the situation had been in Germany, the Austrian government did not collect enough taxes to cover its spending and so produced massive deficits. These deficits were covered by treasury bills the government sold to the Austro-Hungarian bank, and attempting the same solution as Germany had, the bank funded the purchase of these bills by printing more money.

Between 1919 and 1923, the amount of printed money in circulation in Austria increased by a monstrous amount; in March 1919, there were 4.7 billion Austrian crowns in circulation, and by December of 1923, there were 7.1 trillion. From January 1921 to August 1922, the inflation rate in Austria was approximately 10,000 percent per year.[4]

Charles Ohlenberg, or Karl Ohlenberg as he was called then, was born in Vienna, Austria, on February 17, 1922, in the middle of this financial chaos.

Charles's mother and father, Benno and Amalia Ohlenberg, were both originally from Poland, although in their youth, Poland was part of the Austro-Hungarian Empire, so Poland and Austria were united in one empire. Benno was a physician, a general practitioner, who had a private practice near the Ohlenberg's house. Amalia, too, had been in medical school, but when she and Benno met and decided to marry, she chose to start a family rather than continue her schooling.

Charles was the youngest in the family; he had one sibling, an older brother, Paul, who was born in 1919. Their family of four lived in an apartment with 50 units in the building, and at one point in time, the building had belonged to Charles's grandfather, but by the time Charles lived in it, his family had lost the deed in the aftermath of World War I. During the Great War, his grandfather, who had been a diamond merchant, lost nearly everything he owned by throwing his savings into the purchase of war bonds for the empire. When the empire lost the war, he lost his savings, along with the apartment building. The Ohlenberg family was extremely patriotic and thoroughly assimilated, and so, while the loss of the apartment building was certainly upsetting, it was a sacrifice that was made for the nation.

Because of this love for their country, no one in the family expected the changes that soon swept over Vienna and the drastic effects these changes would have on their lives. Nor did they realize that all this would happen just 15 years after Charles had been born. They were Austrians and they suffered with their country. Tragically, however, they soon would suffer at the hands of their country.

But it was not just they who were shocked by what would take place in the ensuing years. In 1922, the same year that Charles was born, the *New York Times* published its first article ever about Adolf Hitler—a man whose political ideas, along with the financial crisis, were becoming some of the most discussed topics in Germany. Yet his virulent antisemitism was something that was simply dismissed:

> The keynote of his propaganda in speaking and writing is violent anti-Semitism. . . . But several reliable,

well-informed sources confirmed the idea that Hitler's anti-Semitism was not so genuine or violent as it sounded, and that he was merely using anti-Semitic propaganda as a bait to catch messes of followers and keep them aroused, enthusiastic and in line for the time when his organization is perfected and sufficiently powerful to be employed effectively for political purposes.[5]

Charles was nine months old when this article was published. He had only 15 more years to live with his family—before Hitler's antisemitism, and the antisemitism of his followers, would tear the family apart, never again to be reunited.

## Childhood

The Ohlenbergs' flat in the apartment building had three bedrooms and was located on the fourth floor. The neighbors in the building were mostly Austrians, but Charles's friends from the apartment were Jewish. One of Charles's fondest memories in this building was of playing games with these friends. Sometimes they played soccer, chess, or marbles, and on Sundays they went exploring in the Vienna woods—but Charles's favorite pastime was ping-pong. He and his friends actually put together their own table; one of their fathers was a manufacturer, so he created the tabletop for them, and they simply placed the top over a typical table. Charles's greatest triumph in the ping-pong world was when he defeated all of his family at once—a memory that still has not left him even decades later.

Charles cherished his family. They were a close-knit, middle class family of four. Even the extended family was quite involved in his life: his uncle (his father's brother) lived nearby, and his mother had three siblings, one of whom had moved to France and to whom Charles attempted to flee at one point in the late 1930s. Many of his relatives lived in Vienna, and the Jewish holidays were celebrated together, with one of Charles's uncles leading the prayers and rituals.

As far as the Jewish traditions, Charles remembers his family as being "conservative."[6] They celebrated all the holidays, and Charles enjoyed the time with family immensely. They were also particular about what they ate—oftentimes refraining from ham—but they did not keep the laws of *kashrut* (kosher).

Charles attended school in Vienna until 1938, when the *Anschluss*, the German annexation of Austria, took place. His primary and secondary schools were connected to two famous names: his elementary school was called the "Schubert School,"[7] and it was where Franz Schubert had taught prior to devoting all of his time to music. Charles's secondary school was quite close to where Sigmund Freud had his office. Charles had a few memories of this school—there he took Latin and Greek, but he recalled that he did not do very well with either of them. He also remembers being taunted, even before 1938. There was one particular student there who always called Charles a Jew, and although he was indeed a Jew, Charles saw himself as an Austrian and did not appreciate his heritage being used in a derogatory way. In an attempt to quiet this other student, Charles vaguely remembers resorting to his fists. Charles was quite an imposing and strong young man, so his strategy proved to be successful—until the *Anschluss*.

### Anschluss

In 1938, after the *Anschluss*, things in Vienna changed in an instant. Charles remembers the day that Hitler arrived in Vienna. Charles had been at his uncle's coat factory that day, and as he began to walk home, he suddenly realized that things were extremely different from what they had been only hours and days before. Now, swastikas covered the front of the

Parliament building, and before it stood a large crowd. Charles was surprised—and as he stared at the building and the people, trying to get his bearings, a man opened the door of the Parliament building and stepped outside. It was not Hitler, but it was Rudolf Hess, Hitler's Deputy Führer.

Everyone immediately saluted.

Charles, in a split-second, needed to make a decision. Hess was a man who represented violent antisemitism, and unbeknownst to Charles, this venomous ideology would annihilate his entire family in just a few years. But everyone else in the crowd was saluting—and the Nazis did not take kindly to nonconformity. Charles explained:

> If you don't raise you own hand, they chop it off. I was a bit scared, looked around if anybody knew me. Just tried to get out of it . . . even Americans had to wear a swastika with an American flag.[8]

It was March 1938. And that was when Charles knew that his life was going to change irrevocably.

Thus, after the *Anschluss*, that same student who had taunted Charles suddenly arrived at school in a Hitler Youth uniform, and that changed everything significantly. The situation no longer centered on just him and Charles. Now this student was part of a menacing group. Throughout the school, students and even professors saluted this student, and Charles knew that he was in trouble.

It was soon after this that Charles left school.

At the same time, there was a park that Charles and his friends used to frequent. After the *Anschluss*, signs were posted on the benches, making it clear that Jews were not allowed to sit on them—and Charles knew that these signs were not to be ignored: "If you did, you took a big chance."[9]

March 1938 marked the time when the entire atmosphere changed:

> There was no need to leave Vienna. We had more money, more friends than enemies. . . . Before Hitler, the Jews were fairly well treated.[10]

> It was pretty scary. . . . The climate actually changed after Hitler. . . . We were aware all the time.[11]

Charles and his family were no longer allowed to feel like typical Austrians. They were Jews, and that indeed would be held against them.

## The Polish Expulsion

With the Nazi takeover of Austria, the Jews lost one of the nations that had been a refuge to them from the Nazis for the last five years. Because of this, a number of European nations feared an influx of Jewish emigrants seeking asylum. This fear led the Polish Parliament on March 31, 1938, to pass a law that worked against its own citizens. All Polish citizens who had lived exclusively abroad for five years or longer were deemed to have lost their connection with Poland, and therefore the government could withdraw their citizenship.

This law went into effect in October 1938 and is partly connected with the events of *Kristallnacht*. It was the reason that Herschel Grynszpan, the young Jewish man whose murder of Ernst vom Rath preceded the November pogrom, had parents who were stateless and homeless on the Polish border.

The Polish government stated that all Polish citizens living abroad needed to get in touch with the appropriate consulate by October 30, 1938. If their papers were in order and their cases deemed acceptable, their passports would be marked with a check mark, and they would retain their citizenship. If they failed to obtain a checkmark by October 30, their passports expired, and they were made stateless—they had no citizenship and were forbidden from entering Poland.

This problem was compounded, however, when the German Embassy in Warsaw contacted Berlin to notify the Nazi government of Poland's policy. The Polish government had hoped that this policy would prevent a mass deportation of emigrants—but the Nazi government acted before the Polish law went into effect. Between October 27 and October 29, 1938, thousands of Polish Jews in the German Reich received an expulsion order, were arrested, or were forcefully expelled to the German/Polish border.[12]

Charles was one of those who was affected by these policies. His parents were Polish, and yet he had lived in Austria all of his life.

Shortly before *Kristallnacht*, therefore, the police arrived at the door to Charles's apartment. Many of his extended family members were there at the time, and the Nazis arrested Charles, Paul, and their grandfather. The three of them were taken to the police station and, from there, were transported to a military compound where, ironically, his father and his uncle had both been stationed as cavalry officers in the Austrian Army during World War I. He, his brother, and his grandfather were all searched by the Nazis, and everything of value that they had in their possession was taken. But that was not the worst of it.

Soon after the searching, the Nazis decided that these Jewish men needed a little bit of roughing up. Charles was specifically struck on his eye—and afterward, his eye swelled and would not focus correctly. For about three days, the three of them were locked in that compound, wondering what would happen. It was only a few blocks away from where they lived—they were so close to everything they loved but had no idea when or whether they would be reunited with the rest of the family.

Finally, they were told that they could leave the compound—but only after signing a form stating that they would leave the country.

Thus, these three men were three of the thousands of Jewish Poles who were affected by the events leading up to *Kristallnacht*. And now, upon returning home, they had to leave both their family and their country.

Where would they go? They absolutely could not go to Poland, and they had always lived in Austria.

For about a week, Charles and his family anxiously pondered their situation—and then came another request from the police. This time, fortunately for Charles and Paul, the police did not arrive at the apartment but instead sent them a form requesting that Charles and Paul present themselves at the police station to be interviewed. Though they had just had a terrible experience with the police, they thought it wise to do what was requested of them, so they walked to the police station.

There was a lineup of people there waiting to be interviewed. Charles and Paul watched closely and noted that once people were called in for their interviews, they did not come back out.

It was the same type of thing that had happened just one week prior.

Seeing the writing on the wall, Charles and Paul fled the station and went into hiding—still continuing to live in Vienna but now living illegally and secretly with an uncle. It was dangerous, but they did not know what else to do.

At times, the police stopped by the old apartment where the rest of Charles's family continued to live and asked about the two's whereabouts. There was no way that Charles and Paul could return home.

Then came *Kristallnacht*.

### *Kristallnacht* and Escape

While living illegally with their uncle, on November 9, 1938, Charles and Paul decided to travel to Linz, a city about an hour west of Vienna. The two of them flagged down a Nazi in an attempt to hitchhike—Charles had blonde hair and blue eyes, so he assumed that his appearance would not turn him in as long as he did not meet anyone he knew. They went to Linz and then hitchhiked back to Vienna. When they returned to Vienna, they saw the destruction:

> It was just like a revolution type of thing. People just took to the streets, plundered Jewish shops, and took everything for themselves.[13]

> They were breaking the shop windows, they were putting people . . . scrubbing the pavement the following day . . . they were laughing.[14]

Charles's uncle and aunt owned a jewelry store, and the store's windows were broken and inventory was stolen. There was also a synagogue on his street, and he saw it in flames:

> It was like a bonfire, and all the Nazis were yelling around. . . . You realize, if anyone recognizes you, it's not so good . . . of course we were frightened.[15]

Paul and Charles knew that they needed to escape: they had been arrested, and now they had experienced *Kristallnacht*. But whom could they trust? They had always seen themselves as Austrians and felt a solidarity with their countrymen. But it was the police officers from the police station near their house who had arrested them. It was Austrians who had participated in *Kristallnacht*. Even Austrians who were not sympathetic with the Nazis were afraid to help for fear of being called "Jew-lover."[16] Charles described the hopelessness the Jews felt in Vienna at the time:

> They were practically taking the place apart—breaking windows, people commit suicide . . . they took over the business, some people shot themselves, friends of ours.[17]

After all that they had witnessed, Charles and Paul decided to run away.

First, they went to Saarbrücken in Germany, a city right on the border between Germany and France. They had an uncle in France, and they were hoping that somehow they would be able to escape into France and find asylum there. In Saarbrücken, they stayed on a farm and then attempted to cross the border. They were stopped by a German policeman, who demanded to know why they were crossing into France. In a desperate attempt, they offered him some jewelry and some money, hoping that he would simply let them pass.

At first, he refused. And then he changed his mind.

After being bribed, the border guard turned out to be helpful. Not only did he allow them into France, but he also told them the way to go to avoid being caught. They crossed the border, following his instructions.

After all their suffering in Vienna, Charles and Paul had made it to France—a nation where Jews were free. But because of the new Polish law, by this time, their passports were worthless, and they had no citizenship. As such, they were not necessarily welcome in France either.

From the border, they took a tram and then a taxi to Paris where they hoped to find their uncle—but unfortunately they made an unexpected stop.

The taxi driver drove them to the French police.

They were put in custody and kept in jail for a night, where Charles remembers not being treated well at all. The jail was quite small, and there were no restroom facilities.

The next day, the French police gave Charles and his brother an ultimatum: Paul was old enough to join the foreign legion, but Charles was not; therefore, Paul could stay in France, but Charles had to return to Germany. Their requests to contact their uncle were refused. Paul was not willing to be separated from his brother, so they were put on a train and told to leave the country—with one of the police officers making it very clear that Jews like them were unwanted in France: "Don't come back; our provinces are polluted from your type."[18]

After all of their efforts to get to France, they were insulted, jailed, and sent back to whatever awaited them in Vienna.

But it was not just what awaited them in Vienna that was of concern. The journey back itself was also extremely dangerous. On the train from Paris to the German border, they were confronted by a French detective: he told them to get off the train because otherwise he would have to shoot them. They escaped from the train and returned to Germany as quickly as they could. At the border, they were confronted by the SS and were searched—and once again, they were in trouble. This time, because they had more money on them than they were permitted to have. The SS men had a stern message for them: get back to Vienna on the next train or be sent to Dachau.

Needless to say, they returned to Vienna on the next train, and in Vienna, they went back to living secretly with their uncle.

## The Kindertransport

It was December 1938. Charles had heard about the Kindertransport, and he knew he needed to somehow leave Austria. He started filling out all kinds of forms related to emigration and was finally accepted to travel to England strictly for education purposes. Regardless, Charles simply wanted to get out, so he accepted whatever would help do so.

However, when he attempted to secure a place on the first Kindertransport out of Austria, Charles was informed that he was just barely over the age limit; he was about to turn 17. Upon learning of this, Charles relayed his story. He had been living illegally in Vienna, and he had escaped to the German border and into France only to be turned back. Now he had very few options.

Upon hearing his story, the one who had initially told Charles that he was too old dismissed the concern and offered him a place on the train.

Charles left Vienna on December 12, 1938.

The journey was uneventful. There were a few Nazis who rode on this train full of children, but they did not give Charles any trouble. As with almost all the other Kindertransport stories, Charles went to Holland first and then traveled by boat to England.

## Charles's Family

Charles attempted to rescue both his mother and his brother. He escaped Vienna before any of his family did and came to live with the Greens, who were Christadelphians. While living with them, he looked for a way to bring Amalia and Paul over the channel. At the time, most adult emigrants from Germany or Austria had to come over as domestic servants, so Charles needed to apply for a work permit for his mother. A few Christadelphians who were friends of the Greens were willing to sponsor her. Eventually, her papers came through, and it looked as though his mother would be able to escape.

But tragically the war then broke out, and emigration from Austria to England was no longer possible. Both Benno and Amalia perished in the Holocaust. Charles believes that his mother was deported to Theresienstadt and does not know what happened to his father.

Paul Ohlenberg was too old for the Kindertransport. He had, though, been able to escape Austria illegally, but was only able to flee as far as Belgium. Charles presented his plight to the Greens, who were "a modest family,"[19] but who pooled their resources, along with those of others, to pledge enough money to sponsor Paul. And then Germany invaded Belgium: "I remember being in England and hearing about the invasion of

Holland and Belgium and realizing how bad it was. And then later on I found out . . . "[20]

In those days, Charles and Paul had written letters to one another—but after the invasion, the letters simply stopped. Charles later found out that his brother had been deported to Auschwitz-Birkenau extermination camp on April 19, 1943.[21] Paul Ohlenberg was killed in Auschwitz. He was 24 years old.

For many, Auschwitz is a name that symbolizes the Holocaust. It was the largest of the camps, and it was divided into three sections: Auschwitz I, which was established in April 1940; Auschwitz II, which is also called Auschwitz-Birkenau; and Auschwitz III (also called Auschwitz-Monowitz). Auschwitz-Birkenau was an extermination camp, and most of the prisoners who arrived there went straight to the gas chambers to be murdered. But at the same time, all three of these sub-camps used forced labor. Thus, while Auschwitz II was indeed an extermination center, if upon arrival one was deemed fit to work, it was possible to avoid the gas chambers. It is thought that the SS and the police deported at least 1.3 million to the entire Auschwitz complex (all three camps) between 1940 and 1945. Of those 1.3 million, approximately 1.1 million were killed.[22]

For Charles, the story of his family ended in the calamitous way that it did for so many other survivors of the Holocaust: "[In] my family, no one survived."[23]

**Arrival in England**

But Charles escaped.

When Charles arrived in England, he was taken to live in a camp called Butlins Holiday Camp, which was vacant at the time, because it was winter. Charles remembers that while he was at the camp, the Nazis who had traveled with the children on the Kindertransport train, and later the boat to England, were caught for being out at night with flashlights trying to scope out the coast. The English police caught them and sent them back to Germany.

Additionally, at this camp, Charles's life also took another turn, as this was where he met the Christadelphians.

## The Christadelphians

One day, two Christadelphians visited the Butlins Holiday Camp—a man named Sydney Laxon and his wife. They were looking for children they could place in Christadelphian homes throughout the Coventry and Rugby area. Charles was 16, almost 17, and it was unlikely that he was going to be placed quickly.

Nevertheless, Mr. Laxon approached Charles and asked him a question: "He wanted to know if I wanted to come to Coventry."[24]

However, at that point, Charles was still quite new to English, so he did not really understand what Mr. Laxon had asked: "I thought [he meant] the country, so I said 'yes.'"[25]

With that, Sydney Laxon and his wife took Charles and placed him with the Greens, a Christadelphian family from Coventry. Jack and Winnie Green were a young couple who had been baptized into the Christadelphian faith just a few years earlier. Mr. Green worked for the Singer Sewing Machine Company, and Mrs. Green was a homemaker. At the beginning of World War II, they had one young daughter, Valerie, who was born in the mid-1930s. And now, with Charles joining them, they also had a 16-year-old son: "I was part of the family. . . . I was treated well, they were just working people, they had a small house, and they were good Christadelphians."[26]

Elisabeth Ohlenberg, Charles's wife, conveyed the same idea: "Charles remembers that they treated him as one of the family and found him a job with a church member who owned a garage and bicycle shop. Charles knew no English."[27]

Eventually, with all of the bombing that took place in Coventry, Valerie Green was evacuated to live in Stratford-upon-Avon with another Christadelphian couple. Charles continued to live with the Greens throughout the bombing. In Coventry, he worked first in the bicycle shop and then eventually was given a job manufacturing Jaguar cars.

*The Green family, 1942. From left to right: Mrs. Green, Mr. Green, Betty Talbot (who married Mrs. Green's brother), and Charles Ohlenberg.*

Being old enough to work, Charles was also old enough to stay at home on Sundays when the family went to the Christadelphian meetings. Therefore, unlike a number of other children who came to live with Christadelphians, Charles was given the choice either to come to the meeting or to stay home. Frequently he chose to stay at home; however, sometimes, when Mr. Green delivered the address, Charles attended the services. He was clear, though, that despite living with Christadelphians for two to three years, he did not feel as though they pressured him to become one himself. They considered him part of the family and recognized that at this point he was old enough to make his own choices.

One thing that he did not have much choice about, however, was his job with Jaguar. Soon after taking that job, the war began, and as an Austrian, he was not permitted to manufacture cars any longer:

> Later on when the war was a little bit too intense, they told me that I could not work in a car factory because I was born in Vienna . . . then I went and worked in a rescue squad, that was, you know, we were helping first aid repairs, helping people who got bombed.[28]

Charles recalled kicking unexploded firebombs away and attempting to pull out bodies from the wreckage—the living along with the dead.

The Blitz made life quite difficult, but despite the dangers in Coventry, Charles was thankful to the Laxons for finding him at the camp and bringing him to live with the Greens and was grateful for his time with the Christadelphians. His feelings toward the Christadelphians, and toward the Laxons, are still overwhelmingly positive, even though he is now 94 years old:

I have only good things to say about them, they were good people. Mr. Laxon himself was exceptional, he was a real old English gentleman. In fact, during the war after we had the bombing, he had a house like a mansion . . . he gave it to the town as a hospital . . . it was used as a hospital during the war.[29]

Charles's wife Elisabeth continued:

Charles . . . admired the sincerity and dedication of the Christadelphians, and those feelings remain with him. . . . He talked with great admiration of the Laxons. . . . They adopted an 8-year old Czech child and Charles sometimes helped interpreting for them—she spoke no English.[30]

Charles's feelings toward the Greens are similar. Commenting on their willingness to make him a part of their family, Charles

*Left: Charles Ohlenberg at work as a maitre d', around 1965.*
*Right: Charles Ohlenberg as a maitre d' about 10 years later, around 1975.*

stated, "It's not easy to . . . take somebody else's kids into their home, and I think it's a very wonderful thing to do."[31]

## Parting Ways

After a few years of living in Coventry, the Greens decided to move back to Rugby, where they had relatives. In Rugby, for a time, Mrs. Green became the housemother of Little Thorn—the Christadelphian hostel there for Jewish refugees.

When the Greens moved to Rugby, Charles moved to London. In London, he continued the gruesome work on the rescue squad. After the war ended, Charles took a position as a waiter on an ocean liner. He traveled back and forth between England and the United States, eventually meeting an English nurse, Elisabeth, marrying her, and moving to New York. They have now been married for over 60 years. They have three children and five grandchildren.

*Ohlenberg family picture, 2004.*

## Conclusion

Throughout all the years that have passed, Charles and Elisabeth have stayed in touch with the Greens. Because of Jack and Winnie's willingness to open up their house and their family to a Jewish refugee, the two families, the Greens and the Ohlenbergs, have been knit together. Elisabeth Briley, Mr. and Mrs. Green's granddaughter, is still in contact with Charles and Elisabeth and said the following about them:

> He [Charles] always kept in touch with my family, sending letters, photographs and gifts for my mother, to whom he was a sort of 'big brother'.

> Charles, and his family, have always been part of my extended family.

*Charles Ohlenberg, 2016.*

It is quite hard to put into words the very deep and special relationship which exists between my family and the Ohlenbergs. . . . Because of their deep conviction in the promises to Abraham, my grandparents chose to open their home to a Jewish refugee who lost all his close family in the Holocaust. . . . Because of their action Charles was able to grow up, find a lovely wife and have children and grandchildren of his own, and to live into his 90s. I find this extremely moving.[32]

Without doubt, she is not the only one who does.

---

[1] Susan Feigenbaum and R. W. Hafer, *Principles of Macroeconomics: The Way We Live* (New York: Worth Publishers, First Edition, 2011), 329.

[2] Ibid.

[3] C. R., "Germany's Hyperinflation-phobia," *The Economist,* last modified November 15, 2013, http://www.economist.com/blogs/freeexchange/2013/11/economic-history-1.

[4] Robert Hall, *Inflation: Causes and Effects* (Chicago: University of Chicago Press, 1982), 48-50.

[5] Cyril Brown, "New Popular Idol Rises in Bavaria," *The New York Times* (New York, NY), November 21, 1922.

[6] Charles Ohlenberg, *USC Foundation Institute Testimony of Charles Ohlenberg,* USC Shoah Foundation Interview, May 13, 1996.

[7] Charles and Elisabeth Ohlenberg, e-mail message to author, April 7, 2016.

[8] Ibid.

[9] Ibid.

[10] Ibid.

[11] Ibid.

[12] "Memorial Book - Victims of the Persecution of Jews under the National Socialist Tyranny in Germany 1933-1945," *Das Bundesarchiv,* last modified January 14, 2016, https://www.bundesarchiv.de/gedenkbuch/zwangsausweisung.html.en.

[13] Charles Ohlenberg, *USC Foundation Institute Testimony of Charles Ohlenberg*, USC Shoah Foundation Interview, May 13, 1996.

[14] Ibid.

[15] Ibid.

[16] Ibid.

[17] Ibid.

[18] Police officer in France, quoted in Charles Ohlenberg, *USC Foundation Institute Testimony of Charles Ohlenberg*, USC Shoah Foundation Interview, May 13, 1996.

[19] Charles and Elisabeth Ohlenberg, e-mail message to author, February 25, 2016.

[20] Charles Ohlenberg, *USC Foundation Institute Testimony of Charles Ohlenberg*, USC Shoah Foundation Interview, May 13, 1996.

[21] "The Central Database of Shoah Victims' Names - Paul Oehlenberg," *Yad Vashem,* accessed April 15, 2016, http://yvng.yadvashem.org/nameDetails.html?language=en&s_lastName=ohlenberg&s_firstName=&s_place=&itemId=7856036&ind=37&winId=-5466662086370935376.

[22] "Auschwitz," *United States Holocaust Memorial Museum,* last modified January 29, 2016, https://www.ushmm.org/wlc/en/article.php?ModuleId=10005189.

[23] Charles Ohlenberg in discussion with the author, March 2016.

[24] Charles Ohlenberg, *USC Foundation Institute Testimony of Charles Ohlenberg*, USC Shoah Foundation Interview, May 13, 1996.

[25] Ibid.

[26] Charles Ohlenberg in discussion with the author, March 2016.

[27] Charles and Elisabeth Ohlenberg, e-mail message to author, February 25, 2016.

[28] Charles Ohlenberg in discussion with the author, March 2016.

[29] Ibid.

[30] Charles and Elisabeth Ohlenberg, e-mail message to author, March 3, 2016.

[31] Charles Ohlenberg in discussion with the author, March 2016.

[32] Elisabeth Briley, e-mail message to author, March 28, 2016.

# INGRID WUGA

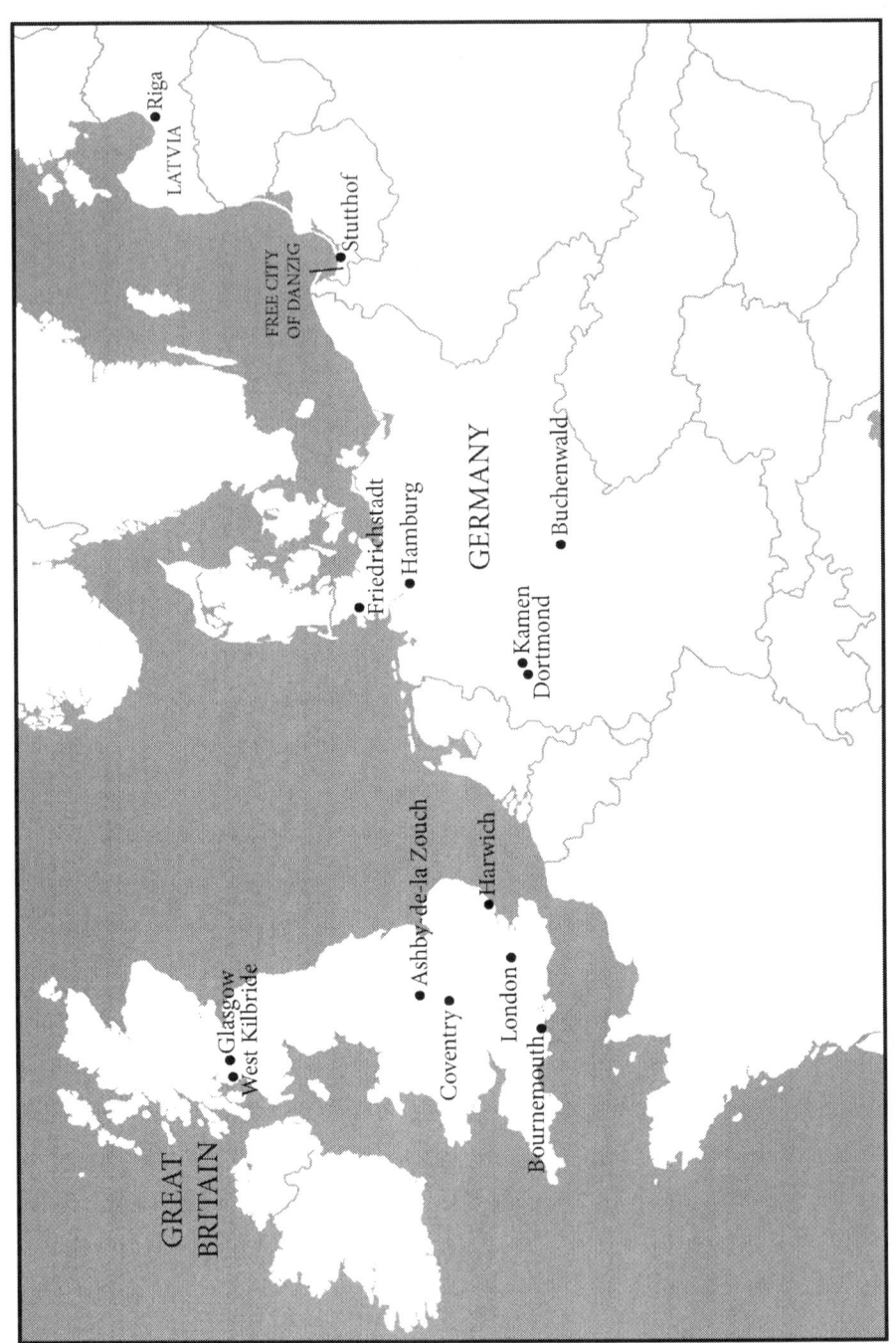

# 2

---

# INGRID WUGA, NÉE WOLFF

B y June 1924, Adolf Hitler had spent one month in prison. In November 1923, he had been sentenced to five years for an attempted coup known as the Beer Hall Putsch. Nevertheless, due to political pressure from friends of the Nazi Party, he was released in December 1924, having served only eight months of his original sentence.

At the time, Hitler's influence on Germany seemed minimal. *Mein Kampf* had not yet been published. Hitler was radical and had been jailed for his views, and it seemed as though many recognized his policies as extreme.

For the Wolff family in 1924, everything seemed just as it always had been—except that in June of that year, their family had added one new member to its ranks.

Ingrid Wolff was born on June 24, 1924, in Dortmund, Germany, a city in Westphalia, approximately three to four hours west of Berlin. She was an only child, beloved by her parents—and as such, despite having no siblings, she never felt lonely. Although her parents were strict, she was raised in an environment where she knew she was cherished: "I had a very happy childhood. My parents, Mutti Erna and Pappi Ascher Wolff, were very loving, caring . . . I have many happy memories of these times."[1]

One of Ingrid's favorite memories of her early years is her family's annual trip to Friedrichstadt—which was very different than Dortmund. It was a hamlet surrounded by rivers, just on the Danish border, and was actually settled by Dutch immigrants in the 1600s as a haven for their Mennonite and Remonstrant religious views. It was a picturesque little Dutch village, with canals intersecting the houses.

This was the town where Ingrid's parents had grown up, so when they visited each summer, they visited family, spending six weeks in the large home of Ingrid's grandparents, Helene and Nessanel Levy. Ingrid's other grandparent, her father's mother, Betty Wolff, lived just on the next street over. Ingrid never knew her father's father, Emmanuel Wolff, as he had tragically drowned when Ascher was just 16. Emmanuel had been a butcher, and when he died, Betty was able to continue the family business with the help of their oldest son, Julius.

Because both sides of the family were from Friedrichstadt, the summer was always filled with exciting games and outings with cousins and aunts and uncles. Sometimes Ingrid would swim in the river or travel to the seaside. Occasionally the town would have some sort of celebration, and children would walk through the streets carrying candle-lit paper lanterns.

Ingrid had a good relationship with both of her grandmothers—with Oma Lene playing cards with her and teaching her how to play "Patience," and Oma Betty always greeting her with warmth. Whenever Ingrid walked one street over to visit Oma Betty, she was greeted with the words, "Oh the dear Lord must have sent you!" and asked to run an errand for her grandmother.[2]

She remembers these visits to Friedrichstadt with great affection. In fact, even after the war, when she was able to travel back to the mainland, she found no pleasantness in

*An etching of the old Friedrichstadt marketplace by Hans Feil circa 1900. The second shop from the left, with the sign "R. Behrend" was the General Store belonging to Ingrid's uncle.*

journeying to her hometown of Dortmund, but did find comfort in a journey back to Friedrichstadt, where she had spent so many carefree days with her parents, grandparents, aunts, uncles, and cousins.

Closer to Dortmund, Ingrid's Uncle Hugo and Auntie Clara lived in Kamen. Clara was Erna's sister, and Kamen was only about 15 minutes northeast of Dortmund. It was a short train trip, so Ingrid made frequent visits. While she was there, she played with her cousin Lore and admired her uncle's skill as a butcher—he would make salami in front of her and sometimes allowed her to taste it and take some home. Seeing Ingrid's delight with the salami, Uncle Hugo told her that she had expensive taste, as salami was one of the most expensive sausages in his shop!

At times, however, Ingrid's visits to her relatives in Kamen were not filled with foods that she enjoyed—particularly when they ate leeks in their soup. Once Ingrid sought to remove the leeks and simply leave them on the rim of her plate, but her subtlety did not go unnoticed by her father. With one stern look at his only daughter, he conveyed his message—she needed to eat whatever was put in front of her. Reflecting on that incident, Ingrid wrote: "Little did I realise at the age of 8 that once you are away from home, you eat what is put in front of you, or you will go hungry."[3]

The lesson was powerfully imprinted upon Ingrid's mind some six years later, when she was living in a different country with different foods and customs than the ones that she found so comforting in Germany.

**Daily Life**

In 1930, Ingrid was six years old, and it was time for her to begin school. Ingrid's parents recognized the antisemitism taking hold in Germany—and so they purposefully sent Ingrid to a Jewish school from the very beginning, hoping that she would avoid any incidents.

At school, Ingrid had classes in all the typical subjects— history, music, and language, but her favorite subject was science. Perhaps, however, the most useful subject to her was one whose importance she would only realize a few years later. When Ingrid was 11 or 12, approximately 1935 or 1936, the headmaster of this Jewish school wisely saw the way in which the country was moving. He realized that a number of his pupils would probably emigrate. Out of concern for their futures, he made a prudent choice about their education, telling them that while they may have wanted to learn French as their foreign language, they could take French privately. Instead, they were all going to learn English—because English could be used in nearly any country to which they would move. Such could not be said of French. Thus, Ingrid took English classes while still living in Germany.

After school ended each day, Ingrid had the afternoon free, and she would often roller skate to wherever her friends had gathered. At one point, she remembers asking her father for a bicycle and being told, "You cannot have everything you want,"[4] a lesson that, just as the others, was essential for what she was about to experience in the coming years.

Ingrid's Jewish culture was a part of her daily life. She went to a Jewish school, and on the Sabbath, she accompanied her father to the local synagogue, where she enjoyed singing in the choir. Her parents' home was kept somewhat kosher, but not entirely—such was not the case for her grandparents' home in Friedrichstadt, where the law was followed to the letter. Ingrid's immediate family enjoyed the celebrations together and kept the traditions alive.

**Antisemitism**

In 1936, Ingrid finished at her Jewish primary school and proceeded to secondary school. While in primary school, she did not experience a great deal of antisemitism, although there were times she was called "Dirty Jew" on the way home from school—which she said was "hurtful and frightening."[5]

In 1938, however, after she had graduated from the first school, she was to experience her first major antisemitic incident—and it was terrifying. By this point, everyone in Germany had had to register his or her address with the police, which made it easy to find anyone whom the Germans wanted to locate. Ingrid's family had registered all of their names with the police, along with the name of a little Jewish girl of Polish descent—because the girl wanted to attend the same Jewish

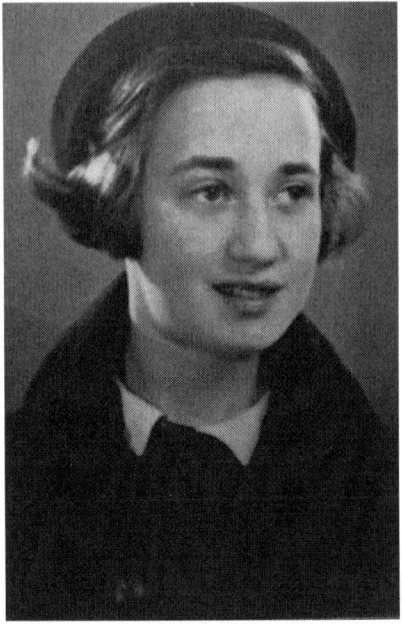

*Ingrid Wolff, 1937.*

school that Ingrid had attended and was not able to do so without a local address. Ingrid's parents, happy to help, allowed her to register her name at their address.

However, October 1938 was when Hitler demanded that all Jews of Polish origin, including their children who had been born in Germany, like this little girl, be expelled from Germany.[6]

On the night of the Polish expulsion, the storm troopers arrived at the Wolff household—they had looked at the lists at the police station, and they knew that a little girl lived in the house. They entered and searched, looking for the little girl who no longer was welcome in Germany. Finally, they found her—she was in Ingrid's room, lying on Ingrid's bed. They ordered her to get out bed, which she did, and were preparing to drag her away.

There was just one problem: The Polish girl did not actually live at their house, and the little girl they had found in Ingrid's room *was Ingrid!*

Ingrid, only 14 at the time, was terrified. What was going to happen to her? Where would they take her? Would she ever return to her parents?

Finally, her father was able to persuade the men that they had the wrong girl. The one they had ordered out of bed, who was sleeping in Ingrid's room, was not the little Polish girl, but was Ingrid, his own daughter.

Astonishingly, the men let Ingrid go and then left the house.

Ingrid described her feelings at that time: "This was our first skirmish with the SA Brown Shirts. I will never forget that night of terror."[7]

More and more restrictions were placed on the Jews. When they were forbidden from working as professionals or running businesses, Ascher was put out of work. The Jews were also not allowed to employ non-Jews, so all of their domestic help had to be let go. Ingrid recalls being barred from the cinemas, theaters, and opera houses as well.

Then, November 9 and 10, 1938 arrived: *Kristallnacht.*

Ingrid described the destruction and the fear from that night:

> With Kristallnacht . . . the horror became even more apparent. Marauding gangs of Nazi brownshirts systematically smashed Jewish flats and houses up.

Miraculously, our flat remained untouched. My grandparent's houses and businesses in Friedrichstadt were completely destroyed. My father and uncles were arrested and transported to Buchenwald concentration camp. A frightening time for all the family. Released after six weeks, they were traumatised but glad to be home. Others were not so lucky; they never returned.[8]

The story of Ingrid's father is particularly sad—though she mentioned that he had been sent to Buchenwald, his arrest was a bit different from that of many of the other Jewish men. As Ingrid said, her flat remained untouched. Both her mother and her father woke up the next morning, along with Ingrid, without knowing what had happened. Ingrid was sent to school, and as she walked along the streets and saw all the destruction in the shop windows, she thought at first that there had been some type of mass burglary (which, indeed, there was). But then she realized that it was *only* the Jewish shops that had been attacked.

When Ingrid arrived at school, she was informed that some of the children's fathers had disappeared; but she, thankfully, had not lost hers. Tragically, though, this information about the arrest of the Jewish men made its way to her parents' house, where it was accompanied by a warning for Ascher: if he did not go to the police, he would be sent to a concentration camp. In an attempt to avoid this, Ascher reported to the police station—where he was promptly arrested and sent to Buchenwald, along with the other fathers who had been torn from their families that night.

Buchenwald was one of the largest concentration camps constructed within the old German borders (1937; before the annexation of Austria and occupation of the *Sudetenland* in Czechoslovakia), and was located about five miles northwest of Weimar in east-central Germany. As a result of the roundups at *Kristallnacht*, approximately 10,000 Jewish men were brought to the camp and detained. Their treatment upon arrival was so poor that 255 of them died shortly thereafter.[9]

Ascher survived, but it was six weeks before Ingrid and Erna saw him again.

## Hamburg

After Ascher returned to the family, it was decided that they would leave Dortmund and move to Hamburg. It was not that they thought that Hamburg was any safer than Dortmund but they moved primarily because Ingrid's parents hoped that living in a larger city would make it easier for them to obtain visas, which would allow them to emigrate. After Ascher's experience in Buchenwald, emigration was the family's main goal.

They moved in 1939—but they did not all move together. Ingrid was sent ahead, for reasons unknown, and she had to live with her aunt Gerta until he parents followed her a few weeks later. Ingrid was apprehensive about the idea—she did not want to be separated from her parents, and she did not really know Gerta. Ingrid was not sure whether her aunt would be kind or whether she would be strict and demanding. However, Ingrid stated, "I need not have worried, she was the kindest and most understanding aunt you could have wished for."[10]

In Hamburg, while first living with her aunt and then with her parents, Ingrid attended another Jewish school, where she continued to take English lessons. But her attendance at the school did not last very long. In preparation for emigration, Erna felt that it was more important for Ingrid to have domestic skills, and so Ingrid enrolled in a school for domestic science where she had some cooking lessons and took care of children. The school turned out to be an orphanage, the Paulienestift Jewish Orphanage, and while Ingrid enjoyed working with the children, she hated the institution itself.

Then one day, life changed dramatically. Up until this point, the changes had been incremental. But on this day, Ingrid's life took a drastic turn. After filling out application after application, the family learned that Ingrid, Ascher and Erna's only child, had found a guarantor in England. A family, the Dixons, in Ashby-de-la-Zouch, had agreed to sponsor Ingrid to come to Great Britain. Ingrid, therefore, via the Kindertransport, could flee from the horror Germany had become.

Immediately, Ingrid's mother set herself to preparing Ingrid to leave—buying her clothes into which she could grow, so that

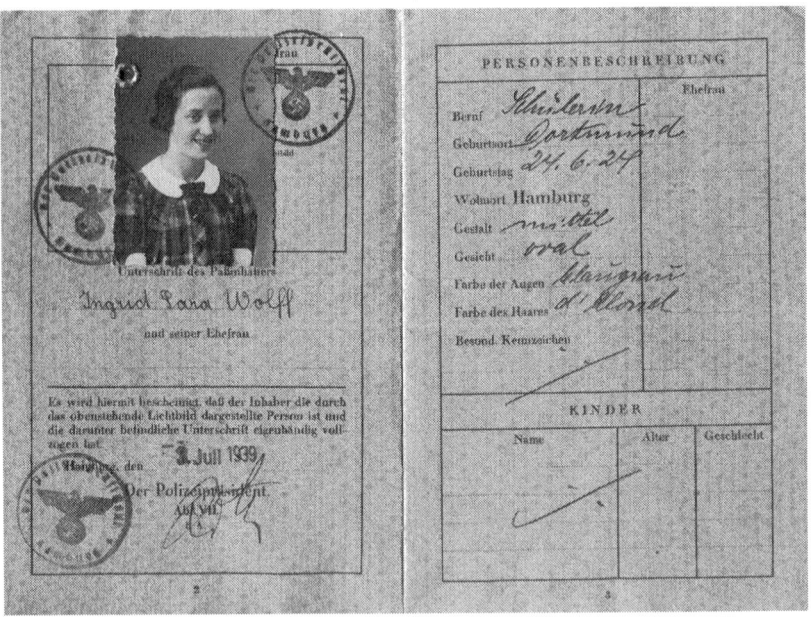

*Ingrid's German passport from 1939. Note her middle name: "Sara." By January 1, 1939 all Jewish men and women who had first names deemed "non-Jewish" were forced to add "Israel" or "Sara," respectively, to their name.*

she would be prepared for many years to come. Because in reality, Erna did not know if she would be able to buy clothes for her little girl ever again.

## Leaving

Ingrid left Hamburg by train in early July, 1939. She had just turned 15 years old.

She remembers the parting vividly—she was on the train, waving to her parents, and they were on the platform outside, running alongside the train:

> I found it very traumatic to say goodbye to my parents at the train station. I will never forget waving till I could not see my parents any longer. Going into the unknown was extremely difficult. Little children were crying bitterly. I remember one father not being able to part from his daughter and lifting her out through the window.[11]

> My parents ran alongside the departing train waving until we could no longer see each other. When would we ever be reunited? My parents had applied for a visa to work as a domestic couple in Britain. It had not yet arrived.[12]

From Hamburg, Ingrid traveled to Holland. Again, the experiences on her journey are best described in her own words: "The 8-hour train journey on the Kindertransport was distressing to say the least. Children were crying, little girls clutching their dolls. At the Dutch border we all sat silent with fear."[13]

The Dutch border was the children's last encounter with the Nazis—so the stakes were high. Would the Nazis somehow force them to turn around? Freedom was so close, but would it slip from their fingers?

Finally, after the German customs officers had completed their check, the train entered Holland, and the children were free. In Holland, they were welcomed by kind women who gave them fruit and sandwiches. From there, Ingrid boarded an overnight ferry bound for Harwich, England. She arrived in England on July 4, 1939—a day that she has always called her "Independence Day."[14] But Ingrid's journey was not over yet. From Harwich, she took another train to Liverpool Street Station in London where she waited, wondering who would come fetch her: "We sat in a large hall waiting to be collected by someone from the refugee committee or a guarantor. . . . Uncertainty again, would someone really come for us?"[15]

Finally, a man approached Ingrid and introduced himself as Mr. Overton. He had come to take her to the Dixons in Ashby-de-la-Zouch. Mr. Overton and the Dixons were Christadelphians.

## Ingrid's Family

As the train pulled away from Hamburg, Ingrid could not stop waving—because for all that she knew, it was the last time that she would ever see her parents.

After reaching Great Britain, Ingrid continuously worried about their fate. One day, she received distressing news: her father had been taken into custody again. This time, it was not because of a nationwide roundup but rather because Ascher Wolff had been accused of spying on Germany.

The situation seemed dire. Ingrid's parents had applied for British visas and had hoped to join Ingrid in England—but what would happen to her father now? And would it make any difference if the visas did arrive? The Nazi government acted with such unpredictability that no one ever really knew what to expect. And espionage was a serious crime.

Day after day went by. And then, for some unknown reason, Ingrid's father was set free.

He had been in prison for just over a week.

Immediately after he was released, the visas arrived. Ascher and Erna were given permission to come to Great Britain to be reunited with their daughter—and to be free from the deadly fate that awaited so many Jews.

Ingrid's parents escaped Nazi Germany in late August, 1939, just *one week* before Great Britain declared war on Germany. If they had endeavored to leave only a few days later, they would not have been able to enter England.

They came as domestic servants for British families, giving up nearly everything they had owned in Germany. Both were well educated and were upper-middle class, having employed servants themselves. The shift in status was unsettling for them, but at least they were alive.

Tragically, the same could not be said for Ingrid's aunt and uncle.

Though Ascher had urged his brother-in-law to humble himself and apply for work as a servant in England, he was too proud and responded curtly, "No way will I expose my wife to this kind of work."[16]

Ingrid's uncle was separated from his wife and child and deported to Riga,[17] where he was murdered. Her aunt, along with her cousin, were sent to Stutthof concentration camp.[18]

They survived; however, her aunt perished from typhus, a common disease contracted in the camps, only two weeks after being liberated.

Other aunts and uncles along with cousins also found asylum in Great Britain, and one cousin, Emil Wolff, survived by immigrating to Paraguay.

## The Christadelphians

Though Ingrid nor her parents had never met Mr. Overton or the Dixons, these Christadelphians were willing to go out of their way to save her—once again, because of what they believed. In a conversation between the author and Hilary Hodsman, Ingrid's daughter, Hilary stated that her parents had taught her that it was indeed these beliefs that had in part served as the impetus for the Christadelphians' actions: "Dad [Henry Wuga] said that part of the reason for giving Jewish children a refuge was that the Christadelphians believe the Jews are the chosen race."[19]

Acting on their beliefs, Mr. Overton and the Dixons did what they could to help the suffering Jewish people. Therefore, not only did they offer help to the Jews, but they also sought to offer this help with kindness. One of these thoughtful acts is still remembered by Ingrid today, even though it may seem so small:

> Mr. Overton was very kind, and he took me to Lyons Corner House, and he said 'You might want something to eat,' and I was very shy. . . . He said, 'Just eat whatever you think.' He made me very welcome, and I had tea.[20]

At that meal, Ingrid was given her first lesson in British table manners. Mr. Overton showed her that in England you broke bread with your hands rather than cut it with a knife. In addition, Ingrid was surprised to watch Mr. Overton cut his potato with a knife rather than break it with a fork. In all of this, Ingrid remembers Mr. Overton being extremely gentle and patient.

After the meal was over, Mr. Overton handed Ingrid a penny and looked at her with a "you will need that" type of smile. Ingrid was surprised, as she had always been taught never to take money from people she did not know, and she did not understand why she would need it. Thus, she politely refused and returned the penny to him.

Unabated, Mr. Overton slid the penny back to Ingrid and insisted, "You will need it."

Little did Ingrid know, in this new culture and this new place, that to go to the ladies' room at the time, one needed to insert a penny into the door, or it would not open. Mr. Overton, Ingrid explained, was just too polite to tell her why she would need the coin.

Mr. Overton's kindness in taking Ingrid to the corner house, offering her whatever she would like to eat and drink, and urging her to take a penny, is a story she has told to her children time and again to emphasize the kindness was shown to her by one Christadelphian when she was scared, alone, and unsure of her new surroundings. She and her family insisted on the inclusion of this story as a tribute to what Mr. Overton had done for her.

Afterward, Ingrid traveled with Mr. Overton to the Dixon's house in Ashby-de-la-Zouch.

The Dixons lived in a large house in which they were the only occupants. At one time, Mr. and Mrs. Dixon had had one son,

*The Dixon's house in Ashby de la Zouch.*

but he had tragically died before Ingrid arrived. Mr. and Mrs. Dixon, in an attempt to create good from tragedy, chose to take a portion of the money they had put away for their son and use it to sponsor Ingrid.

For a little over a week, Ingrid lived with them.

She described her first night and some of the small cultural issues that are generally overlooked when describing the Kindertransport:

> My first night there had its problems. I was used to downies, here there were blankets tightly tucked in. As I did not dare to make a mess of the neat bedding, I spent a jolly uncomfortable night. I soon learned how to deal with blankets.[21]

Unfortunately, it seems that though they wanted to do something good for the Jewish people, their nerves from the loss of their son were still a bit raw. Ingrid described both of them as "kind,"[22] remembers Mr. Dixon with great fondness, and appreciated his gentle disposition. Mrs. Dixon, however, had a difficult time coping with all of the changes—losing her son and now having another child, a girl, in the house.

Though she did express kindness toward Ingrid, telling her one day, "You're very welcome, we wanted to help you,"[23] Mrs. Dixon, perhaps overcome by her circumstances, also told Ingrid that she had seen her picture on the application, and though it was nice, she would rather have had a boy.

It was a strange remark considering that there was a far greater need for homes for Jewish boys than for Jewish girls—which is why the hostels were initially opened. Perhaps it was a comment that simply came out one day when Mrs. Dixon was pining for her only son and perhaps Mrs. Dixon regretted it later. It was as though she *wanted* Ingrid to become part of the family but that it was simply too much for her.

Reflecting on what Mrs. Dixon had said, Hilary Hodsman, Ingrid's daughter, explained:

> I think that we will never know. . . . Mrs. Dixon was obviously bitter, which . . . if you've lost a child, I mean, I don't think any of us can even imagine what it was like for her, so I think they did the good thing, they did the right thing, but she was happy probably not to have Mummy in front of her all the time. . . . You've got to forgive her for whatever she said, did, and felt . . . to pledge their £50 to somebody else is amazing.[24]

*Top: Mr. and Mrs. Dixon on a trip to Scarborough.*
*Bottom Left: Ingrid working as nanny for Patrick.*
*Bottom Right: Mr. Dixon on the Scarborough trip.*

Despite the circumstances, the words were said, and they had their effect. Ingrid felt unwanted, and only later did she find out about the Dixons' son.

Adding to this difficulty, Ingrid had hoped that she would be able to continue her education; it had ended in Germany when she was sent to the orphanage to learn domestic skills. Mrs.

Dixon, however, felt that it would be better for Ingrid to continue using those domestic skills, and so instead of sending Ingrid to nursing school, which is where she had wanted to go, Mrs. Dixon asked whether Ingrid would "like to earn some pocket money."[25]

Ingrid answered in the affirmative and was given a job as a live-in nanny for a local family, taking care of an 18-month-old baby named Patrick. She was given a half-day off every week. On those half-days, Mr. Dixon stopped by and picked her up to visit him and his wife. Mrs. Dixon also took her out shopping if Ingrid needed anything.

On those half-days, she also attended the Christadelphian meeting with the Dixons. There she met a few other Jewish refugees who had been brought in by other Christadelphian families. She stated that she felt "no pressure" to become a Christadelphian. In fact, she was the one who *asked* the Dixons whether she could go with them to their meetings: "No pressure . . . I said . . . I'd like to come to meeting with you and say thank you for being able to be in this country and free."[26]

For about 10 or 11 months, while she was living in Ashby, Ingrid attended the Christadelphian ecclesia there. When asked what she thought about the Christadelphians as a group, Ingrid responded: "[My] feelings towards Christadelphians . . . [are] very good. It's a very good religion . . . they did a good job for me—all they ever did was tried to do good things."[27]

**Her Parents**

While all this was happening to Ingrid, her parents were still in Germany. Eventually, Ascher and Erna were able to flee to Great Britain, just two months after Ingrid had left on the Kindertransport. It was a huge relief for Ingrid to know that they too were able to escape.

111

On one of Ingrid's half-days, the Dixons, anxious to meet Ingrid's parents and to reunite mother and father with daughter, drove Ingrid to Coventry, where Ascher and Erna had found positions as a butler and a maid.

Their troubles, however, were not yet over. Ascher and Erna's circumstances prevented them from having Ingrid live with them, and Ashby-de-la-Zouch was not as close to Coventry as Ingrid would have liked. More troubles arrived too when, after working for a few weeks, both of Ingrid's parents were dismissed from their jobs because of their German nationality—with the war going on, all Germans were viewed as the enemy. Moreover, being intimately aware of the situation for the Jews in Germany, Ingrid's family was terribly worried about their relatives' fates.

Eventually, Ascher and Erna were able to secure new positions, as a cook and a butler in a large house in West Kilbride, Scotland. This, however, was quite far from Ashby. As such, Ingrid asked whether they could find a job in West Kilbride for her too. They were successful in securing her a position as a mother's help in a nearby village. Finally, the family was more or less together again.

But it was wartime. So in 1941, her family had to move to Glasgow, as all people deemed enemy aliens were forbidden from living near the coast in case they should attempt to send coded messages to the Germans. That same year, Ingrid met Henry Wuga at a refugee club. He, too, had come to Great Britain via the Kindertransport. She was only 17, but three years later, on December 27, 1944, the two of them were married.

*Ingrid Wuga, 1949.*

## Conclusion

Ingrid and Henry have been happily married for over 70 years, and still reside in Scotland. They have two daughters, Hilary and Gillian, and four grandsons. They feel extremely blessed to be alive and to have been able to come to live in the United Kingdom.

Ingrid and her family feel an enormous debt of gratitude to the Christadelphians and to Mr. Overton, whom they later learned had helped organize much of the Christadelphian activity for Jewish refugees. In addition, they feel extremely grateful to the Dixons. Even after she left Ashby to live closer to her family, Ingrid continued to keep in touch with her foster family. After the Dixons had retired and moved to Bournemouth, Ingrid

*Top and Right: Ingrid and Henry Wuga, 2013.*

*Bottom: Wuga Family picture at a 90th birthday celebration for Ingrid and Henry, 2014. Back row (from left to right): David Field, Richard Field, Alastair Hodsman, Peter Hodsman, Jonathan Field, and Paul Hodsman. Front row (from left to right): Gillian Field, Henry Wuga, Ingrid Wuga, and Hilary Hodsman.*

and Henry went to visit them—their act of kindness had made such a lasting impression upon her: "I kept in touch with them of course, oh yes, I was grateful for the things they had done for me: after all, they saved my life."[28]

Ingrid feels as though she owes them everything: "The Dixons . . . as Christadelphians . . . wanted to save a child from persecution, and for that I am forever grateful."[29]

---

[1] Ingrid Wuga, "Ingrid's Story," Typescript, July 2002, 1.

[2] Ibid.

[3] Ibid., 2.

[4] Ibid.

[5] Ibid.

[6] See explanation of the Polish expulsion in Charles Ohlenberg's biography.

[7] Ingrid Wuga, "Ingrid's Story," Typescript, July 2002, 2.

[8] Ibid., 3.

[9] "Buchenwald," *United States Holocaust Memorial Museum,* last modified January 29, 2016, http://www.ushmm.org/wlc/en/article.php?ModuleId=10005198.

[10] Ingrid Wuga, "Ingrid's Story," Typescript, July 2002, 3.

[11] Ingrid and Henry Wuga, "Wednesday 23rd January Fettes College Historical Society," Typescript, January 2013, 5.

[12] Ingrid Wuga, "Ingrid's Story," Typescript, July 2002, 4.

[13] Ibid.

[14] Hilary Hodsman, e-mail message to author, February 10, 2016.

[15] Ibid.

[16] Ingrid Wuga's uncle, quoted in Ingrid and Henry Wuga, "Wednesday 23rd January Fettes College Historical Society," Typescript, January 2013, 5.

[17] See description of this ghetto in Ursula Meyer's biography.

[18] See description of this camp in Ursula Meyer's biography.

[19] Ingrid and Henry Wuga, and Hilary Hodsman in discussion with the author, February 6, 2016.

[20] Ibid.

[21] Ingrid Wuga, "Ingrid's Story," Typescript, July 2002, 4.

[22] Ibid.

[23] Ingrid and Henry Wuga, and Hilary Hodsman in discussion with the author, February 6, 2016.

[24] Ibid.

[25] Ibid.

[26] Ibid.

[27] Ibid.

[28] Ingrid and Henry Wuga, and Hilary Hodsman in discussion with the author, February 6, 2016.

[29] Ingrid Wuga, "Ingrid's Story," Typescript, July 2002, 4.

# URSULA MEYER

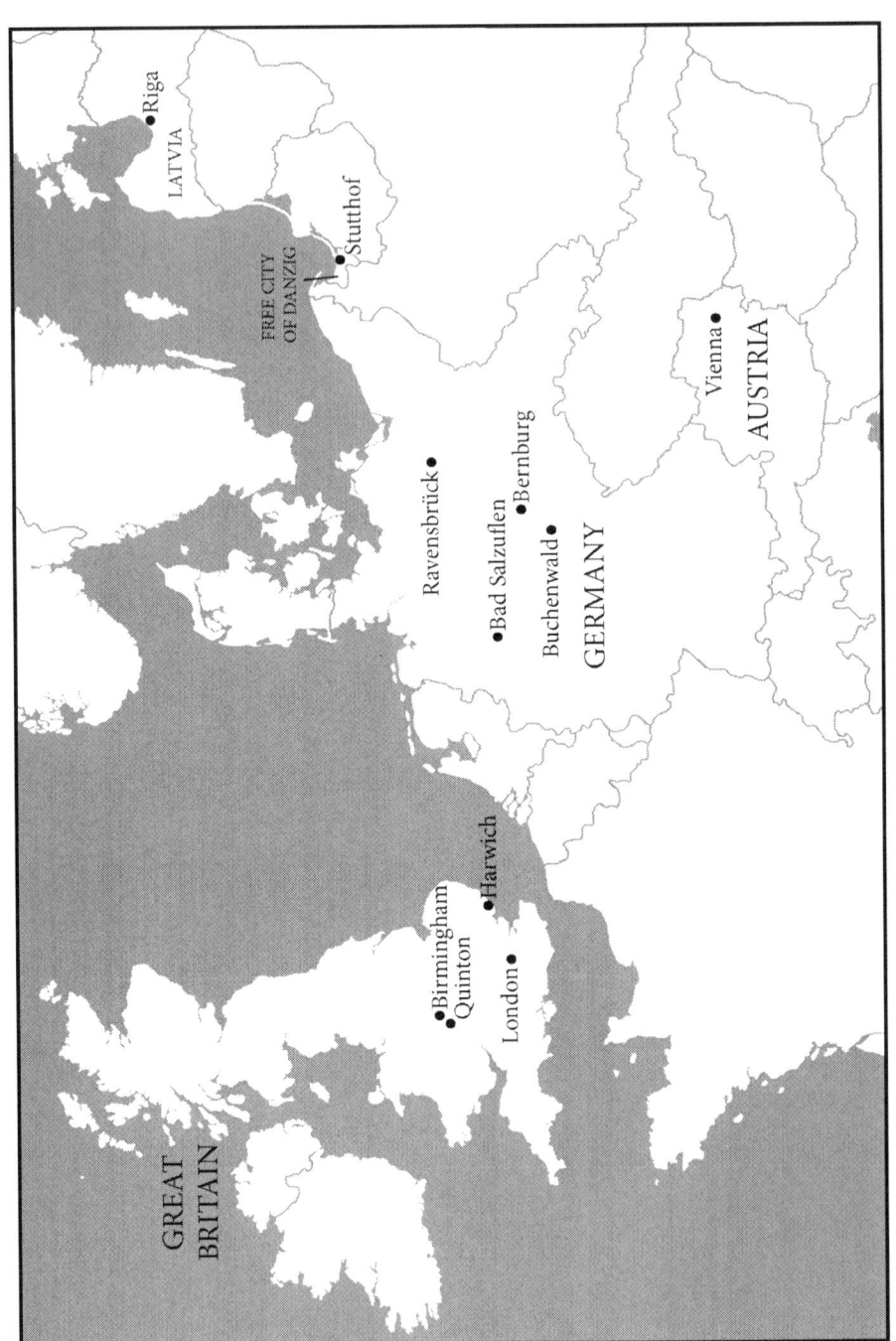

# 3

## URSULA MEYER, NÉE EICHMANN

In 1924, Germany accepted the Dawes Plan. It was an agreement between the Allies and Germany with a twofold purpose: to help Germany repay its war debt and to end the Allied occupation of German territory. Germany had defaulted on its reparation payments in 1923, and as a result, French and Belgian troops had been sent to occupy the Ruhr River Valley. Essentially, the agreement reduced the immediate payments owed by Germany and increased them over time as the German economy improved. The plan appeared to be successful, and because of its success, its main architect, Charles Dawes, won the Nobel Peace Prize in 1925.[1]

Though the Dawes Plan helped to bring about stability in the German economy, and the money that subsequently flowed into Germany via U.S. loans ushered in a few years of prosperity, by 1928 it was recognized that Germany was struggling once again to make the increasing payments, and that a new agreement was needed.[2] This new plan was adopted in 1929 and was called the Young Plan.[3] Unfortunately, regardless of the various payment plans that the German government accepted, reparations were simply a reminder to the German people of the enormous debt that was forced upon them by the victors of World War I through the Treaty of Versailles. Though the reparation plans helped the German economy to recover, they could not fully heal the frustration that had been brought about by Versailles.

It was into this environment that Ursula Eichmann was born. She was born on August 19, 1924, in the Bad Salzuflen community of Westphalia, Germany, to Bruno and Ilse Eichmann. Bruno was born in 1900 and later became a cattle dealer, and Ilse was born in 1902. Ursula's aunt and uncle, Hans and Gertrud Eichmann, lived nearby. Eventually, as the Jewish population became more and more excluded, Hans closed his business (he was also a cattle dealer), and came to work for his younger brother Bruno, Ursula's father, in the summer of 1937.

When describing her life in Germany, Ursula remembered that she had been born into a religious house—one that observed all the holidays. The family was careful with the food that they ate, avoiding pork and shellfish, but did not keep all the laws of *kashrut*.

When describing how they lived at the time—especially as the regulations became more and more stringent, Ursula's memories became darker and darker. Here is how she described that time:

> It was a very difficult life in Germany. Very difficult . . .

> It was more than regulations. It was frightening. My father, they took him to Buchenwald concentration camp very, very early already . . . just after *Kristallnacht*. . . . He came back an old man.

> Quite frankly, I don't know how we lived. Because they took everything from us. . . . I can't remember how we lived. I really don't know.

> When you're young, you don't realize as much as when you get a little bit older.

I had to leave school when I was 12 years old, so you can imagine what happened.[4]

In 1938, during *Kristallnacht,* six Jewish men from the community were arrested. Bruno and Hans, the Eichmann brothers, were among them. They were arrested and taken to Buchenwald.[5]

Ursula's father and uncle both survived. Eventually, they were released from Buchenwald, but they came back as different people. As Ursula said, her father returned "an old man,"[6] yet he was only 39. When he returned home, he was forced to close his business.

At the time, in August, Ursula had turned 14. She was an only child—and for a few months, she was an only child without a father who had no idea where he had gone and when or whether he would return.

Upon his return, he and Ilse arranged for Ursula to travel to England via the Kindertransport. It was only because of this that she was saved—if she had stayed with her parents, it is unlikely that her fate would have been any different from theirs. For her sake, her parents sent their only child to a new country, a new family, and a new culture.

**Ursula's Family**

Shortly before Ursula left for England, the relocations began:

> Two nights before I left, they took all the Jews, took them out of their homes, put us in a house with six families. We had one room . . . to eat in, to sleep in, to bathe in, to do everything in. And then two days later, I left for England.[7]

In December 1941, after living in this situation for three years, her parents were deported to the Riga Ghetto. Riga had been the capital of independent Latvia, with a population of approximately 40,000 Jews. The ghetto was created in October 1941 with about 30,000 of these Jews. In late November and early December, 26,000 of these people were taken into the Rumbula Forest and shot.[8] Just days after these mass killings, Bruno, Ilse, and Hans, Ursula's uncle, arrived in Riga.

The ghetto was divided into multiple sections—one section became the Latvian ghetto, where the few remaining Latvian Jews were kept. After the initial mass murders, a German ghetto was created, where the prisoners from Germany and Austria, such as Bruno and Ilse, were taken. Many of those in the German ghetto shared the same fate as that of the initial Latvian Jews. They were taken into the forest and murdered.[9]

Tragically, Ilse was killed in Riga,[10] when she was 39 years old, along with Hans.[11]

Gertrud, Ursula's aunt, was deported to Ravensbrück concentration camp in 1941 and then to Bernburg Euthanasia Center, where she was murdered.[12]

Bruno survived for at least another three years. On October 1, 1944, he was transferred to Stutthof concentration camp.[13] This camp was created in 1939 in the town of Stutthof— approximately 22 miles east of Danzig (Gdansk). It was originally a civilian internment camp and then became a "labor education" camp, and finally, in 1942, it became a concentration camp. It is believed that perhaps 100,000 people were sent there.

Life in Stutthof was brutal. Though it was not an extermination camp, those who were deemed unfit to work were gassed in Stutthof's small gas chamber. Gassing with

Zyklon B began in June 1944. Typhus epidemics broke out multiple times and took many lives. Of the 100,000 who came to this camp, approximately 60,000 died. Those who lived were used as forced labor—working in various businesses, such as German Equipment Works or Focke-Wulff, which produced airplanes. Others were made to work in local brickyards, agriculture, or private industry.[14]

There is no further documentation of Bruno Eichmann after his arrival to Stutthof from Riga on October 1, 1944. As such, it is believed that he was murdered there. He was in his early 40s.

## Leaving

It was August 2, 1939. Ursula's younger cousin Susanne Eichmann (born 1926), the daughter of Hans and Gertrude, was with Ursula. They first traveled to Holland, and then to Harwich, and finally to Liverpool Street Station in London. Ursula remembers extremely little about leaving her parents—although she does remember that they brought her to the train in Germany. Ursula brought only one small suitcase.

It was almost too late. It was early August—and war was declared on Germany by Britain on September 3, at which point all Kindertransports out of Germany ceased. After Ursula left, it would only be possible to leave Germany for Britain for another few weeks.

At this time, Ursula was 14 years old, about to turn 15. She would celebrate her 15th birthday after living with her foster family for just a few days. She was a typical teenager—thinking about all of the things that an early teen would consider, and yet, added to all this was the burden of arriving in a new country, saying goodbye to her parents, and wondering whether she would see them again.

She would not.

Yet, perhaps weighing on her mind most heavily at this point was the new family with which she would be living. How would the family treat her? What would her life be like? Would the family accept her?

**Arrival in England**

When Ursula arrived at Liverpool Street Station, she was met by Elsie Craddock—a Christadelphian. Elsie was Norman Sawyer's sister, and had come to meet Ursula to take her to the Sawyers' home. Ursula described her arrival in this way:

*Elsie Craddock, who met Ursula at Liverpool Street Station in August 1939.*

[I] remember the ship leaving from Holland to England, and then arriving in a big hall, where our names were called out. A lovely little lady greeted me. I liked her on sight. She was the sister-in-law of the Sawyers, the family who took me in. She took me to Birmingham, where I lived till war's end.[15]

Though the language barrier prevented them from speaking to one another, Ursula immediately felt a bond with Elsie. From Liverpool Street Station, Elsie took Ursula to another train station in London (Euston or Paddington) where they caught a train and rode for an additional two-and-a-half hours, before arriving in Birmingham. At that point, it was just a short journey to 14 Thuree Road, Warley, on the outskirts of Birmingham, where Ursula met Norman and Mabel Sawyer and their young son, Mark, who was two years old.

This was her foster family—the family with which she would live for the next few years.

*Left: Norman and Mark Sawyer, August 1939, shortly after Ursula's arrival.*

*Right: Mark and Mabel Sawyer, August 1939, shortly after Ursula's arrival.*

**Life with the Sawyers**

Speaking with Ursula about her arrival and her feelings toward the Sawyers is heartwarming. In the history of the Kindertransport, there have been so many tragic stories—stories about children being taken and put in homes of highly unsuitable families who did not relate well to them or who simply wanted to have someone to act as a maid around the house. This is not one of those stories. Perhaps it is best to allow Ursula to describe the Sawyers in her own words:

> The Sawyers, who were Christadelphians, who were truly the Righteous Gentiles. Not by words but by deeds . . . I was constantly worried about my parents and the Sawyers tried to get them into England too; but then war broke out and that put an end to their efforts.[16]

> I was very lucky to come to this wonderful family . . . Sawyer. . . . They were just wonderful people. Very kind

*92 Gower Road, Quinton—the house with the bay windows.*

to me, very patient. And they were like family to me.
. . . They absolutely felt like home.[17]

When Ursula was asked whether she felt welcomed by the
Sawyers, she was effusive. She could not say enough positive
things about this Christadelphian family. In fact, after stating
that she felt, ". . . very welcome. Very, very welcome,"[18] she
went on to relate an incredibly moving and astounding story.

Sometime between June and November in 1940, the Sawyers
moved to 92 Gower Road, Quinton, a house on the corner of
the road. It had large bay windows, and when cars would drive
by, their lights would shine on the windows and reflect off one
of them. While this had never really been a problem, there was
one exception—it was a night sometime after the German
bombing raids began. Birmingham was under blackout
regulations: all lights had to be off (to protect from enemy
bombing). Each house had to have thick lined curtains to
prevent all traces of light from leaving the house. If any light
were visible, air raid wardens would knock on the front door
and make the offense known. Unfortunately, in this particular
house, when a car drove by, its headlights would light up the
bay windows of the Sawyer household, and it looked as though
some of their lights had turned on for a brief second.

This "suspicious" activity caught the eye of one of the Home
Guard sergeants—who was convinced that the blinking lights
he saw coming from the Sawyer house were some type of
signaling to the German Air Force. The lights appeared to be
going on and off, so this Home Guard sergeant became
determined to put a stop to it.

Approaching their house, he broke down the door and looked
for the one who had been making the signals. When this man
burst into the Sawyer household and saw Ursula, a German, he
was certain that he had found the enemy agent. He was armed,

and he was ready to shoot—he had to rid Birmingham of this German spy.

It looked as though Ursula had fled all the way to England, left her parents and her hometown, only to be killed by the British.

And that's when something simply astonishing happened—something that has remained indelibly imprinted on Ursula's mind, from that time until now—at the age of 91. This act showed her the love that this Christadelphian family had for her. She was not merely someone living in the Sawyer's house. She was family.

As the Home Guard officer prepared to pull the trigger, Norman Sawyer stood between him and Ursula and said, "You shoot me first."[19]

After that dramatic moment, Ursula was able to produce her documentation, proving that indeed she had been brought into England legally and was allowed to be there. She was not a spy. Thus, the Home Guard sergeant left them in peace, and Ursula was left to contemplate the love of this family—this family that had taken her into their house without ever knowing her, all because of their beliefs, and that had just saved her life again. She will never forget that kindness.

But it was not just Norman Sawyer's kindness that moved her. Ursula felt as though she had been accepted and loved by the entire family *and* the extended family.

## The Difficult Times

Although Ursula loved her time with the Sawyers and could not say enough good about them, the war years were extremely trying and difficult. Not only had Ursula left her own family, but also, once she had settled in with the Sawyers, war was declared on Germany just weeks later. She was now a German, living in the country that was fighting against her own people! On top of that, for those first few weeks, the Sawyers had begun looking into ways they could help Ursula's parents immigrate. Those efforts were cut short when war was declared.

However, as the weeks passed, the difficulties continued.

As another challenge, Ursula had to learn English—she needed to be able to communicate with everyone around her. Simply being around so many people and having to speak with them really propelled her learning forward. But to supplement her learning further, she read voraciously. She would take one book and read it repeatedly until she understood it, and slowly her understanding of the language grew.

At the same time, in those earlier years of the war, Ursula was also subjected to a few restrictions, one being that she was not allowed to travel more than 4 miles without reporting to the police. Mark Sawyer wrote about this regulation. He said, "I remember walking down to the local police station with her to check in and have [a] movement record signed."[20]

Elaborating on that, Mark explained, "Visits to the police station . . . had to be made during WW2 if she travelled more than 4 miles I believe because she classed as an 'enemy alien.'"[21]

Indeed, it would have been difficult for Ursula to forget that, for many people in Britain, the Germans were the enemy.

Moreover, life would soon become even more difficult. By November 1940, the Sawyers had moved out to 92 Gower Road, the house on the corner where the lights from the cars reflected and looked like signals to the Germans. The German bombing raids had intensified that year. Not only was this frightening, but it was also another reminder to Ursula that she was a German and living in a country at war with Germany.

As part of the Blitz, the strategic German bombing of the United Kingdom, between November 1940 and May 1941, the Birmingham area was bombed heavily. Because of this, Ursula and the Sawyers had to evacuate their house twice, and one of those occasions was a potential near-death experience. Mark Sawyer described those events:

> We had to leave our house on two occasions: during one of those very heavy raids and also when a landmine made a soft landing on the opposite side of the road and did not explode but was safely disarmed by bomb disposal soldiers the next day. Had it gone off when landing I would probably not be here to write this and nor would Ursula be likely to be alive. We moved to my father's aunt's house until allowed to return later the next day.[22]

Such was wartime. While Ursula and the Sawyers were at Norman's aunt's house, a powerful explosion made them think that the landmine had exploded while the crew had attempted to disarm it:

> An unexploded landmine at nearby Woodgate did go off while being disarmed and killed the bomb disposal crew, and the blast was powerful enough to project me from my mother's knees to the other side of the room, making her and Ursula think that 92 Gower Road was in ruins. Happily this was not the case.[23]

The months of the bombing were months of uncertainty. Each day brought a question—what would happen that night?

Ursula had fled one scene of danger, and during the bombing, she was in another. Mark stated that while at Gower Road, "There were many disturbed nights when we all 'sheltered' in a cloakroom under the stairs."[24]

The intensity of the air raids lessened after 1941. However, perhaps one of the greatest tragedies came at the beginning of 1942: Norman Sawyer contracted meningitis—and antibiotics were not available then. On January 30, 1942, he passed away. He was only 35.

For Ursula, this was quite a blow. This was the man who had saved her life—not only indirectly when he had opened up his family to her so she could flee the horrors of Nazi Germany, but directly and literally when he had stood between her and the barrel of a gun. As Ursula recalled, it was not simply trying for Mabel and Mark (who was 4), "It was a hard time for all of us."[25]

Adding to all of those difficulties, during this entire period, Ursula was never able to return to school. It was not that the Sawyers did not want her to be educated. Ursula explained that various circumstances in the years that had led up to the war, and in the years during the war, simply prevented it. Back in Germany, Ursula was forced to leave school when she was 12. That was her last year of education. Upon moving to England, there was so much upheaval with the war, and she was so far behind (as she had not been to school for 3 years), that education was just not really possible.

Thus, Ursula's years in England were spent with many changes and numerous trials. Nevertheless, though the times were dark, Ursula found light and hope in the love and the support she received from the Sawyers. They were her friends, they were her encouragement, and they were her family.

## As the War Progressed

Eventually, as the war progressed, Ursula was given a few options by the British government. She needed to serve her adoptive country, and to do so, the choices were as follows: she could join the army, work in munitions, or become a nurse. The first two options were not terribly appealing, so Ursula chose to become a nurse.

The hospital in which Ursula worked was in Birmingham although it no longer exists today. At that hospital, Ursula saw the horrors of war. Soldiers were brought there from the front. To care for them, she had to get up early and work late, but she enjoyed the work. She felt this was finally an opportunity for her to give back to the country that had opened its doors to her and saved her from Nazi extermination:

> The war years were very hard and I trained as a nurse and enjoyed my work. We had troop trains constantly coming in and being able to help, even a little, in the fight against the Nazis gave me great satisfaction. I worked hard and many long hours in a hospital dealing with broken bones and burns, especially when troop trains arrived with wounded soldiers.[26]

Once again, even though she was working in the hospital and getting older and more independent (she turned 18 in 1942), she continued to return to the Sawyers' house whenever she had spare time. She did so because for her, that was where she belonged and where she was accepted. She stated, "Whenever I was free, I came back to the Sawyers' for the weekend, because my home was there."[27]

For Ursula, the Sawyers' house, though it was English and Christadelphian—rather than German and Jewish—was where she felt at home. In fact, writing about this period and Ursula's experiences, Barry Turner, in his book about the Kindertransport, . . . *And the Policeman Smiled*, described this exact phenomenon. Typically, when Christian families took in Jewish children and started to inculcate Christianity in them, the children were quite glad to be able to move to a different residence. Nevertheless, this generally was not the case with those who lived with Christadelphians—as Ursula's story, documented in Barry Turner's book, supports:

> The chances of transferring young people to Jewish hostels were greatest when foster parents set about inculcating Christian values with a sledgehammer. Thus Edgar was only too happy to depart from a Methodist family who 'insisted on him attending church on Sundays three times, and various weekly meetings'. But Ursula had no wish to leave her Christadelphian foster mother, even though she did have to go to Sunday school. Everything else about her home she liked very much and, according to one RCM visitor, she was 'well instructed in the Jewish religion.'
>
> Orthodox critics were liable to generalise. All Jewish children who shared a home with a Christian family were at risk, they argued; but they were frequently proved wrong.[28]

For Ursula, even though she had to attend Sunday school when she lived with the Sawyers, and even though they lived by Christadelphian values, which were slightly different from Jewish ones, she had no desire to leave the Sawyers. It was with them that she had found safety, support, and the comfort of having a home. What's more, her Jewish heritage also was not forgotten—with the Christadelphian emphasis on the Hebrew Bible, she remained "well instructed in the Jewish religion."[29]

**The Christadelphians**

Throughout this time, Ursula attended Sunday School and went to the Christadelphian meetings with the Sawyer family. Yet, in her attendance there, she did not feel as though the members were pressuring her to join their congregation—which she emphasized twice in her interview.

As such, though she attended Christadelphian Sunday school throughout her years with the Sawyers, Ursula chose to hold to her Jewish heritage. It was for this heritage that her parents had lost their lives—so it was this heritage that she would accept and carry forward.

This choice was not based on her feelings toward Christadelphians—which remain extremely positive, even today. When asked to describe her feelings about Christadelphians, Ursula replied:

> I think they're wonderful people. I really think so. They do good. They do anything they can for other people, and I admire them. . . . Absolutely, I admire them, because what they did—some people I know they had a boarding house, they took in 5 children…You know they couldn't really afford it, but they did that. They were really really wonderful.[30]

**Conclusion**

After the war, Ursula left England in 1947, moving from there to Rhodesia, where one of her aunts had found sanctuary. After a few months, she moved to South Africa where her grandfather and an aunt and uncle had been able to flee before the war had begun. There she met Max Meyer, who had also fled from Germany, and whom she married in 1948. Max was an architect, and the two lived a successful and happy life in

South Africa, building a family together. Their two children eventually both moved to the United States—and Ursula, not wanting to separate again from family, followed them in 1981. She and Max now live in Florida; Ursula is 91, and Max is 93.

Despite the distance, the Meyers and the Sawyers have stayed in contact. Mabel visited Ursula and Max twice in South Africa—staying with them in their house for three months on each visit. Ursula and Max also went to visit Mabel numerous times. They remained in touch until Mabel's death in 1983.

*Ursula Meyer and Max Meyer, revisiting Cape Town, South Africa with Mark Sawyer, 2003.*

Ursula and Mark speak on the phone every month, and Mark, along with his wife, Rachael, has come to visit her. While the Sawyers were still living in England, they came twice to Florida. Ursula and Max came to England twice to visit them. After moving to Australia, the Sawyers visited the Meyers while they were on holiday in Cape Town, South Africa, in 2003.

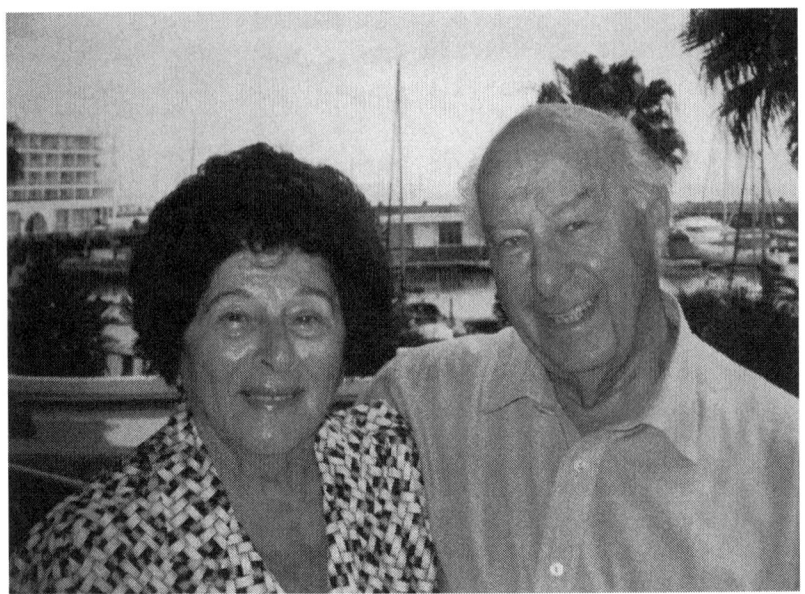

*Ursula and Max in Cape Town, South Africa, 2003.*

For years, whenever Max would hear about Christadelphians, he was generous in his praise. It was because of the willingness of this group that he has "the love of his life."[31] Indeed, it was not just Ursula's life that was affected when this Christadelphian family joined with their community in sheltering Jewish children from Hitler's onslaughts. Ursula now has two children, four grandchildren, and one great grandchild. Truly, the love that was shown her—and the future generations that will come from her—will not be forgotten. Ursula repeatedly said of the Sawyers, "They were wonderful people,"[32] and elaborated on all that they had done for her. Even her cousin, Susan Clapper, née Susanne Eichmann, who came to England on the same Kindertransport train (and whose story will be included, Lord willing, in Volume 2), knew of the Sawyers' kindness. Speaking of Ursula and her foster family, Susanne said, "She also stayed in Birmingham, she went to a family, and they were very good to

*Ursula and Max Meyer, 2016.*

her . . . they were also not Jewish. But they were very good to her."[33]

As for the Sawyers, this feeling of love was certainly mutual—they will not forget Ursula and her family either. As Mark stated in a letter to Max on his 90th birthday:

> I find it pretty emotional to think, as I frequently do, of these ties of friendship and the length of time over which they have lasted. . . . You and Ursula mean a great deal to us and I feel so blessed that our paths in life have crossed, albeit originally in such poignant and terrible circumstances.[34]

---

[1] "The Dawes Plan, the Young Plan, German Reparations, and Inter-allied War Debts," *Office of the Historian, Bureau of Public Affairs, United States Department of State,* accessed May 6, 2016, https://history.state.gov/milestones/1921-1936/dawes.

[2] John M. Carroll, "American Diplomacy in the 1920s," in *Modern American Diplomacy,* ed. John Martin Carroll and George C. Herring (Lanham: SR Books, 2004), 69-70.

3 "Dawes Plan," *Encyclopedia Britannica Online,* accessed May 6, 2016, http://www.britannica.com/event/Dawes-Plan.

4 Ursula Meyer, in discussion with the author, January 26, 2016.

5 More details about this concentration camp in both Ingrid Wuga's biography and the glossary.

6 Ursula Meyer, in discussion with the author, January 26, 2016.

7 Ibid.

8 "Riga," *United States Holocaust Memorial Museum,* last modified January 29, 2016, http://www.ushmm.org/wlc/en/article.php?ModuleId=10005463.

9 Ibid.

10 "Gedenkbuch - Opfer Der Verfolgung Der Juden Unter Der Nationalsozialistischen Gewaltherrschaft in Deutschland 1933-1945," *Das Bundesarchiv*, accessed April 15, 2016, http://www.bundesarchiv.de/gedenkbuch/de854559.

11 "Gedenkbuch - Opfer Der Verfolgung Der Juden Unter Der Nationalsozialistischen Gewaltherrschaft in Deutschland 1933-1945," *Das Bundesarchiv*, accessed April 15, 2016, http://www.bundesarchiv.de/gedenkbuch/de854544.

12 "Gedenkbuch - Opfer Der Verfolgung Der Juden Unter Der Nationalsozialistischen Gewaltherrschaft in Deutschland 1933-1945," *Das Bundesarchiv*, accessed April 15, 2016, http://www.bundesarchiv.de/gedenkbuch/de854556.

13 Archivist at Stutthoff, e-mail message to author, February 24, 2016.

14 "Stutthof," *United States Holocaust Memorial Museum,* last modified January 29, 2016, http://www.ushmm.org/wlc/en/article.php?ModuleId=10005197.

15 Kirsten, Hanus, and Anita Grosz, *Kindertransport Memory Quilt* (Kindertransport Association of North America, 2000), 79.

16 Ibid.

17 Ursula Meyer, in discussion with the author, January 26, 2016.

18 Ibid.

19 Norman Sawyer, quoted in Ursula Meyer, in discussion with the author, January 26, 2016.

20 Mark Sawyer, letter to Max Meyer, March 23, 2012.

[21] Mark Sawyer, e-mail message to author, January 20, 2016.

[22] Mark Sawyer, e-mail message to author, February 22, 2016.

[23] Ibid.

[24] Ibid.

[25] Ursula Meyer, in discussion with the author, January 26, 2016.

[26] Kirsten, Hanus, and Anita Grosz, *Kindertransport Memory Quilt* (Kindertransport Association of North America, 2000), 79.

[27] Ursula Meyer, in discussion with the author, January 26, 2016.

[28] Barry Turner, . . . *And the Policeman Smiled* (London: Bloomsbury, 1990), 246.

[29] Ibid.

[30] Ibid.

[31] Mark Sawyer, "My Big Sister Ursula," *Christadelphiansisters.org,* accessed April 15, 2016, http://www.christadelphiansisters.org/URSULA.HTM.

[32] Ursula Meyer, in discussion with the author, January 26, 2016.

[33] Susan Clapper, *USC Shoah Foundation Institute Testimony of Susan Clapper,* USC Shoah Foundation Interview, November 23, 1995.

[34] Mark Sawyer, letter to Max Meyer, March 23, 2012.

# HANA HOLMAN

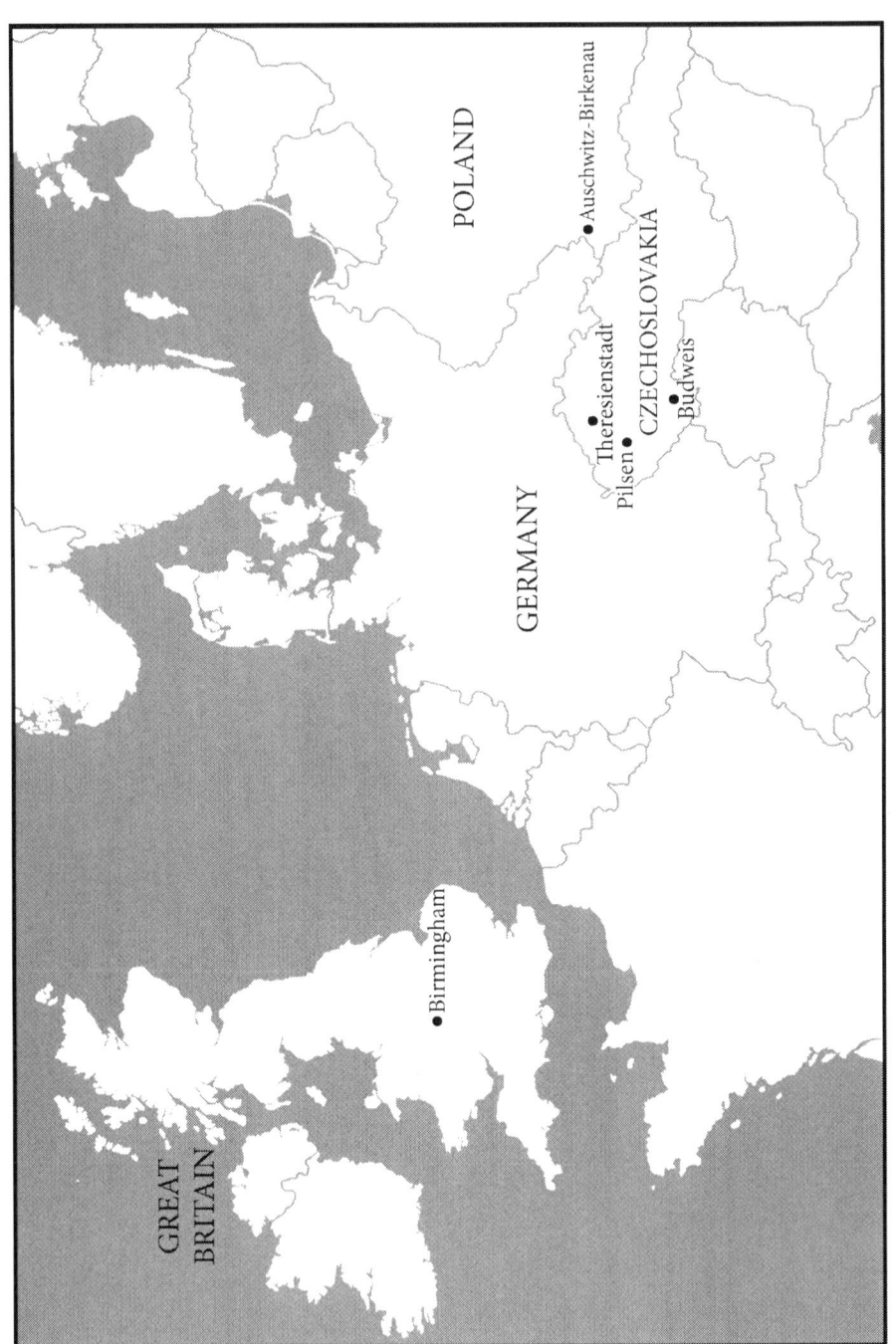

# 4

***

# HANA HOLMAN, NÉE OFNER

In January 1925, Hitler's influence appeared to be slowly increasing. The failure of his Beer Hall Putsch, and his subsequent imprisonment had taken Hitler from being a relatively obscure name to being a well-known figure.[1] Adding to that, by January, he had already been released from prison, having only served eight months of his five-year sentence.

His eight months in jail had been far from terrible. Landsberg Prison, a detention center that resembled an old medieval castle, featured an inner courtyard, meetings rooms, a lending library, and even soccer matches. In prison, Hitler was allotted a suite of rooms on the second floor, giving him a central sitting area, and private bedrooms, which were assigned to his fellow revolutionaries.[2] These eight months also provided Hitler with the time to write up his poisonous thoughts and create a book—the notorious *Mein Kampf*—published in 1925, the year following his release.[3]

In the ensuing months, Hitler's influence, while rising, was curbed by a public speaking ban that was levied upon him by a number of German states throughout 1925 and 1926.[4] As the year progressed, things began to look worse for the Nazi Party.

Hitler was a radical figure, who was gaining notoriety, yet whose potential for danger and control in Germany appeared to be in check.

143

But, the Ofner family did not even live in Germany. In 1925 Czechoslovakia, Hitler's influence was miniscule. For a Jewish family such as the Ofners, life was happy and comfortable, and in 1925, it brought the blessing of a firstborn daughter.

*Hana and her father, Ernst Ofner.*

Hana Miriam Ofner[5] was born on January 23 in the city of Budweis, Czechoslovakia, to Ernst and Marta Ofner. Her childhood was joyful, as was her relationship with her parents. Though her parents required obedience and respect from their children, both were also full of kindness.

Four years later, in 1929, the family celebrated the birth of another girl, Ruth Ofner. Ernst and Marta loved their two daughters immensely.

*Ernst Ofner*

Their house in Budweis was an apartment above the Kafkas—who were Marta's parents. As such, Hana grew up surrounded by family. Not only did they live above one set of grandparents, but her other set of grandparents, the Ofners, also lived nearby. The Kafkas were coffee importers, so whenever one went into their basement, the smell of coffee would permeate the air. It was there, in that basement, that Hana first learned to ride her bike and where she and her sister loved to go to get little treats from their *babička,* the Czech word for grandmother.

The Ofner side of the family was quite religious. Hana's grandfather, Jacob Ofner, kept the Jewish traditions and passed on that reverence of God to his son Ernst. Every week, Ernst and Marta attended synagogue. Every Friday night and Saturday, they kept the Sabbath. In fact, one of Ernst's cousins, Rudolf Ferda, was a rabbi. He taught Hana's religious classes in school, and even after he was deported to the Theresienstadt ghetto in 1942, he continued to perform his religious services—conducting weddings and bar mitzvahs and offering spiritual encouragement until he was sent to Auschwitz in 1944.

For Hana, Judaism was both a religion and a culture. As her daughter, Susan Waite wrote:

> Life was full and happy with many family gatherings, celebrations, outings, and visits to the synagogue. At Budweis, the synagogue was very close to where they lived. Every Sabbath, they put on their best clothes,

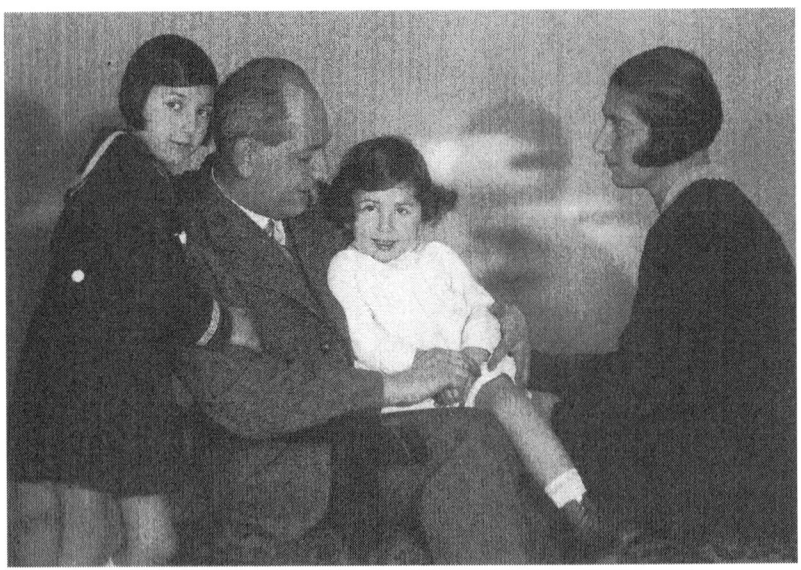

*An Ofner family photograph: Hana, Ernst, Ruth, and Marta.*

146

Ernst picked up his prayer shawl and they walked across the narrow road to the old stone synagogue. There, Ernst walked to one side, to sit alone, as women and men were not allowed to sit together. Marta and the two girls sat upstairs and listened quietly to the mellow singing of the Cantor.[6]

Even today, Hana Holman begins her prayers in Hebrew, *Sh'ma Yisrael Adonai Eloheinu . . .*

Hana's days in Budweis were filled with child-like simplicity and enthusiasm. She and her sister spent their summers walking in the surrounding forests. This was something that Marta, their mother, encouraged and something that Hana and Ruth greatly enjoyed. Children, Marta fervently believed, needed to walk to get enough exercise, so she made sure that Hana and Ruth walked as much as they could. It was in these walks through the forest that Hana formed some of her fonder memories—memories of looking for berries and mushrooms. In fact, years after the war, Hana was in her late 60s and traveled to the Czech Republic. There she found herself drawn to recreating the memory—so one of the main things that she wanted to do while in the country was walk through the forest and look for mushrooms. Indeed, these were happy and carefree days.

When the girls were not walking through the forest, they frequented a few other places. They sauntered along the Moldau and Malse river banks, or visited Samson's Fountain in the large town square. In the summer, they loved to swim in the river and play in the nearby park called *Hajecek*, where they were amused by small animals frolicking in a cage.

During the winter, the ground was always covered in snow. Instead of walking from place to place, Hana and Ruth took advantage of the weather. They grew up ice skating and skiing with their parents—Hana could even remember pushing a small wooden chair in front of her on the ice to help her keep her balance before she grew accustomed to the slipperiness of ice skating. Once she could keep her balance, she kept her hands warm by skating with a tiny hot water bottle inside her fur muff—just another small, yet sweet, memory she had of her early years.

At the same time though, another aspect of her childhood was different from what might be expected. Hana did not have any chores. Many household tasks in the Ofner home were done by the family's live-in help, a young girl named Sofie. Sofie made most of the meals, washed and ironed the clothes, and tidied the apartment. This too added to the carefree nature of Hana's childhood.

Indeed, the first ten years of her life were both memorable and fun. Hana's parents loved her dearly, and life was good.

**Pilsen**

In 1935, when Hana was 10 years old, Ernst and Marta moved the family to Pilsen—a move that brought them closer to Prague, the capital of Czechoslovakia. However, this was also a move that would bring them closer to Hitler and his Nazi violence.

In 1938, after the *Anschluss*—the sudden German occupation of Austria—Hitler set his attention to what was called the *Sudetenland,* or portions of Czechoslovakia, mainly in the northern, southern, and western regions of the country, where the population was primarily German speakers.

Later in 1938, through the Munich Pact, negotiated with Hitler by the French and the British (but not by the Czechs), these portions of Czechoslovakia were "given" to the Germans in

*Hana Ofner at 14 and Ruth Ofner at 10.*

order to reunite ethnic Germans with the Fatherland. Thus, while the world looked on, Hitler marched his troops into Czechoslovakia and redrew the country's borders.[7]

The city of Budweis was not part of the *Sudetenland*. Pilsen, however, was right on the border.

It was at this point that Hana's peaceful and comfortable life— along with that of her sister Ruth—was about to change in a way that no one then would have ever expected.

In just one year, Hana and Ruth would say goodbye to their parents, their grandparents, and their aunts and uncles for what they did not know would be the last time. They would board a train and travel to a country whose language they had never spoken, and they would live with two separate families—families they had never met.

Yet despite the agony and the loneliness that was to come, Hana Ofner has been able to look back and see the hand of God leading her through it all.

## The German Occupation

When Hana and Ruth lived in Pilsen, their apartment was directly opposite the old synagogue, which was not in fact all that old at the time. Completed in 1893, the synagogue is today known as the "Great Synagogue," is the second largest in all of Europe, and the third largest in the world.[8] Being almost totally destroyed during the Nazi era, the building underwent extensive renovation during the late 20th century. Thus, the building that stands today almost perfectly resembles building that stood across the street from Hana Ofner's childhood

*A modern photograph of the synagogue in Pilsen.*

*Top: A modern view of the Pilsen synagogue from the Ofners' apartment building.*
*Bottom: A modern photograph of the Ofners' apartment building.*

home. As Hana's daughter, Susan, recounted, Hana and Ruth could lie in bed and see the engraving of the Ten Commandments that had been placed between the synagogue's two towers.

Unfortunately, life in Pilsen was not the same as life in Budweis. It was not carefree. After the family's move, Ernst took a position as a lawyer with the Pilsen Council, and Hana attended the Girls' Higher Elementary School. A few months after the move, however, the Germans arrived.

Hitler annexed the *Sudetenland* in October 1938.

Between the time that the *Sudetenland* was annexed and when Hana and Ruth left for England in June, the Nazis overran Pilsen. No longer could Hana look out the window of her bedroom and simply see the synagogue and its engraving of the Ten Commandments. After the occupation, Hana also saw tanks stationed outside the building: the synagogue had been transformed from a place of worship into a place of violence.

All this took place only a few months before Hana and Ruth Ofner would depart for England.

**Preparing to Leave**

Though Hana and Ruth did not know it, their father had been working behind the scenes. After losing his job when the German occupation began, Ernst started traveling to Prague and working with a young English stockbroker named Nicholas Winton. Ernst, working for the British Committee for Children in Prague, helped organize the children's departure on the Czech side, while Nicholas Winton led the effort to organize the departure of the children on the British side.

Ernst's involvement in this work ultimately helped save his children.

On a pleasant day in June, a young boy sped down the street on his bicycle. He was carrying a telegram for Marta Ofner, Hana's mother. The girls were unaware of what awaited them, but with Ernst's involvement in the movement for refugee children, Marta already knew what the telegram said. Her two daughters—her only children—were about to leave. And for their sake, she would have to allow it.

The train was scheduled to leave on June 30, 1939.

As the day drew closer, Ernst and Marta sought to prepare their two children as best as they could for the new world that awaited them. Ruth was given her father's *tallit,* or prayer shawl, and Hana was given her mother's fur muff. As a final token, Marta took her little wristwatch with a red leather strap and put it on Hana's wrist.

Hana was selected by a family named Warre. They were Christadelphians. Ruth was selected by the Browns. They were not. Neither of the girls knew, however, that they would not be together. Before they left, the girls were assured that their parents would do everything in their power to follow them in a few months' time. Though they would be separated, it would not be for long.

Thus, when June 30 came, Hana and Ruth were put on the train with 669 other children and began their trip for Britain.

The only thing Hana remembered about the train trip was waving goodbye to her parents.

She would never see them again.

She was 14 years old, and Ruth was 10.

## Hana's Family

After leaving Pilsen, Hana and Ruth continued to write to Ernst and Marta and received letters from them in return. This correspondence ended, however, when their parents were "resettled" in Theresienstadt (Terezin)—a ghetto within the Czech border that the Nazis used primarily as a transit camp for deportations to extermination, concentration, and forced-labor camps. It had characteristics of both ghettos and concentration camps and was a facility the Nazis used to deceive the world. This is the camp that was infamously visited by the Red Cross—the ghetto that the Nazis cleaned up, decorated, and beautified for that visit. But the whole thing was a sham. Life in Theresienstadt was sordid, cramped, and diseased. Approximately 140,000 Jews were deported to Theresienstadt. Nearly 90,000 of those were deported east—to almost certain death. And about 33,000 of them died in the camp itself.[9]

After the war, Hana and Ruth learned of their parents' fate. From Pilsen, Ernst and Marta were sent to Theresienstadt, along with other family members. After two years there, they were deported to Auschwitz where they perished.

This terrible truth was revealed to Hana when one day, sometime after the war, she received an official-looking letter. It stated the facts simply: Her parents had been killed at Auschwitz in October 1944.

The camp was liberated in January 1945.

One of the only tangible memorials that Hana has of her parents is the following letter—written by Ernst Ofner on July 7, 1939, one week after Hana and Ruth left Pilsen. It was written in Czech and then translated into English in Czechoslovakia. Below is that exact English translation:

Remark written at the top: "Hanna should not be allowed to read this letter."

Esteemed Mr. and Mrs. Warre,

As the father of your present foster-child Hanna from Pilsen, I beg to express to you my deepest gratitude for your generosity and kindness with which you have received our child. I assure you that my child Hanna is all that I have and she represents all my happiness in life, and this, what is my life, is now with you. Whereas my other child, which means to me as much, is now with Mr. Brown, 54 Hannon Rd, Kings Heath. You, as gentle people, will understand what it means to send beloved children into a strange world. How much pain and tears are in this. You will imagine under what pressure such a step could be resolved. I assure you that since, my eyes have not been dry and I had no sleep in the night, (but my child must never know this). My sense of duty only could compel me to save the children from a life which would be for them without honour and dignity.

They shall grow up to become straight and believing and they should not lose their human dignity and a surrounding which would deprive them of it.

They shall not live in fear and flight for being Jews, of the people described in the Bible. And so I am crying daily tears for my beloved children.

But I trust in the Lord that all our sacrifices shall not be in vain because I know that good and gentle people have taken care of my child, and they will educate and care for it in my stead. Our Lord did not wish that humanity should be disgraced, he has provided angels which will not leave them and such angels are you Mr. and Mrs. Warre and Mr. and Mrs. Brown. I beg you with all my might not to leave our children Hanna and Ruth in whatever chance in life as long until we shall be again reunited. It is our daily and hourly prayer to the Almighty Lord.

We shall try either to have the children follow us or to follow them, wherever fate may drive us to. Not until then our life shall be again happy.

You cannot imagine how happy our family life has been and how all this has now been destroyed. Please protect our children before needs and disgrace, in peace and in war. Make them happy, satisfied and fit for life and leave them to remain Jews because we all love our suffering nation which we will not deceive against all persecutions. To be Jew is also to be humane and this is how we have also educated our children. You will convince yourself that they are made of good material. To make this good in them grow, will be your task, difficult but not ungrateful and you may be sure of the Lord's benediction for it.

And as long as we live, you may be sure of our deepest gratitude. By taking care of my children you have proved that you belong to a large and wise nation which will live forever and always win. We are the grateful parents of Hanna and Ruth. I request you to kindly send this letter on to the address of Mr. Brown too.[10]

## In England

After two days and many tears, the girls arrived in London. It was July 1, 1939. And here, after separating from their parents, the girls' hope of staying together as sisters was shattered. It was in London that Hana and Ruth learned that each would indeed be alone in this new country. From London, both girls were taken to Birmingham. Mr. and Mrs. Warre ran a haberdashery and millinery shop on Coventry Road; Mr. and Mrs. Brown lived a few miles away.

Hana knew five words in English: "Yes," "No," and "I am hungry." The first day she met the Warres, she was asked to fetch a bucket of coal—something which she had never been asked to do in Czechoslovakia. Sofie had always taken care of these types of tasks.

Certainly this new life was not going to be the carefree one she had known back in Budweis.

*A Warre family photograph. From left to right: Maud Warre, Joan Warre (daughter), Herbert Warre, Hana Ofner.*

**The Warres' House**

Nevertheless, though her first day with the Warres may have been a bit foreboding, Mr. and Mrs. Warre were extremely kind to her. They were Christadelphians, moved by their beliefs to open their house to a 14-year-old Jewish refugee. Though they were elderly, they brought Hana into the family and treated her like their own daughter. In fact, when they later found out that she had a sister, they, just as Hana had been, were quite upset that they had not been given the opportunity to care for both girls. Eventually, they attempted to bring Ruth into their family as well, so that Hana and Ruth would no longer have to be separated, but the Browns had grown too attached to their foster daughter and refused.

Despite this refusal, Hana and Ruth were still able to see each other (although the Browns forbade them from speaking Czech). Hana worked in the Warres' shop and during the war became a bus conductress. Through her jobs, she was able to earn some extra money, with which she visited her sister. As often as she could, Hana left two shilling pieces with Ruth.

*Ruth at age 10 and Hana at age 14 in England.*

Life was by no means easy. Along with being separated from her family, Hana had to work hard, and Great Britain was at war. There were food shortages, and the Germans dropped bombs on the city of Birmingham. Hana sold many black gloves and hats in those years—a testament to all the women who had become widows. At one point, an incendiary bomb destroyed the house next to the Warres, but by God's providence, Hana and her foster parents were spared. They spent the air raids underneath the large oak table in their dining room, sleeping there on the floor. The family suffered through the bombing together.

*Hana as a bus conductress in England.*

## The Christadelphians

But it was not only the difficulties that they faced together. Because they treated her as their daughter, Herbert and Maud Warre involved Hana in one of their daily family activities: the daily Bible readings. Each day, many Christadelphian families around the world read from a Bible reading planner; this planner allows them to read through the entire Bible in one year. The Warres did their Bible readings together as a family—thus, as their daughter, Hana participated in this. On Sundays, as a family, they all attended the Christadelphian meetings, and though Hana was Jewish, she "loved to sing the hymns."[11] It was partly this daily Bible reading and the weekly singing of hymns that Hana credited with her learning English.

Hana Ofner felt as though living with the Warres and being introduced to the Christadelphian community was a blessing. Though she had parted with her natural family, she found among the Christadelphians a spiritual family. In the words of her daughter:

> Although Hana missed her parents, she received much love from the Christadelphian community. She attended the Meetings, had invitations out for meals and was surrounded with friendship and loving-kindness.[12]

> She especially remembers how kind they were to her ... putting a hot water bottle in her bed ... [at] night.[13]

And even more than finding a community, as the years passed after the war, Hana found that her Christadelphian family and her belief in both the Hebrew and Christian portions of the Bible helped to bring her a feeling of peace. Again, her daughter Susan stated:

> My mother's Christadelphian faith certainly helped her get over losing her parents in the Holocaust. She has always felt that God has looked after her in her life, but the big thing is the ability to forgive. . . .

My mother never blamed the Germans. . . . She had friends from Germany. She has always had the attitude of helping others because somebody took her in. She had two foster children (one in England and one in Australia) and looked after them for quite a few years. All this was a healing time for my mother. By doing things for others, it helped her get over what had happened. . . .

Whatever happens she says it is in God's hands. So this attitude helped her get over losing her parents and her old way of life, and she was grateful to have found the Truth.[14]

Hana's Christadelphian community and her Christadelphian beliefs are extremely precious to her. Not only did these give her a feeling of belonging and a family, but also they helped her heal. Through these beliefs, she was able to overcome animosity and was able to feel as though all of her life, no matter what it was that happened, was "in God's hands."

Thus, after a few years of living with Herbert and Maud Warre, Hana decided to join the Christadelphian body through baptism. It was a special night for her. A few months later, *The Christadelphian* magazine printed an announcement of her baptism:

BIRMINGHAM (Small Heath) ...We had a unique pleasure in baptizing on Dec. 20 a Jewish and a Gentile candidate, Miss Hana Miriam Ofner (17), who came from Czechoslovakia as a refugee child some four years ago and has been under the loving care of sis. Warre and has attended the Sunday School; also Gerald William Griffin (17), son of bro. and sis. H. Griffin and grandson of bro. and sis. Fell (Central), all three generations being present. May our young bro. and sis. endure to the end.[15]

Hana Ofner and Gerald Griffin—a Jew and a gentile—were baptized together on December 20, 1943. Hana had lived in England and with the Warres for three-and-a-half years and was 17 years old. At the time of writing this publication, she is 91 and is still a fervent Christadelphian (having been baptized for 73 years), even attending the daily Bible readings at the Christadelphian care home in which she lives.

Nevertheless, she was clear that she never felt pressure from the Warres to join their faith. Her father had requested that she hold to her Jewish heritage—and so she was not forced to become a Christadelphian. Instead, Hana later stated that the Warres' beliefs and their faith were simply a "way of life."[16] When she joined their family, she saw that way of life in action, and then, a few years later, she made the choice to make that way her own.

## Conclusion

Two years after her own baptism, in 1945, Hana Ofner married Kenneth Holman, a man who had also chosen to join the Christadelphian community (ironically, through the efforts of the Christadelphian family who had met Hana when she first arrived in England). Together, they raised their children in that same "way of life." For Hana Holman, what she learned at the Warres' house is something of eternal value. Susan wrote:

> The ecclesia and her family have been the most important things in her life. At Olivet Aged care she attends the Bible Readings group every day. . . . She has attended the Breaking of Bread meeting every Sunday . . . [and also enjoys] listening in via her computer to

*Top: Ken and Hana Holman*
*Bottom: The Holman family, just before their move to Australia, 1961. From left to right: David, Ken, Hana, and Susan.*

Canterbury's memorial service. She always says it's her life. . . . and a way of life.[17]

Today, many of Hana's children and grandchildren have also made that choice to join the Christadelphians—a religious body whose beliefs about the Jews compelled them to act during the tragic years of the 1930s and 1940s, and specifically caused Herbert and Maud Warre to open up their home to Hana.

*Hana Holman at the Olivet care home in Australia.*

Through that action, not only was one life saved, but the possibility of many more was preserved. Thus, as Hana reflects today upon her 91 years, she certainly feels as though God has had a plan for her life—and that although it was not at all what she had expected when growing up, indeed He has been working all along.

---

[1] Nicholas John Cull, David Holbrook Culbert, and David Welch, "Mein Kampf," in *Propaganda and Mass Persuasion: A Historical Encyclopedia, 1500 to the Present* (Santa Barbara: ABC-CLIO, 2003), 243.

[2] Timothy Ryback, *Hitler's Private Library* (New York: Alfred A. Knopf, 2008), 63.

[3] Ibid.

[4] Detlef Mühlberger, *Hitler's Voice: Organisation and Development of the Nazi Party* (Oxford: Lang, 2004), 110.

[5] Hana spells her name with only one "n," despite the fact that it occasionally is spelled with two on documents she did not author.

[6] Susan Waite, "How My Mother, Sis. Hana Holman, Learnt the Truth," *Christadelphiansisters.org,* accessed February 14, 2016, http://www.christadelphiansisters.org/HANA.HTM.

[7] "Sudetenland," *Encyclopedia Britannica Online,* accessed April 16, 2016, http://www.britannica.com/place/Sudetenland.

[8] "The Great Synagogue," *Municipality of the City of Pilsen,* accessed May 3, 2016, http://www.pilsen.eu/tourist/visit/top-tourist-destinations/the-great-synagogue/the -great-synagogue.aspx.

[9] "Theresienstadt," *United States Holocaust Memorial Museum,* last modified January 29, 2016, http://www.ushmm.org/wlc/en/article.php?ModuleId=10005424.

[10] Ernst Ofner, letter to Herbert and Maud Warre, July 7, 1939. In possession of Susan Waite. Translated into English in Czechoslovakia.

[11] Susan Waite, "How My Mother, Sis. Hana Holman, Learnt the Truth," *Christadelphiansisters.org,* accessed February 14, 2016, http://www.christadelphiansisters.org/HANA.HTM.

[12] Ibid.

[13] Susan Waite, e-mail message to author, January 22, 2016.

[14] Susan Waite, e-mail message to author, February 6, 2016.

[15] F. G. Owen, "Intelligence," *The Christadelphian*, February 1943, 38.

[16] Susan Waite, e-mail message to author, January 22, 2016.

[17] Susan Waite, e-mail message to author, January 22, 2016.

# CHARLES BORGER

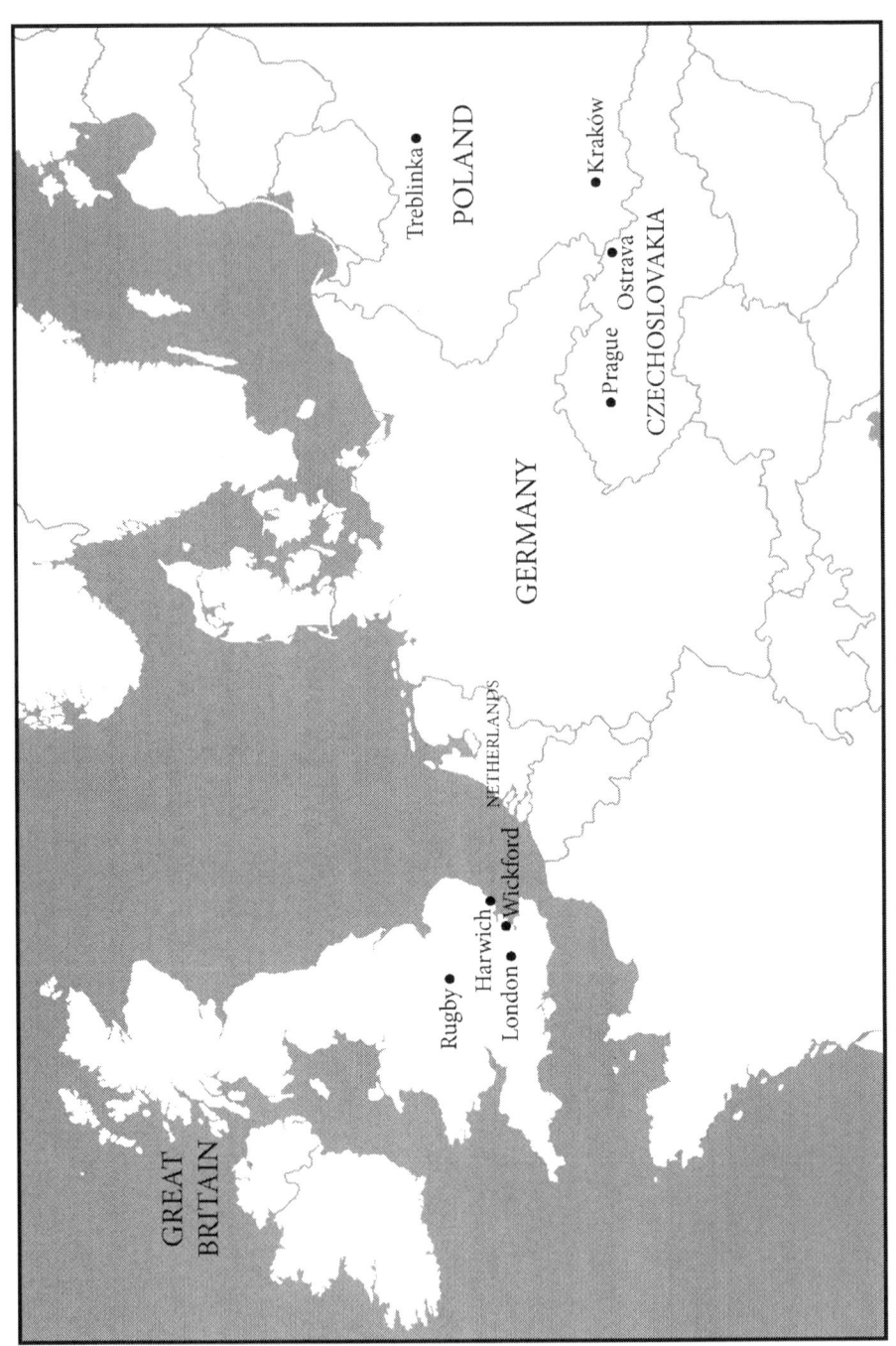

# 5

---

# CHARLES BORGER

In October 1925, the nations of Europe came together to negotiate the Pact of Locarno—a series of agreements, signed in Locarno, Switzerland, which were meant to guarantee peace to the nations of Western Europe. In the agreements, it was declared that the German-Belgian and Franco-German borders were fixed and would not be moved. Germany, Belgium, and France would never attack one another except in "legitimate defense" or in response to a League of Nations obligation.[1]

The peace affirmed at Locarno was deemed a genuine one. In contrast to Germany feeling forced to sign a treaty, as it had with Versailles in 1919, the Locarno agreements were negotiated with Germany as an equal. For the next six years, before Japan invaded Manchuria in 1931, Locarno became a symbol for peace in world politics, and it felt as though the world had finally achieved lasting peace. In fact, whenever two countries were able to work together in the spirit of cooperation, it was typical to speak of "Locarno spirit."[2]

At the same time, though the nation of Czechoslovakia had been created with the dissolution of the Austro-Hungarian Empire at the end of World War I,[3] the country's borders were not included in this pact of inviolability. Rather, the Locarno Pact provided for arbitration between Germany and Czechoslovakia—leaving the latter's borders open to discussion. Additionally, it was clear that Great Britain was

169

prepared to defend either Belgium or France, but not those nations on Germany's eastern border: Poland and Czechoslovakia.[4]

The agreements, although providing a semblance of peace for approximately 10 years, were unfortunately only a foreshadowing of the way the *Sudetenland* of Czechoslovakia would be given over to Germany via the Munich Pact in the late 1930s.

On October 8, 1925, the very same month that this treaty was signed, Charles Borger, or Karel Borger as he was named at that time, was born.

Four years later, on March 30, 1929, the Borger family welcomed another child, this time a girl, and named her Edit.

Charles and Edit were born to Hermine and Alfred Borger in Ostrava, Czechoslovakia, a city only a few miles from the Polish border, approximately two hours west of Kraków, Poland, and three hours northeast of Vienna, Austria. Charles and Edit both lived there for their childhood years until leaving for England in 1939.

Alfred Borger was a bookkeeper, and Hermine was a homemaker. In thinking back on his childhood, Charles harbors pleasant feelings about those 14 years that he spent with his mother, father, and sister in Ostrava: "My first 14 years were spent there, so very many family memories. I don't remember anything specific, but we had a very middle class, very happy household until 1939 . . . a pleasant and happy household, that's all I can say."[5]

These convivial years were spent without the interference of antisemitism—at least, before the Germans invaded the non-*Sudetenland* portion of Czechoslovakia on March 15,

1939. The Germans had occupied the *Sudetenland* for six months by then, since October 1938. Charles attended a school with Jewish and non-Jewish students, and most of his friends were not Jewish. Charles was simply Czech—he did not feel he was different from his peers, nor did they seem to feel that they were different from him.

Because the atmosphere was so different in Czechoslovakia than it was in Germany, Charles had no experience of *Kristallnacht*, which took place in November 1938, before the Germans came to Ostrava in March 1939. Nevertheless, on that fateful day in March, when the Germans overtook the *Sudetenland*, everything changed, just as it had in Austria with the *Anschluss*. Charles explained how life was dramatically altered:

> As soon as the Germans walked in, there were some attacks on shops, and all the synagogues in our town were burned down the day after they walked in. After, the restrictions came in on what the Jewish people could participate in. [Students] finished their schooling in June of 1939, but after that, you would not have been allowed to go back in September of the new school year. We were not allowed to go to swimming pools. There were some restrictions on transport and such like. In time, in between the German invasion in March and before I left in the end of July, things were coming in that were not very pleasant.[6]

## Winton's List

There were only five months between the German occupation of Ostrava and Charles and Edit's escape to the United Kingdom. With the occupation, life deteriorated so rapidly, that the Borgers quickly recognized the grim future for Jews in

Czechoslovakia, and sought to send both of their children out of the country.

At that time, Charles had an uncle, Alfred Gedudig, who lived in Prague—the base of operations for Nicholas Winton and his team. Winton, along with those who worked with him, brought 669 Czech children out of Hitler's clutches. Charles and Edit, through the determination and efforts of their uncle Alfred, fortunately found themselves on Winton's list.

Charles and Edit's names were eventually passed on, probably via Nicholas Winton, to Alan Overton. Overton worked to find homes for these two children amongst his Christadelphian contacts. Initially, he could only find a home for Edit, who was chosen by the Fawcett family because they sought a young girl as a companion for their young daughter Hazel. Dr. Chana Revell Kotzin, in her doctoral thesis on "Christian Responses in Britain to Jewish Refugees from Europe: 1933–1939," read through several of the letters sent between Mrs. Fawcett and Alan Overton:

> Sister Fawcett offered to take a Jewish girl around 11 years old to be a companion and friend to her daughter Hazel. Asking to choose from several girls she concluded that considering the situation she would also 'take whatever he has'. Overton replied by enclosing the particulars of one girl that he thought would be suitable.[7]

The "one girl" was Edit Borger. At the same time, however, Overton needed a place for two children, not just one. Therefore, when he sent information to the Fawcett family about Edit Borger, he also made an enquiry:

> [He asked] whether she knew of anyone who would be interested in a boy. 'If there is no one you know likely,

*Top: Mr. and Mrs. Fawcett, 1939.*
*Bottom: Hazel and Aidan Fawcett, 1939.*

please let me have the enclosure back soon as the time is very short.' Fawcett, in turn, took up the issue of the boy Overton wanted to place. As the brother of the girl they had already agreed to take, Fawcett asked him to 'send a form to us at once, we will fill it in and so not part brother and sister. They have enough parting to suffer without that and a little extra sacrifice will not kill us—when we work for Him that gave his life for us.'[8]

Both children were taken by the Fawcett family—because the Fawcetts were moved by a desire to do good for the Jewish people, working for "Him that gave his life for us." They also had a son, Aidan, who was approximately Charles's age, and so their two children could be playmates with the Borger children.

After hearing that the Fawcetts would sponsor their children, Hermine and Alfred Borger prepared Charles and Edit to leave. They purchased new clothes and gave them bedding to take with them. They also made sure to supply them with food for the journey.

At midnight, on July 31, 1939, Charles and Edit Borger, ages 13 and 10, said goodbye to their parents and stepped onto a train in Prague.

They would never see their parents again.

## The Journey

The train left Czechoslovakia, traveled through Germany, and then stopped in Holland. In Holland, they were met with a welcome reception: "I remember when we went to Holland and crossed the Dutch border, we were greeted by ladies with fruit and drinks. . . . I was quite excited about the ferry journey from Holland to England."⁹

After Holland, they took a ferry to Harwich, England, and from Harwich, they took a train to London, where they were met by Mrs. Fawcett. Mr. and Mrs. Fawcett lived in Wickford, about 30 miles east of London.

## Charles and Edit's Family

A little over one month after the children had arrived, Hermine Borger wrote the following letter to Mr. and Mrs. Fawcett. In it can be seen a mother's struggle to take care of the immediate concerns regarding their diet and their linens, but at the same time, agonizing over the future of her only two children. This letter was sent to the Fawcetts in English, and therefore, likely translated into English in Czechoslovakia:

7th August 1939

Dear Mrs. Fawcett,

I received your kind letter. I thank you very much for the hearty reception you have given my children Karel and Edit and it is a great consolation to me that both children are together. Our dear God will reward you for your deed.

We had never sent away our children if the situation had not forced us. Unfortunately there was no possibility for them to learn something.

My husband is a clerk, until now he works, but I don't know how long he will keep his position. We have always lived under modest conditions and we were only anxious to care for the future of the children. They have both learned very well and I should like to ask you to write me if there is a possibility for them to attend the school. At the beginning they will have perhaps difficulties with the language but I hope they will overcome them very soon.

Referring to the food I should like to ask you to have patience with the children and I would be very glad if they would accustom to eat vegetables; they didn't like it here too. In reply to your question about the food, I will tell you that they had meat 3 or 4 times weekly, the most they liked was chicken with rice, potatoes and stewed fruit. But they like also sweet dishes, for inst. all sorts of dumplings. For supper they liked best bread and butter or fat /in winter/ and fruit. But I hope they will accustom also very soon to your food, not to cause you so much trouble.

Besides I should like to ask you to leave at first the children sleep together until they will get more acquainted with your children. At home they slept in one room but each in his own bed. I shall write later the children they must sleep parted.

Referring to the linen I must tell you that I have done that all in great hurry because I was informed very late and had only two days time. Will you kindly excuse, if something will not suit or should not be in order. One part is made in a bigger size so that the children should wear it later too.

I thank you very much for your words, which were a great comfort to me. You as a mother can imagine and feel it very well, how hard it was to me to send the children abroad and how much I care for them.

Now I ask you very heartily to inform me, if the children are good and if they are longing home.

Again, my heartiest thanks and many regards to you and your husband,

Yours faithfully

Hermine Borger[10]

On October 5, 1942, Hermine and Alfred Borger were deported to the Treblinka extermination camp. Treblinka was split into multiple camps, much like Auschwitz-Birkenau, although Treblinka was only composed of two camps rather than three. Treblinka I was established as a forced labor camp in November 1941. As part of the so-called "Final Solution," Treblinka II was set up in July 1942. Unlike Treblinka I, Treblinka II was an extermination camp. Those who arrived, unless chosen to work as part of the small staff, were gassed upon arrival. The Germans murdered between 870,000 and 925,000 Jews at the killing center.[11]

Both Hermine and Alfred Borger were gassed at the Treblinka killing center.[12]

Hermine was 41 and Alfred was 47.

Uncle Alfred, who had helped organize the children's escape to England, was deported to Auschwitz in 1944, where he was murdered in the gas chambers. He was 45.[13]

After the war, Charles attempted to find out about his family's fate: "As soon as a transport became available, I went back to my home town, to see any news, but there was no news of any member of the family. They all perished in the camps. Everyone. There was not a single person who survived."[14]

## The Christadelphians

Charles lived with the Fawcetts until mid-1940. Edit continued to live with them for another 15 months, after which she went to live with Hermine Borger's cousin, who had managed to escape Czechoslovakia and start a home in England. Charles described his few months with the Fawcett family:

> They were kind, originally they only wanted a girl as a companion to their daughter. . . . They did have a son about the same age as me, so they decided to sponsor me as well. It was a bit hard for them . . . Mr. Fawcett was just a salesman in a shop, so it was quite a strain on their finances and things, to look after us, but they did look after us very kindly.[15]

*Edit and Charles Borger, 1939.*

While living with the Fawcetts, Charles attended the local school at the beginning of the school year in 1939. He attended that school until his 14th birthday, in October of that year, when he was sent to be an apprentice to an agricultural company. However, repairing agricultural machinery was not work that he enjoyed. Rather than doing manual work, he had always been interested in furthering his education. As such, around April 1940, after living with the Fawcetts for about 10 months, Mr. and Mrs. Fawcett arranged for Charles to stay at Little Thorn, the Christadelphian hostel in Rugby, where it was easier for him to continue his education.

All throughout his time with the Fawcetts, Charles attended the Christadelphian meetings, just like so many others:

> As far as living with the Fawcetts, we had to go every Sunday . . . to attend the Christadelphian meetings . . . but certainly there was no other pressure. There were some other Christadelphians living nearby who also were kind to us, they donated a bicycle to me, and a few other things . . . they were very sympathetic.[16]

**Rugby Hostel**

At the hostel, Charles was surrounded by a number of other Jewish boys. It was a good experience for him, and he enjoyed his time there:

> It was a good atmosphere of course, we were about a dozen boys . . . most of them were Czech, some were German, and Alan Overton was very much involved. And most of the boys went to various schools. Because it was the end of the school year, I initially went to Coventry . . . a friend of Overton's, another Christadelphian, who was running a shop, and manpower was very short at the time, so I was sent to

*Top: A reunion of the "boys" who lived in the Rugby hostel, 1998.*
*Charles is third from the left.*
*Bottom: Charles and his wife visiting Hazel Fawcett, 1998.*

help in the shop, and I stayed there for quite a while, and continued my studies at night school. . . . We were a close-knit community.[17]

We kept in touch with the boys from the hostel and the Overton family . . . we had a reunion of the boys in 1998 in which the Overton family also took part . . . we went to Rugby for the reunion . . . it was quite an eventful event.[18]

At the time of this writing, Charles, now in his 90s, is the only one of the boys who lived in this hostel who is still alive, the last two others having passed away in 2015.

Charles lived in this hostel for three years, from 1940 to 1943. There, he was well aware of the Christadelphian influence, but unlike his time at the Fawcetts, he did not attend the Christadelphian services.

**After the War**

Charles turned 18 in 1943 and volunteered to join the Czech Army. He was assigned to a special mission that took him through Iran, Iraq, and other parts of the Middle East. Eventually, he came to Prague, arriving there in May 1945, only five days after the war had ended. Edit also made her way back to Prague, returning there three months after Charles had.

In 1947, Charles returned to England, where he met the woman who would become his wife. They married, and then in 1949, they moved to Australia. Just one year earlier, soon after the new nation had been declared, Edit moved to Israel.

After the war, Charles and Edit lost contact with the Fawcetts. Nevertheless, Charles did not forget them, though he only lived with them for 10 months. In 1984, when Charles and his wife went back to visit England, they tried to trace the Fawcett family and were able to establish contact once again with Hazel, Mr. and Mrs. Fawcett's daughter. From then on, with every trip the Borgers made to the United Kingdom, up until Hazel's death in 2009, Charles and his wife made sure to stop and visit with her.

**Conclusion**

Charles and Edit Borger's lives were saved when their parents made an agonizing choice. But, moved by their belief that the situation in Czechoslovakia would not soon improve, Hermine and Alfred chose to do what they could to spare their two children. At the same time, Charles and Edit found a home through the efforts of faithful Christadelphians who also felt compelled by their beliefs, despite the hardships that having two extra children entailed, to do good for these young people. Indeed, these are stories that stand upon the foundation of belief—and the way in which beliefs bring about actions.

Perhaps, then, one of the most important questions to ask ourselves is how our own beliefs affect our actions—and whether these beliefs are truly influencing our actions for good.

---

[1] "Pact of Locarno,"*Encyclopedia Britannica Online,* accessed April 22, 2016, http://www.britannica.com/event/Pact-of-Locarno.

[2] V. N. Khanna, *International Relations, 4E* (Vikas Publishing House, 2009), 72.

[3] "Czechoslovakia," *United States Holocaust Memorial Museum,* last modified January 29, 2016, https://www.ushmm.org/wlc/en/article.php?ModuleId=10005688.

[4] "Pact of Locarno,"*Encyclopedia Britannica Online,* accessed April 22, 2016, http://www.britannica.com/event/Pact-of-Locarno.

[5] Charles Borger, in discussion with the author, February 4, 2016.

[6] Ibid.

[7] Chana Revell Kotzin, "Christian Responses in Britain to Jewish Refugees in Europe: 1933-1939" (doctoral thesis, University of Southampton, 2000), 145.

[8] Ibid., 146.

[9] Charles Borger, in discussion with the author, February 4, 2016.

[10] Hermine Borger, letter to Mrs. Fawcett, August 7, 1939. Copy in the author's possession. Likely translated into English in Czechoslovakia.

[11] "Treblinka," *United States Holocaust Memorial Museum,* last modified January 29, 2016, https://www.ushmm.org/wlc/en/article.php?ModuleId=10005193.

[12] "The Central Database of Shoah Victims' Names - Hermina Borger," *Yad Vashem*, accessed April 22, 2016, http://yvng.yadvashem.org/nameDetails.html?language=en&s_lastName=borger&s_firstName=hermine&s_place=&itemId=6705895&ind=76&winId=6418920438816 116318.

"The Central Database of Shoah Victims' Names - Alfred Borger," *Yad Vashem*, accessed April 22, 2016, http://yvng.yadvashem.org/nameDetails.html?language=en&s_lastName=&s_first Name=&s_place=&itemId=6705894&ind=1&winId=-4962800414323544064.

[13] "The Central Database of Shoah Victims' Names - Alfred Geduldig," *Yad Vashem*, accessed April 22, 2016, http://yvng.yadvashem.org/nameDetails.html?language=en&s_lastName=&s_first Name=&s_place=&itemId=6705899&ind=7&winId=3173333848311561686.

[14] Charles Borger, in discussion with the author, February 4, 2016.

[15] Ibid.

[16] Ibid.

[17] Ibid.

[18] Ibid.

# MAX RUBINSTEIN

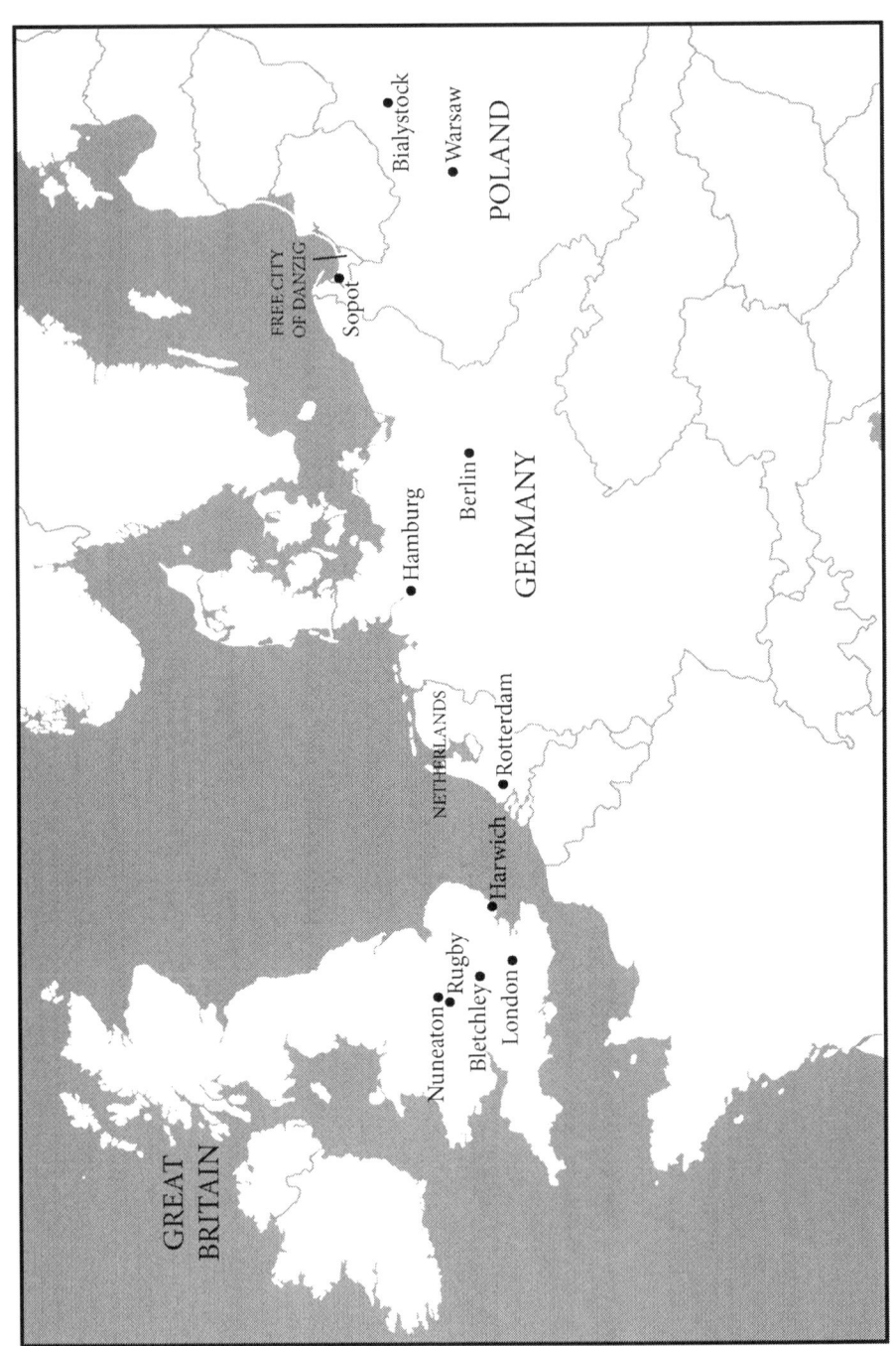

186

# 6

---

## MAX RUBINSTEIN

After the Great War, Sopot, a beautiful tourist destination on the Baltic Sea, became a part of the Free City of Danzig. The Free City of Danzig was a small, semi-autonomous city-state that was created on paper by the Treaty of Versailles in 1919, but really came into existence in 1920. This city-state was composed of the major city of Danzig (now Gdańsk) and about 200 surrounding towns and villages. It had its own government, but it was sandwiched between Germany on the east and Poland on the west. The League of Nations was its overseer, and Poland had a number of economic ties to the region[1]—it was to serve as Poland's seaport, and Poland was to develop the city's transportation and communication facilities.[2]

The majority of the population in the Free City of Danzig was German—and the nation of Germany very much resented that they had been separated from the Fatherland. William Shirer, in his classic history of this period, wrote:

> Even more than France, Poland was the hated and despised enemy in the minds of the Germans. To them the most heinous crime of the Versailles peace-makers had been to separate East Prussia from the Reich by the Polish Corridor, to detach Danzig and to give to the Poles the province of Posen.[3]

One of Hitler's fundamental beliefs was that all ethnic Germans should be united. Because the population of this area was primarily composed of ethnic Germans, and there was only a Polish minority, the "crime" of separating Danzig from Germany would not go unnoticed or unaddressed. In 1933, the Nazi Party became the dominant party in the city's government. In January 1939, Hitler gave a chilling message to the Polish foreign minister: "Danzig was German, would always remain German, and sooner or later would return to Germany."[4]

Poland, backed by the Soviet Union, refused to give up the territory that had been legally made its possession. But when the German-Soviet Nonaggression Pact was signed on August 23, 1939, the tables were turned. Poland's powerful eastern ally suddenly became allied with Germany—and secretly agreed to carve up Poland after the nation was conquered by Hitler.[5] Thus, as Poland was invaded by Germany on September 1, 1939, the Free City of Danzig was taken, that very day, and incorporated into the German Reich.

**Beginnings**

Max Rubinstein was born in Sopot on June 24, 1929. His sister, Pauline, was born in Danzig on March 8, one year earlier. Their births were both in the midst of the chaos of this political environment—with Germany vying for Danzig and Poland refusing to give it up.

Max is the youngest of four children born to Saul and Vera Rubinstein. His older brothers were George and Robert. George was born in 1921 in Mena, Ukraine, the same city as his mother, and Robert was born in 1922 in Bialystock, Poland. Around 1927, the family moved to Danzig, and shortly after Pauline's birth, they moved to Sopot. Max's childhood was spent in Sopot, and it was from there that he would leave his parents' household in 1939.

Saul Rubinstein was a machinery salesman and traveled around the world to meet clients and sell his machines. Vera was a dentist.

Max remembers having had a happy childhood. He often played with his sister, as she was only a year older than he, and his older brothers generally busied themselves with their own work. Sometimes, however, he remembers them acting as typical older brothers: teasing their younger siblings.

Though the Nazi Party ruled over the Free City of Danzig, Max remembers his early years as being no different from any of the other children's in the area. He went to school and had his friends, just like everyone else. And he had his favorite sport, tennis, just like everyone else. He can even recall sneaking under a fence in Sopot to watch tennis matches. In some sense, Max grew up in an idyllic setting: his house was just across the street from the beach, allowing easy access to relaxation and fun in the water.

## Antisemitism

However, this normal childhood was about to take a dramatic turn. Though the first Nazi president of the Danzig Senate sought to put a moderate tone on Nazi views towards the Jews, antisemitism was working behind the scenes, pressuring Jews, or even using executive actions to force them to leave public offices and professional associations. Worse yet, some Jews were also physically assaulted.

When this "moderate" president of the Senate left office in 1934, antisemitism became much more public. Gerson C.

Bacon, in his work *Danzig 1939: Treasures of a Destroyed Community* wrote:

> Officially, the new president Greiser promised to uphold the constitution, but in practice the government permitted the continuation of boycott actions, public display of the anti-Semitic newspaper *Der Sturmer* and the public singing of songs calling for the spilling of Jewish blood.[6]

As time went on, the conditions for the Jews in Danzig worsened. The only mitigating force was Germany's desire to avoid a direct confrontation with Poland; therefore, while attacks occurred against the Jews, the official government sought to distance itself. In fact, when Jewish businesses and homes were attacked on October 23, 1937, the Nazi government of Danzig even imprisoned some of those who took part in the rioting. But despite its "official" stance, the government continued to make the situation worse for Jews and introduced further antisemitic legislation. Because of these terrible circumstances, many of the Jews in Danzig fled. Mr. Bacon continued to explain:

> By 1937, some three thousand of the more than ten thousand resident Jews had already left Danzig, and for the first time some community leaders began considering an at least partial evacuation of Jews from the city. Administrative pressure for the Aryanization of businesses coupled with stormtrooper-enforced boycott activity made things harder and harder for Jews. From November 1937 to the summer of 1938, another two thousand Jews left the city.[7]

Then came *Kristallnacht*. Though the "Night of Broken Glass" specifically occurred in Germany, Austria, and areas of Czechloslovakia,[8] the violence spread to the Free City of

Danzig. *Kristallnacht* took place throughout the Reich on November 9–10, 1938. In Danzig, it was just a few days behind, occurring on November 12–13, 1938.[9] Max remembers the experience: "We were in our living room, and somebody threw a rock through the window and broke the window. . . . My parents wouldn't let me go out of course. I was in the house. You heard all the noises going on outside."[10]

But in describing the aftermath of *Kristallnacht,* Max had the typical resilience of a young child:

> When it comes to shopping, 'No Juden allowed.' No Jews allowed in stores to buy anything. My mother gave me a list to the grocery store; I had blonde hair, looked like a German anyway, and I did the shopping. And I wasn't afraid, because I didn't know any better.[11]

Despite the passing of antisemitic legislation and the hatred focused on the Jews, because Max was a young child, he recalls his childhood days as being happy and carefree. But though Max did not notice the highly fraught situation, his parents certainly did:

> My life between 1937 and 1938 was no different from any other child at the time. . . . Antisemitism started to become a way of life for the Poles openly in the early 1930s. As conditions worsened in 1938 for the Jews, my parents sent George (age 17) and Robert (age 16) to England, knowing that trouble was just around the corner.[12]

As 1939 began, Max and Pauline were now alone with their parents in Sopot. Max did the shopping because he did not look Jewish, yet he still found himself the target of German hatred.

At one point, after he knew that he would be going on the Kindertransport, he was confronted by four German boys: "And they said Germany is the biggest country in the world. . . . I was nine years old, so I said England is the biggest country in the world because I knew I was going there."[13]

The result of this confrontation was extremely unpleasant for Max. The fists of these four boys found their mark on his nine-year-old frame. He was left beaten and injured, and he returned home with a burning desire for vengeance. Before he left for England, Max got his revenge upon them—and he recalls that in his escape from them, one boy's mother yelled, "Jew! Jew!"

Though he was just a child, and though he attempted to hold to his childish innocence, the circumstances compelled Max to leave his childhood behind: "I had to be very strong after that, with all the things going on. You had to be tough to survive."[14]

However, things were going to get much worse.

**Leaving**

Max was nine and Pauline ten. It was May 3, 1939. They were frightened and alone—frightened of the journey that lay ahead of them and frightened of the prospect of living with complete strangers. Before they had been allowed to leave for the United Kingdom, pictures had been sent by his family to England and he and Pauline had been selected by the Whittaker family.

That day, Max said his last goodbye to his parents, Saul and Vera Rubinstein—though he did not then know that he would never see them again. Now, he was only with Pauline, and he was on a bus, driving through Germany, on his way to Holland, and from there to England:

We went through Hamburg, and I saw the Nazis marching. We were on the bus, and then we wound up on the train, stopped in Berlin about a half hour, and when the train moved, I was very happy. And when I looked out on the windows, there was Hitlerstrausser [Hitler Street] with big flags all over the place with huge swastikas.[15]

Finally, Max and Pauline reached Rotterdam in Holland. They were taken into a big hall, where a large meal had been prepared for them. Max especially remembers the Dutch apple pie. Nevertheless, though this would have seemed to be a bright spot in a dark journey, Max ate so much of the food that was in front of him that he became sick and had to run outside and throw it up.

The next day, they boarded a ship and went to Harwich, England. From Harwich, they took a train to Liverpool Street Station, where they were met by Alan Overton and taken to Rugby. In Rugby, they met a woman Max called "Auntie Pam" (many of the Christadelphians encouraged the Jewish children to call them "auntie" and "uncle"), who had driven Harry and Phyllis Whittaker from Nuneaton to Rugby to pick up Max and Pauline.

This was the first time the Rubinsteins met the Whittakers.

**Max's Family**

Both George and Robert survived the war, having previously fled to England in 1938. It is not fully known, however, what precisely happened to Saul and Vera. According to the existing evidence, Saul and Vera Rubinstein eventually lived in Poland, perhaps fleeing Sopot like so many of their fellow Jews. In Poland, it is believed that they were rounded up into the Warsaw ghetto, where they perished.[16] Max explained: "My

*Max and Pauline's Kindertransport group, 1939. Max is number 71 and Pauline is number 50.*

parents left, the last I heard they moved to Poland. . . . We never heard anything again, never."[17]

And that was the end.

Like so many others, Max's family was torn apart by Nazi hatred and antisemitism. Yet, in their love for their children, Saul and Vera's sending all four children to families they had never met enabled Max and his siblings to survive the war. Esther Rubinstein, Max's wife, described the agony: "You had to have parents who loved their children beyond love to send their children to strangers...they went into the arms of strangers."[18]

## England

For Max and Pauline, those strangers were the Whittakers. The Whittakers were Christadelphians—and quite dedicated Christadelphians. Harry Whittaker was a prolific author on Bible subjects, and by the end of his life, he had written something on nearly every book of the Bible. He was an oft-requested speaker at Christadelphian gatherings, and the Christadelphian faith was his life. In a book Harry wrote on Abraham in the 1960s, he spoke about this specific period, putting forth part of the Christadelphian position toward the Jews:

> I will bless them that bless thee.—This was doubtless true concerning Abraham himself in a material sense, although the record does not strongly emphasize this in the story of his life. There is good biblical reason for believing that God has carried over the same principle to the nation which is Abraham's seed. . . . The thing has proved its truth in history scores of times over, and in every generation dictators and statesmen have been blind to the simple best policy for the true well-being

of their peoples. The Battle of Britain was won not by the skill and daring of a handful of highly-trained young men but by the kindliness which received Jewish refugees into homes in this country, because they were the distressed seed of Abraham. . . . The stage of history is peopled with the ghosts of Jew-hating nations. Rapid decay or sudden catastrophe was the 'inevitable hour' of them all, whilst Israel lives on . . . beloved for the fathers' sakes.[19]

Convinced of the truth of what God had promised to Abraham: "I will bless them that bless thee, and I will curse him that curseth thee," Harry and Phyllis Whittaker heard the BBC's radio appeal for the Jewish refugee children, and they responded by writing a letter to the Refugee Committee. They received a response telling them that Pauline Rubinstein "should suit you fine," and asking whether they perhaps knew of another family that would be willing to take her brother Max. Harry Whittaker wrote in his diary: "We looked at each other, and decided to have them both. There was room in the house."[20]

Just like that, the Whittakers chose to have not one, but two Jewish refugees living in their house. Their generosity in undertaking something like this is compounded by the fact that at the time, their son Timothy was only 18 months old. With their hands full with a little child, they opened their house—moved by their beliefs about the "seed of Abraham."

Thus, on May 5, 1939, Harry and Phyllis got into the car with "Auntie Pam" and drove to Rugby where they met Mr. Overton and his carload of Jewish refugees. They loaded Max and Pauline into the car, at which point Max promptly fell asleep from the exhaustion of the journey and all the massive life changes he had experienced in the course of just two days. Harry's description of the two of them is quite moving:

Never did I see such wretchedness, made worse by plenty of sickness. Pauline was just a pair of large wet eyes. Max looked like a corpse. She had had a few months English lessons. He hadn't a word of English. So I was hard driven swotting up my very meagre German, to be able to communicate.[21]

From Rugby, they drove to Nuneaton, a town a few miles north of Birmingham and Coventry. Harry Whittaker was a math teacher, and Phyllis was a homemaker, spending much of her time taking care of Timothy. Max and Pauline spent their first few months focusing on learning English; they did not go to school, as they had arrived in May, quite close to the end of the school year. They quickly picked up the language, learning it fairly fluently before they began attending school in September. The main thing Max remembers about learning the language was that "you put your tongue out as you talk"— apparently something that does not happen when speaking

*Max Rubinstein, George Buckler (a good friend of Harry Whittaker's), Timothy Whittaker, and Pauline Rubinstein.*

*Top: Max celebrated his 10th birthday soon after arriving in England. The Whittakers threw him a birthday party.*
*Bottom: Max and Pauline Rubinstein while living at the Whittakers' house.*

German. His first words in English were "mug, jug, this, and that."[22]

Life with the Whittakers was very different from life back in Sopot. As it was in so many cases, as part of the family, Max and Pauline were expected to go to Sunday school. And, as it turned out in so many of those cases, Max declared that he actually enjoyed it. In his diary, Harry Whittaker wrote that from the beginning, both Pauline and Max refused to go to bed without Harry's telling them a Bible story. Pauline even began to talk about joining the Christadelphians through baptism. Max very much enjoyed the time that he spent, not just at Sunday school, but with the Christadelphians in general:

> The Christadelphian people all were very nice, nice people. I have nothing bad to say about them. They're great. And I went to Sunday school every week. . . . I knew what I was. . . . They wanted to adopt us, but my brothers wouldn't let us.[23]

The Whittakers wanted Max and Pauline to officially become part of the family—and though they could not legally adopt them, they treated them like their own children, and they loved them. In his diary, Harry wrote of a "specially pleasant" memory of Pauline, and in this, you can see how highly he thought of the child:

> One day I took her to the swimming baths. She could swim only a few yards, but was fearless in the water. I tried out with her all the water tricks I knew. She screamed and squealed with delight—to such an extent that everybody else stopped their own fun to watch her enjoying life so much.[24]

In a similar vein, in our interview, Max, and his wife, Esther, repeatedly mentioned the care that he received from the Whittakers and how well they treated had him:

> Well they were so nice to me. . . . They bought me a bicycle, and I taught myself how to ride it. I fell down a few times, and I became very good at it. I went to school by bicycle; I think my sister did the same thing.[25]

> The Whittakers were very kind to him. . . . He always spoke very kindly of them.[26]

> The Whittakers were very good to me because they gave me a part of their garden. I was to grow things, radishes, potatoes, tomatoes. I did all that. And then every Saturday I had to clean all the shoes in the house. They made me do that, but they made a man out of me![27]

Even though he was given chores and perhaps did not appreciate those chores at the time, Max looks back on those days, recognizing that the tasks were actually good for him. In a similar type of incident, there was one main rule that young Max did not appreciate. Like many Christadelphians at that time, Harry and Phyllis adamantly believed that the cinemas were not an appropriate place for children: the influence of the movies and the values shown in them were not always very good. As a result, they told Max that he was not to go to the movies, even if his friends did so.

> In my day, the Whittakers didn't want me to go to the movies. I went to play cowboys and Indians with my friends outside on a Saturday. Then one day I decided to go to the movies. Because I delivered newspapers early in the morning . . . I was ten years old at the time

and made a little money. So I went to the movies. I came home, and I got caught, and I was sent to bed early with no supper. About a month later, I said, 'I'm going to the movies again,' because we didn't have a TV; nobody had a TV, but we didn't even have a radio on. I didn't understand that part . . . my family did all that.[28]

Though he loved them and was treated quite well, there were some things that he simply did not understand—their strictness about the movies was one of them.

Nevertheless, Max looks back today on the years he spent with the Whittakers, and he appreciates the values and the ethics they taught him: "They wanted to teach me, you know, to be a good person. . . . I really missed them when I left."[29]

## Tragedy

Sadly, Max had to leave the Whittakers sooner than any of them expected.

> Then came tragedy. [Pauline] lost her colour and her appetite and her zest for work. Often she was tired out. A queer little cough developed, and also stiffness in her legs. Our doctor could diagnose nothing specific. A few weeks later (precious time lost), Phil insisted on another opinion. Still a mystery, but a strong recommendation to get her into the hospital. Then all at once the crisis with rheumatic fever! She was desperately, unbelievably ill. 'Little hope,' said the doctor, 'and in any case, she's doomed, for we've x-rayed her, and she has TB.' We didn't give up. A few joined us in prayer for her recovery, the ground for what we asked being solely that she might live to be one of the New Israel.

> Behold! Within two days, an amazing recovery occurred, startling everybody. At the end of a week, we were talking about where she should go for convalescence. Then she seemed to wilt. I came back from a [Bible preaching] campaign to find her fretful. She died suddenly that night.[30]

The Whittaker household was in tears. She and Max had lived with the Whittakers from May 1939 until August 1941—just over two years—certainly long enough to become part of the family. Moreover, not only was Pauline dead, but what about Max and Timothy, who had been exposed to the disease?

> Of course immediately we had both Max and Timothy tested, and both gave a positive reaction to the 'ring test' (I think they called it). This sent Phil nearly frantic. Somehow the two must be kept apart! But it was impossible. And Max developed a cough . . .[31]

But there was more: not only was it possible that the two boys had tuberculosis, but the Whittakers had been given orders by the doctor. For November 1941, the archives of the Refugee Committee read: "Mr. Whittaker has asked for Max to be removed, as the doctor will not give consent for him to be with his infant son Timothy."[32]

What was to be done?

Already shaken from the loss of Pauline, fearing what might happen to Max, and wondering whether the disease would spread from Max to Timothy, the Whittakers made the agonizing choice to send Max to another family. He first went to Bletchley, the city in which the German Enigma code was broken, stayed there for a couple of months, and then went to a Jewish family in London. Max said that it was the most difficult for Phyllis: "She couldn't handle the pressure. When my sister died, she just couldn't handle it. And then with me maybe dying from TB, she just couldn't handle the pressure."[33]

Harry's diary seems to agree with Max's take: "Phil was nevertheless determined to hold onto Max, but [the] anxiety of it was getting too much for her. So at last I said, 'Max is going,' and I wrote to the Refugee Committee telling them the story."[34]

As such, in February 1942, Max said goodbye to the family that had treated him so well. After he moved from the Whittaker's home, he missed them terribly.

Two months later, after seeing doctor after doctor, the London Chest Hospital wrote a letter to the Refugee Agency, declaring that indeed something was not right: "It is probable that he has some tuberculosis glands of the lung roots and he has been recommended for admission for observation and diagnosis."[35]

*Max and Esther Rubinstein's wedding day, 1963.*

Later, however, after even more examinations, Max was declared to be completely free of TB.

## The United States

Max recovered and moved from house to house until eventually, in 1948, he moved to the United States. Two years later, he was drafted, and found himself fighting in Korea. Trained as an engineer, and not as an infantryman, he thought that he would be free from combat. Nevertheless, while on a ship in Korean waters, an announcement was made that everyone on the ship from that point on would be part of the infantry. Max was not pleased.

Soon afterward, Max heard that the army was looking for volunteers to become medics. He turned to his two friends and urged them to stand up. Perhaps by becoming medics, they would be trained, and because peace talks were already underway, he thought that by the time they were actually deployed, the war would be over. Unfortunately, such was not the case. There was no training:

> We went to the front lines right away . . . it was on-the-job training. I was attached to the infantry. I carried two hand grenades, a carbine . . . and I got shot. . . . I still got a bullet in my back . . . a sniper got me . . . when they operated, I thought they took it out, and I never knew until I was a civilian when I had a stomachache, I went to my doctor . . . and he showed me the x-ray.[36]

After Korea, Max returned to New York, where he eventually met his future wife, Esther. They had their first date together at a dance, and the rest, as they say, is history.

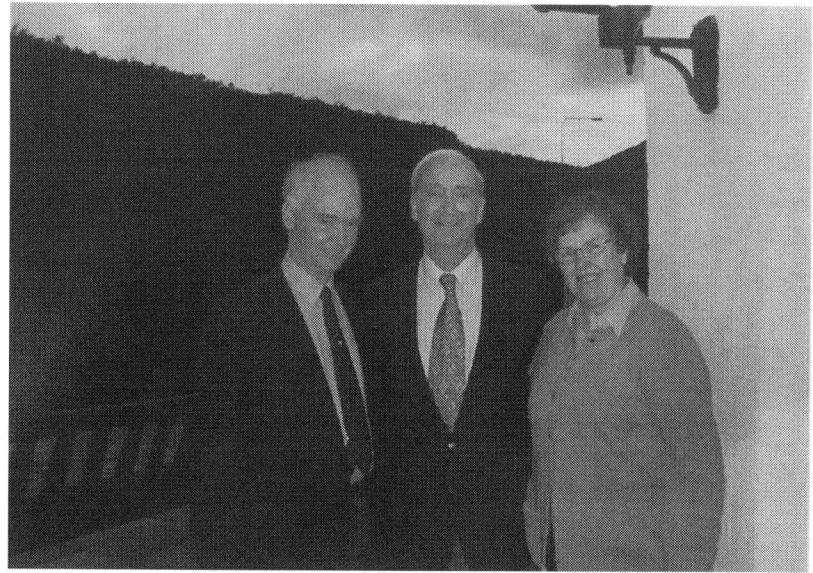

*Timothy Whittaker, Max Rubinstein, and Muriel Whittaker, 2002.*

## Conclusion

Though Max had to leave the Whittakers' house after Pauline's death, he continued to hold the family in high esteem, enjoying the time he had spent with them more than that spent with any of the other families with whom he had lived in England. In fact, decades later, when Timothy Whittaker, then an adult with his own children, traveled to the United States to speak at a Christadelphian conference, he was quite surprised by an invitation he received. George MacDonald, Timothy Whittaker's brother-in-law, explained:

> When Harry's son Timothy was visiting [the] USA . . . to speak at one of the Bible Schools, he and his wife (my sister Muriel) were invited to call in on this family in New York and found themselves feted as guests of honour at a big family gathering.[37]

Though he had only lived with them for a couple of years, those years made a lasting impression. Thus, when I asked Max what he would say to the Whittakers if he could say one final thing to them, he wished that he could continue to express his thanks for what they had done: "Thank you for saving our lives, me and my sister. That's what I would say. If they didn't take me . . . I would have been dead."[38]

Compelled by their beliefs, this Christadelphian family took in Max Rubinstein and his sister Pauline. For that kindness, and the kindness that he received during the years he lived with them as their son, Max is infinitely grateful.

*Max and Esther Rubinstein, 2016.*

---

[1] "Danzig," *United States Holocaust Memorial Museum,* last modified January 29, 2016, https://www.ushmm.org/wlc/en/article.php?ModuleId=10005438.

[2] "The Avalon Project: The Versailles Treaty June 28, 1919." *Yale Law School*, accessed April 22, 2016, http://avalon.law.yale.edu/imt/partiii.asp.

[3] William Shirer, *The Rise and Fall of the Third Reich; a History of Nazi Germany* (New York: Simon and Schuster, 1960), 188.

[4] Michael Fry, "Danzig and the Beginnings of World War II," *Nat Geo Education Blog,* last modified August 28, 2014, https://blog.education.nationalgeographic.com/2014/08/28/tbt-danzig-and-the-beg innings-of-world-war-ii/.

[5] "German-Soviet Nonaggression Pact," *History.com,* accessed April 22, 2016, http://www.history.com/topics/world-war-ii/german-soviet-nonaggression-pact.

[6] Gershon Bacon, "Virtual Jewish World: Danzig (Gdańsk), Poland," *Jewish Virtual Library*, accessed April 22, 2016, http://www.jewishvirtuallibrary.org/jsource/vjw/Danzig.html.

[7] Ibid.

[8] "Kritallnacht," *United States Holocaust Memorial Museum,* last modified January 29, 2016, https://www.ushmm.org/wlc/en/article.php?ModuleId=10005201.

[9] Gershon Bacon, "Virtual Jewish World: Danzig (Gdańsk), Poland," *Jewish Virtual Library*, accessed April 22, 2016, http://www.jewishvirtuallibrary.org/jsource/vjw/Danzig.html.

[10] Max and Esther Rubinstein, in discussion with the author, February 9, 2016.

[11] Ibid.

[12] Max Rubinstein, "My Life, Max Rubinstein," Typescript, 2002, 1.

[13] Max and Esther Rubinstein, in discussion with the author, February 9, 2016.

[14] Ibid.

[15] Max and Esther Rubinstein, in discussion with the author, February 9, 2016.

[16] "The Central Database of Shoah Victims' Names - Vera Rubinshtein," *Yad Vashem,* accessed April 22, 2016, http://yvng.yadvashem.org/nameDetails.html?language=en&itemId=9348275.

"The Central Database of Shoah Victims' Names - Isser Rubinshtein," *Yad Vashem,* accessed April 22, 2016, http://yvng.yadvashem.org/nameDetails.html?language=en&itemId=9348274.

[17] Max and Esther Rubinstein, in discussion with the author, February 9, 2016.

[18] Max and Esther Rubinstein, in discussion with the author, February 9, 2016.

[19] Harry Whittaker, *Abraham, Father of the Faithful.* (Birmingham: The Christadelphian Magazine and Publishing Association, 1966), 18–19.

[20] Harry Whittaker, "Max and Pauline," Typescript, no date, 1.

[21] Ibid.

[22] Max and Esther Rubinstein, in discussion with the author, February 9, 2016.

[23] Ibid

[24] Harry Whittaker, "Max and Pauline," Typescript, no date, 1.

[25] Ibid

[26] Max and Esther Rubinstein, in discussion with the author, February 9, 2016.

[27] Ibid.

[28] Max and Esther Rubinstein, in discussion with the author, February 9, 2016.

[29] Ibid.

[30] Harry Whittaker, "Max and Pauline," Typescript, no date, 2.

[31] Ibid.

[32] World Jewish Relief case files for Max Rubinstein, note for November, 1941.

[33] Max and Esther Rubinstein, in discussion with the author, February 9, 2016.

[34] Harry Whittaker, "Max and Pauline," Typescript, no date, 2.

[35] World Jewish Relief case files for Max Rubinstein, note for April 25, 1942.

[36] Max and Esther Rubinstein, in discussion with the author, February 9, 2016.

[37] George MacDonald, e-mail message to author, January 30, 2016.

[38] Max and Esther Rubinstein, in discussion with the author, February 9, 2016.

# ELFRIEDE RANSOME

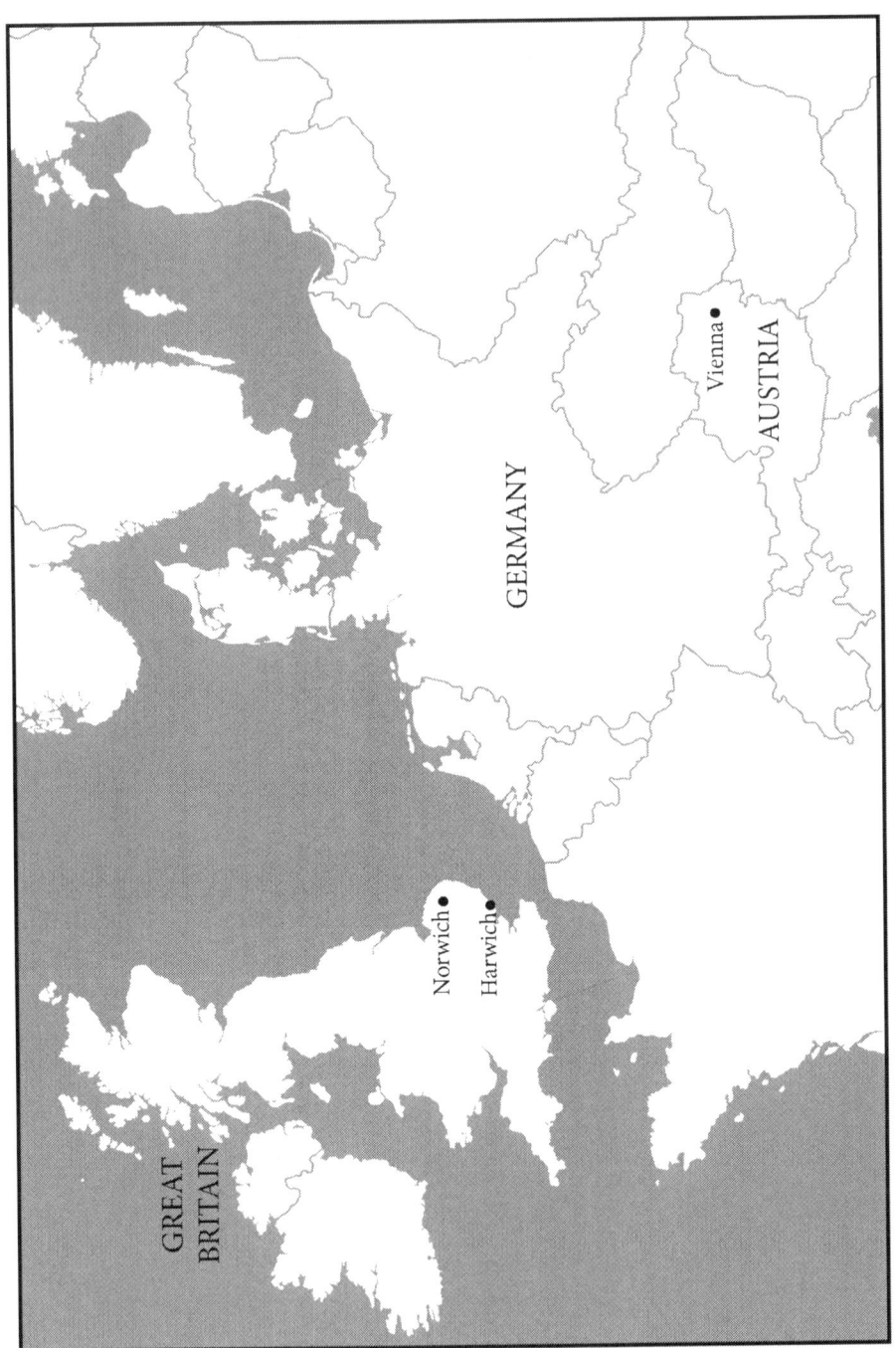

# 7

---

# ELFRIEDE RANSOME, NÉE FISCHER

Elfriede Fischer was born in Vienna, Austria, on April 25, 1930, the year the Nazi Party became the largest political party in Germany. In Austria, however, things were quite different. In 1929, the Austrian Nazi Party could only boast a few hundred members, and in 1930, its ranks were still just as pitiful. Kevin Mason, in his doctoral dissertation, wrote:

> In 1930 . . . unlike Germany, communism and National Socialism in Austria were virtually non-existent . . . the Austrian Nazi Party received 3% of the vote and no parliamentary seats, while its German counterpart had won 18% of the vote and 101 Reichstag seats.[1]

At the same time, despite the Nazi Party's prevalence in Germany, well-known figures and establishments continued to see Hitler as a flame that would soon burn out and as a leader of a movement that would soon lose momentum. In December 1930, *The New York Times* ran an article about Einstein's arrival in the United States. It contained Einstein's view of the man who would eventually become the Führer of the Third Reich:

> Declining to answer a question as to his views on Zionism for fear he might be misquoted, and promising to deal with this problem in a prepared statement later in his visit, he suddenly became grave

and almost vehement when confronted with a query as to what he thought of Adolph [sic] Hitler, the leader of the German fascists. 'I do not enjoy Mr. Hitler's acquaintance,' he said. 'Hitler is living on the empty stomach of Germany. As soon as economic conditions in Germany improve he will cease to be important.'[2]

At the time, many still viewed Hitler as relatively unimportant. He was gaining ground in Germany, but some thought that he would eventually flicker out once the economy had regained strength. In Austria, where Hitler had nearly no influence, there did not seem to be any reason to really care or think about him, particularly in 1930.

Elfriede was the elder of two girls born to Friedrich, although he often went by "Fritz," and Anna Fischer. Elfriede's younger sister was Ilse, who was born only about a year later. Though Fritz was Jewish, Anna was Catholic, and Elfriede and Ilse were both raised as Roman Catholics:

> We were brought up as little Roman Catholics. And I was a very ardent little girl, and I used to go off on the Saturdays to confession. I can't imagine what I confessed—I suppose sticking my tongue out at my sister, or pinching her . . . were about the worst sins . . . that I can imagine that I . . . told the priest. And then the priest would tell you to go and say so many 'Ave Marias' and 'Our Fathers,' and then you were okay, and you mustn't eat anything then—not until you had been to the mass on the Sunday. And I used to go there and do that every week.[3]

As a young girl, Elfriede was very dedicated to this Catholic faith. Even on her last Sunday in Vienna, in the winter of 1939, when it was dreadfully cold, her mother urged her to stay home from mass, but Elfriede told her, at the tender age of eight, that it was something that she needed to do and that she was going to go.

Not only was Elfriede very dedicated to the Catholic Church, but it also helped take care of her and her family. They were not a family of great means, and such were the terms Elfriede used to describe her childhood: "We were very poor indeed, very poor."[4] Their family rented an apartment. Contributing to their financial burdens, after the *Anschluss*, Fritz had lost his job and was forbidden to work. Being an exceptional pianist, however, he was able to make a bit of money by playing the piano and entertaining guests at the local inn. Eventually, even that came to an end when the SS discovered that the owner of the inn had been employing a Jew. A letter was sent to the owner that said, in the words of Elfriede, "I understand that you are still employing that Jew . . . Fischer . . . and you've been warned twice. You won't be warned anymore. If you continue to have him there, there will be dire consequences."[5]

Because of this environment, work was very difficult for Fritz Fischer to find. Elfriede is sure that somehow, the only way that her family was able to afford to survive was because of help that they received from the Roman Catholic Church. She does not know how much help they were given, or how it was given to them, but she is certain that it was.

**Antisemitism**

Just like the others from Vienna, Elfriede does not remember any antisemitism before Hitler. In fact, because of her age and her religion, even after the *Anschluss* came, she did not at first recognize the antisemitism for what it was.

The Fischer family lived extremely close to the local synagogue—being separated from it by only a large courtyard. Every day, Elfriede passed by it on her way to and from school.

One day, when she was running home from school, she saw a large group of soldiers outside of it, and a number of soldiers coming in and going out; those coming out had their arms filled with books. The books were being thrown into a fire outside.

Although this frightened Elfriede—it was not pleasant to have so many soldiers gathered so close to her house, and the burning of books crosses an unspoken boundary in Western civilization—being a faithful Catholic girl, she never once thought that this would ever have any connection to her.

Eventually, though, the antisemitism began to affect her and her family via the difficulties that her father experienced with his work.

Then, all of this was compounded by the terror of *Kristallnacht*. Elfriede was only eight on that terrible night, but she remembers the glass in the Jewish shops being smashed and her father being taken the next day and forced to go outside and scrub the pavement.

Eventually, Fritz Fischer was also forced to wear the infamous yellow star, although Elfriede remembers that her mother continually cut it off his clothes when he arrived home.

It was a terrifying environment in which to be raised. Years later, Elfriede and Ilse's foster father told them that when they arrived in England, there were only two things in life that had filled them with dread—and they were not the typical things many children would say. For them, their greatest fears were defined by their religion and their experiences. Above all else, they feared the devil and Hitler.

Soon they would leave both of these things behind; Hitler could not follow them to Britain, although he tried, and

*The identifying yellow star that Fritz Fischer was forced to wear.*

Christadelphians do not believe in a personal, incarnate devil, but rather understand "the devil" to be a personification of sin.

## The Kindertransport

The Quakers arranged their journey out of Austria, and they were placed on the train that departed Vienna on February 19, 1939. Elfriede and Ilse were able to leave together, so at least in leaving everything they knew, they were not forced to leave one another. In fact, when asked whether she took anything special with her on the journey, Elfriede replied, "I did take with me my sister."[6]

Unfortunately, though it was the day signifying their freedom from Nazism and persecution, it was not a pleasant day. In the book *We Came as Children*, Ilse described the beginnings of their departure: "We left Vienna sometime during the night,

Top: *Elfriede and Ilse's arrival in England. Elfriede is in the front row, second from the right and Ilse is on her left.*
Bottom: *A second photograph of their arrival in England. Elfriede and Ilse are in the front row, in the middle. Elfriede is on the right and Ilse on the left.*

for I remember Mama getting us out of bed, having to dress us, as we were too bewildered and fuddled with sleep to do it properly and quickly."[7]

Elfriede and Ilse said goodbye to their parents, and then went onto the train that would take them away. They were seven and eight years old.

Not only did they say goodbye to their parents, perhaps forever, but also Ilse was quite ill. Just three months prior, Ilse had undergone an operation on her appendix and was still recovering. Moreover, on that specific day, her mouth was full of ulcers—making the journey and the experience even more painful.

When they boarded the train, their father had taken a piece of paper, scribbled on it quickly before the train left, and held it up to their window—this was the message he wanted his eldest daughter to remember: "Look after your sister."[8]

Elfriede took her father's charge very seriously.

At one point on the journey, Nazis came onto the train and inspected the compartments—perhaps checking to see whether anything was being smuggled. Upon arriving at Ilse and Elfriede's compartment, they looked at Ilse, who was sleeping in the corner. One of the Nazis demanded that Elfriede wake her up so that she could be searched. But Elfriede had been given that charge by her father. Her job was to take care of her sister: "I don't know how it worked, but I absolutely refused to let them touch Ilse. I just refused to let them, and they left her alone! A bit surprising when I think about it now . . ."[9]

With that, the Nazis left the girls' compartment and moved on to search the rest of the train.

Finally, Ilse and Elfriede arrived in Holland. Elfriede remembers a great mass of people at the platform in Holland, cheering them on and giving them sweets. Then they quickly boarded a boat and left for England, arriving in Harwich. The next day, February 20, 1939, they boarded a train to Norwich. Ilse described their arrival:

> I was seven years two months, and my sister exactly a year older, on the day we arrived in England, tired, under-nourished, and frightened. The labels hanging round our necks did little to help us look appealing. We had to walk in file up the platform and line up to be photographed by newspaper cameramen.[10]

## Auntie and Uncle

At the station in Norwich, Norfolk, a crowd of people was gathered around the barrier, looking at the children who were arriving. For Elfriede, one particular couple stood out—they were right at the front of the group, and they were smiling. Elfriede remembers poking Ilse at that point and saying, "I hope it's them."[11]

Eventually, Ilse and Elfriede were taken and put into a room, in which they were seated, facing a man and a woman. It just so happened that the man and the woman were that couple Elfriede had seen upon arriving. The girls were told that this man and woman were Mr. and Mrs. Smith and that they would now be living with them.

The Smiths were Christadelphians.

Donald and Enie Smith lived in Norwich, a city about two hours northeast of Liverpool Street Station in London. After being introduced, the two girls eventually took seats in the back of the car and rode to their new home in a suburb of Norwich. On the drive, they held hands, confused by all of the English they heard—of which they understood so very little—and tired from their long journey.

Nevertheless, though they were tired, scared, and confused, they were with a couple who loved them. In describing their meeting, Elfriede stated, "Uncle was absolutely wonderful."[12] He was a chartered accountant and had taken the rest of the day off to come and meet them. In fact, unknown to the girls at the time, Uncle had been so excited to come and meet them that he had accidentally driven through some of the red lights on the way.

This was not a family where the girls would be treated as servants or seen as intruders in the home. This family would care for them and cherish them.

*Donald and Enie Smith, 1939.*

## The Christadelphians

This care was demonstrated immediately.

Elfriede remembers the difficulty of the first meeting because of the language barrier. The Smiths could not speak German, and Ilse and Elfriede could not speak English. Mr. Smith immediately began to teach them English—and there were two important words they needed to know right away. Their first English lesson was as follows: "Uncle immediately started teaching us things. He pointed to himself and said 'Uncle' . . . and 'Auntie,' then he pointed to me and he said 'Elfriede.'"[13]

This was their first English lesson, and it occurred at their first meal together. Elfriede remembers the meal—it was cottage pie and rice pudding, two things she found revolting at the time (although she came to love them!). Ilse hardly ate anything.

But they did learn their two new words: "Uncle" and "Auntie." From now on, they were not simply in a stranger's house. They were in the house of family. In fact, as time passed, it was not just that Ilse and Elfriede were the two nieces of Auntie and Uncle, but they became part of the immediate family: "We were treated very well, as though we were their children . . . and I particularly loved Uncle . . . We were like their daughters to them."[14]

A bond was formed between this couple and these children; a special relationship existed. This relationship can even be seen in the dynamic that existed as the children learned English. Elfriede remembers that for every word they learned in English, Uncle learned the same word in German: he supported them and encouraged them, considering how hard it was for them to be in a new environment and a new culture.

At the same time, Auntie also made an impact on Elfriede. Elfriede remembers that the first night they arrived at the house, they were shown their room and were prepared for bed. Once they were ready, the two of them jumped into their beds, prepared to be tucked in for the night. But Auntie told them that it was not quite time—there was one more thing that needed to be done. She took Elfriede and Ilse, put one arm around each girl, and she prayed with them: "God bless mama, and God bless papa, and help me to be a good girl."[15]

It was their first night together, and Auntie was praying for their parents.

For years, even though Elfriede added her own ideas and thoughts to the prayer, she always began her words to God with those same words that Auntie had said on their first night in England.

It was Tuesday when they arrived, and a few days later, it was Sunday and time for the girls to go to the meeting. Being raised Roman Catholic, the girls did not find going to church on Sundays foreign, although the Christadelphian meeting was quite different from Catholic mass. Nevertheless, this was something that the Smiths did as a family.

Thus, Ilse and Elfriede went to the Christadelphian meetings every week and without being given a choice—something Elfriede feels was good and proper. In raising her own children, she did not give them a choice either. Despite this, when asked whether she felt any kind of pressure to become a Christadelphian, she stated, "I can't remember such a thing at all."[16]

The Christadelphian ecclesia in Norwich was quite small at the time, and Ilse and Elfriede, aside from one other boy, were the only children, so there was no Sunday school. They received

Sunday school lessons by mail, through the Christadelphian Isolation League, and Auntie taught the lesson to them. Eventually, as they grew older, Uncle began to teach the lessons, and Elfriede remembers that he was an excellent teacher.

After Sunday school lessons, they went together, as a family, to the meeting.

One of the more comical memories that Elfriede has of this time was of one of her first meetings. It was only a few days after they arrived, and their English vocabulary was still quite small. When they arrived at the meeting, however, in order to help them follow along, they were given a Bible with pictures—yet it was one of those enormous podium Bibles. She can remember sitting there, with her sister, with this gigantic Bible on their laps, trying to turn the pages and look at the pictures!

Elfriede described her time living with the Christadelphians in the book *We Came as Children*:

> As a girl of eight I went with my younger sister into the home of Christadelphians and we were taught Bible knowledge and Christian behaviour by precept and example. All during the war and our difficult beginnings and readjustments the Roman Catholic representatives completely ignored us. . . . Uncle had obtained my father's permission to bring us up in their religious beliefs, when we first came to England.[17]

## Elfriede's Family

While Ilse and Elfriede were adjusting to life in England, learning a new language, and being introduced to the Christadelphians, their family remained in Vienna.

Throughout the war, Anna Fischer, being non-Jewish, did not run into many difficulties, aside from those associated with wartime and experienced by other Viennese citizens.

The same cannot be said, however, for Fritz Fischer.

Eventually, Fritz Fischer was arrested and taken to a concentration camp near Vienna. He spent his time during the war there, working at a hydroelectric plant. His work group was composed of him and three others. Each day, he was given some pork fat and dry bread to eat—a difficult diet, especially because he had a weak stomach. The problem was compounded, however, because one of the group's men was Orthodox and was extremely averse to eating the pork fat. The three others in their group, including Fritz Fischer, decided to do what they could to help him—trading parts of their bread for his fat. This eventually had terrible consequences for Fritz, who had stomach-related complications arise from the diet. Eventually, he left the group to have his duodenum removed— one of the first portions of the small intestine.

Astonishingly, however, Fritz Fischer survived both the operation and the war. That simple prayer that Auntie had first prayed with the girls was answered.

**After the War**

After struggling to learn English and being immersed in an English society, Elfriede stopped speaking German. After the war in Europe ended, however, in the summer of 1945, she decided to see what she remembered of her native language. The Smith family was on a holiday, staying at a bed and breakfast. Unfortunately, Elfriede had come down with the mumps, so while the rest of the family went out to enjoy the day, she had to stay in bed. Looking for something to occupy her time, she realized that she had a book—*Teach Yourself German*—that Uncle had bought for her.

Nine months later, she passed her exams in German at school. It had all flooded back into her mind. Though she thought she had lost it, the language had been there, hidden in her mind, the whole time.

The next year, 1946, Elfriede chose to become a Christadelphian through baptism. For her, it was something that just made sense: "Well, I just read the Bible, and when I was 16, I said, I want to be baptized. . . . that was it, as far as I was concerned. It was just following what the Scripture said."[18]

Elfriede had grown up reading the Bible, and baptism was what the Bible commanded. She has never looked back and is still a Christadelphian today.

The year 1947 brought with it the greatest shock: Fritz and Anna, after years of silence, sent a letter to their daughters. After the war, Fritz and Anna had been reunited and were looking to be reunited with their two daughters as well. It had been eight years since the girls had seen their parents. In the book, *We Came as Children*, Elfriede described the day they received this news:

> One day when my sister and I got home from school we were told to sit down and were given a letter from our parents. The first news for years! The first intimation that they were still alive. They wanted us home again. It was as though the whole house rocked. We were flabbergasted and horrified. No! We didn't want to go. We belong to you, Aunt and Uncle! We can't go! So it was left to Uncle to write this difficult letter to suggest that we finished our education here

and did not go through another upheaval. To which they agreed.[19]

Many years later, in being interviewed for this book, Elfriede described that day:

> One day, when we got back from school, Uncle said 'I want you to come in the lounge and sit down,' . . . he told us he'd had a letter from Papa, which he'd had translated . . . and it said that he wanted us back. That was absolutely a bombshell. I was baptized, and . . . we were English! . . . we said 'No, we don't want to go back.'[20]

It was not that Ilse and Elfriede were not happy about the news from their parents. It was wonderful to know that they were still alive! Yet at the same time, so many changes had taken place in their lives, and they had grown used to their family and their lives in England. They had been in England longer than they had lived in Vienna. They left when they were 7 and 8, now they were 15 and 16, and did not want to be pulled away after they had become used to their surroundings, only to have to readjust again.

Thus, Ilse and Elfriede continued to stay with the Smiths, and, in fact, later made the choice to remain in England and raise their families there.

Of course, they still very much wanted to see their parents.

Therefore, in 1947, after receiving that letter from Fritz and Anna, Uncle paid for Fritz and Anna to travel to England and see their daughters. Elfriede remembers the day vividly: Uncle had told her parents that Elfriede would come to the station wearing a "blue costume"[21] and that he would be wearing sunglasses—that's how they were to recognize their daughter and her foster father!

On the day that her parents arrived though, it was pouring rain. Nevertheless, Uncle had told them that he would be wearing sunglasses. So, Elfriede has that funny picture imprinted in her memory—of the first meeting with her parents in eight years, with Uncle standing in the pouring rain, wearing his sunglasses.

Her parents looked different. Indeed, it had been eight years, but the war, too, had done its work on them—particularly her father. Both of them were terribly thin. She could still recognize them, but the war years had not treated them well. Regardless, the meeting was joyous:

> It was pouring with rain and Uncle certainly was conspicuous. We waited for hours and ran from platform to platform as different trains arrived. Then

*Fritz and Anna Fischer's visit to England, 1947.*
*From left to right: Elfriede, Fritz, Ilse, and Anna.*

suddenly we saw them! My parents, after eight years of separation from them; I had been eight years old, now I was nearly seventeen. At the first moment we felt strange, then quickly everything was all right.[22]

Here, two families had been brought together because of two children. Both had raised Elfriede for eight years, yet both were extremely different:

> After the summer holidays my parents went home and we carried on with our English lives. We had had a few disagreements with my father and misunderstandings with my mother. Our ways of life were really different. When my father was annoyed with us he said: 'Uncle must smack you.' Of course, by this age we were never smacked—indeed, corporal punishment had been rarely inflicted. There could not have been a greater difference between my father's excitability and Uncle's extremely English 'keep calm and cool' attitude. By inheritance, I have my father's temperament, by environment since the age of eight I had calm, quiet and dignified behaviour shown me.[23]

Such was one of the difficulties created by the Kindertransport—here were two children split between two families. Elfriede loved her parents because they were her parents. Yet she also loved Auntie and Uncle because they had been so good to her and had helped her through all the difficult adjustments and hardships related to her move. Some of the difficulties can again be seen in her words from *We Came as Children*, first published in 1966:

> Although it is rather sad to have grown so much away from my parents, I do feel that Auntie and Uncle are more my parents than my own. We see as much as we can of them and they are always available to give help

or advice if they are asked. I feel that we were very lucky to be sent to them and that we probably had a better education and grounding to face life than we might have done had we not been refugees.[24]

This is not to say, however, that Elfriede ever replaced her parents with Auntie and Uncle. In speaking about their relationship, over 50 years later, Elfriede was extremely clear: "Ilse absolutely took on Auntie and Uncle as Mama and Papa, but I didn't. I never did—they were Auntie and Uncle . . . they were never instead of Mama and Papa, ever."[25]

Thus, throughout the years, though she had decided to stay in England and has continued as a Christadelphian, not a Roman Catholic, Elfriede maintained a relationship with both families. When she was in her mid-20s, in 1956 or 1957, she saved up her money and returned to Vienna to visit her parents.

In 1960, Elfriede had her third child, Susi, and at that time, her parents were able to come to visit them. Elfriede has a photograph that she very much cherishes: a picture of her mother holding Susi.

**Reflections and Conclusion**

Despite the difficulties that the 1930s and 1940s brought upon her and her family, Elfriede remains very thankful for the care shown to her and her sister by Auntie and Uncle. She has remained a dedicated Christadelphian, and she feels that without the Smiths, she would have continued in the Catholic Church and would never have aligned her beliefs with those of the Christadelphians. In 1989, the 50th anniversary of the Kindertransport, she wrote the following note in *The Christadelphian* magazine, demonstrating her thankfulness for the faith that she received while living with the Smiths:

*The photograph taken when Fritz and Anna Fischer visited Elfriede and Ilse after Susi's birth, 1960. From left to right: Ilse, Helen, Margaret, Fritz Fischer, Russell, Anna Fischer with Baby Susi, and Elfriede.*

Fifty years have passed since, in 1939, many hundreds of Jewish and part-Jewish children, left Europe for safety in Britain and elsewhere. In the pages of The Christadelphian during 1938/9, much concern was expressed for the welfare of the Jews and in particular for their children. A number of large-hearted brethren and sisters were moved to 'show their faith by their works'. As one sister, now resting from her labours, said at the time, 'If we believe in the promises to Abraham, we must do something about this'.

There are a small number of brethren and sisters, whom the writer [Elfriede] has been able to contact, whose acceptance of the Truth came as a direct consequence of being taken into the loving homes of generous Christadelphians. Most of these families were poor in this world's goods, but rich in faith. There were many more Jewish children who did not come into the Truth, but went their way, some ending up in Israel. We, who came as refugees from Hitler's horrors, are glad of the opportunity of this 50th Anniversary, to remember our Christadelphian 'mums and dads', and 'uncles and aunts' and to thank God for them. It is fitting that a new generation be made aware of the works of those who went before.[26]

In reflecting on her life and her experiences, Elfriede feels thankful. She is thankful for the willingness of Donald and Enie Smith, she is thankful for the family that she found in the Christadelphians, and she is thankful for the knowledge of the Bible that she gained in living with them. Fourteen years later, in 2003, she wrote an article for *The Testimony* magazine—and in light of her background, her words have a special significance: "We must thank God for overseeing our lives and doing things for our good."[27]

Despite the pain that was caused by leaving Austria and coming to a new culture, new language, and new family, Elfriede believes that God has been working for her "good." She believes that He has been working with her, shaping her, and preparing her for the Kingdom that will one day be set up on this earth. For that, despite the difficulties, she is thankful. This same attitude of thankfulness was expressed in a letter written to the author in 2016: "I wanted to tell you a little more about myself to show how wonderfully God works out His purpose…"[28]

In the letter, she detailed the way in which she first met the man who would become her husband, Russell Ransome, and how he studied to become a Christadelphian. When they were later married, they had three children (Margaret, Helen, and Susi), and they too were baptized as Christadelphians. She now

*Elfriede and Russell Ransome on their 60th wedding anniversary, October 26, 2011.*

has 10 grandchildren—all of whom were also baptized as Christadelphians, and eight great grandchildren, with one more on the way. She closed those thoughts with words that are fitting thoughts for the close of this story:

> Aren't I greatly blessed? All this wonderful company of believers came because Bro. & Sis. Smith took us in as refugees.

> As Jeremiah said in his Lamentations 3:27 'It is good for a man (and woman!) that he bear the yoke in his youth.' I love the previous verses vv. 22–23 'It is of the LORD's mercies that we are not consumed, because his compassions fail not. They are new every morning: great is thy faithfulness.'

> Isn't God wonderful, gracious, merciful, slow to anger?[29]

*Top: Elfriede and Russell Ransome with their children and children's spouses at Elfriede's 80th birthday celebration, 2010. Back row from left to right: Simon Collar, Mark Morris, Russell Ransome, and Richard Baines. Front row from left to right: Helen Collard, Susi Morris, Elfriede Ransome, and Margaret Baines.*

*Bottom: Ransome family picture in Elfriede's garden at Elfriede's 80th birthday celebration, 2010.*

Though she endured such difficulty, sadness, and change at the hands of Nazi Germany, Elfriede has found peace in the teaching of the Bible and a belief that God has always been working in her life. For that, she is truly thankful.

---

[1] Kevin Mason, "Building an Unwanted Nation: The Anglo-American Partnership and Austrian Proponents of a Separate Nationhood, 1918-1934." (PhD diss., University of North Carolina at Chapel Hill, 2007), 321–322.

[2] "Einstein on Arrival Braves Limelight for Only 15 Minutes," *The New York Times* (New York, NY), December 12, 1930.

[3] Elfriede Ransome, interview by Eric Marshall, February 24, 2016.

[4] Ibid.

[5] Ibid.

[6] Elfriede Ransome, interview by Eric Marshall, February 24, 2016.

[7] Ilse Nye in *We Came as Children: a Collective Autobiography*, ed. Karen Gershon (New York: Harcourt, Brace & World, 1966), 25.

[8] Elfriede Ransome and Helen Collard, e-mail message to author, April 20, 2016.

[9] Elfriede Ransome, interview by Eric Marshall, February 24, 2016.

[10] Ilse Nye in *We Came as Children: a Collective Autobiography*, ed. Karen Gershon (New York: Harcourt, Brace & World, 1966), 47.

[11] Elfriede Ransome, interview by Eric Marshall, February 24, 2016.

[12] Ibid.

[13] Ibid.

[14] Ibid.

[15] Ibid.

[16] Ibid.

[17] Elfriede Ransome in *We Came as Children: a Collective Autobiography*, ed. Karen Gershon (New York: Harcourt, Brace & World, 1966), 66.

[18] Elfriede Ransome, interview by Eric Marshall, February 24, 2016.

[19] Elfriede Ransome in *We Came as Children: a Collective Autobiography*, ed. Karen Gershon (New York: Harcourt, Brace & World, 1966), 114.

[20] Elfriede Ransome, interview by Eric Marshall, February 24, 2016.

[21] Ibid.

[22] Elfriede Ransome in *We Came as Children: a Collective Autobiography*, ed. Karen Gershon (New York: Harcourt, Brace & World, 1966), 115.

[23] Ibid.

[24] Ibid.

[25] Elfriede Ransome, interview by Eric Marshall, February 24, 2016.

[26] Elfriede Ransome, "Israel and Their Land," *The Christadelphian,* February 1989, 69.

[27] Elfriede Ransome, "The Prayers of Hannah and Mary," *The Testimony,* May, 2003, 209.

[28] Elfriede Ransome, Letter to author, February 26, 2016.

[29] Ibid.

# SUSANNE WOODIN

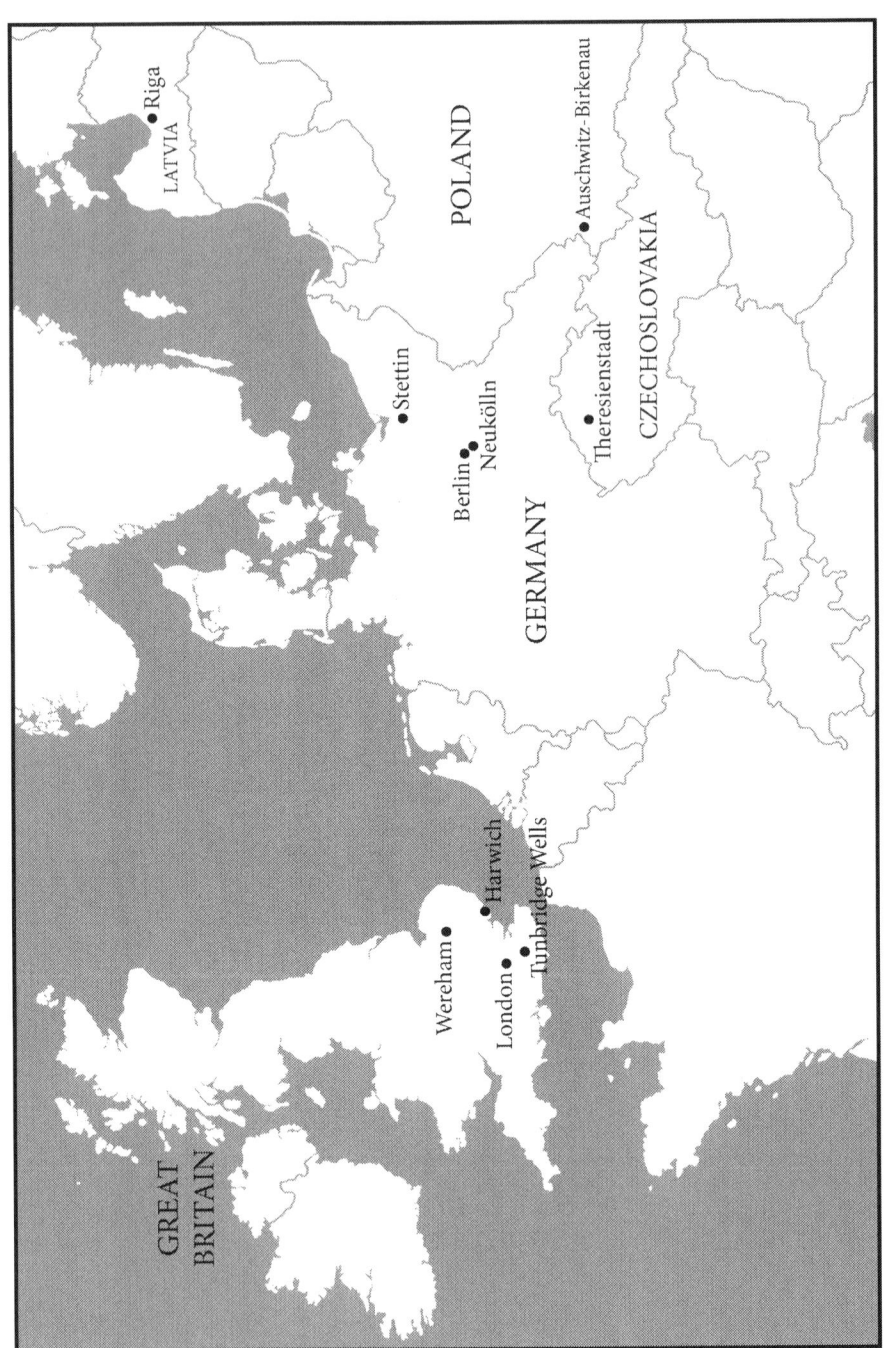

# 8

---

# SUSANNE WOODIN, NÉE SCHLOME

In September of 1930, as noted in the previous chapter, the Nazi Party became the largest political party in Germany, overtaking the Communists. Two months later, on December 13, 1930, Susanne Schlome was born in Berlin.

Susanne's parents were Ruth and Paul Schlome. Ruth was born in 1900, and Paul was born in 1886, making him 14 years older than Susanne's mother. Susanne was an only child. Despite all that happened, she looks back on her childhood with fondness. Her parents gave her a number of happy years, and throughout all of them, she felt well loved. Susanne's best memories were specifically focused on her mother: "I have not a single negative memory of her. I thought she was wonderful and wanted to be like her."[1]

Her memories of her father are not quite the same, though she knew very much that he loved her. He tended to be critical and had very high expectations—wanting her to behave older than her age. Because of this, she too became critical of him. Despite his criticism, there was still a strong bond between them. He could make her laugh and was fun to be around, telling her jokes and teaching her funny songs.

He was a pharmacist and shared a shop with Adolph Cohn, his brother-in-law. Susanne recounted her memories of the shop:

When I was taken there I always liked to see the window. At the top were 4 huge glass bottles with brightly coloured liquids. Down below was the best thing, a model of a large tablet tin, open and upturned to make a tunnel. A row of 4 very fat people passed in on one side and a row of identical but thin people came out on the other side. Very interesting for a small child! I can remember my disappointment one day when the motor was not working.[2]

*Paul Schlome*

*Ruth Schlome*

Her best memory of her father took place around some chocolate liqueur candies that she had. She had finished drinking the contents of the candies and asked her father to refill them. Her father said that this could not be done, but she insisted that as a pharmacist, he should be able to get a substance back inside the little bottles. He accepted the challenge, and together, the two of them sought to insert liqueur into the little necks of the bottles. She does not remember whether they were successful, but remembers the fun in trying.

Family was quite a dominant theme in her early memories. Because her father and Uncle Adolph worked together, their two families grew up in close proximity. Adolph and his wife

Clara had one son, named Walter, who was born in the early 1920s, and one daughter, named Eva, who was born in 1925.

Another early memory was of Uncle Julian and his family. Julian was Paul's younger brother, and he served as a court judge in Berlin until 1933. At that point, the Nazi decrees removed him from his post. Because he had been a volunteer soldier during the Great War, however, he was allowed to serve in a lower position in Stettin, a city about two hours northeast of Berlin. This contributed to the sense of immunity he felt, which ultimately kept him in Germany despite the Nazi advances against the Jews. Nevertheless, in 1935, his position in Stettin was terminated and he returned to Berlin.

Uncle Julian was married to Aunt Kathe, and together they had a little boy named Oscar, born in 1934.

Finally, another family member who had a great influence on young Susanne was her mother's sister, Aunt Alice. Aunt Alice was born in 1892 and was eight years older than Ruth. As a young girl, she had been stricken by polio, so she had to use either calipers and crutches, or a wheelchair. She lived with Susanne's grandmother, and the two of them helped take care of one another. Their house was nearby to Paul and Ruth's, and Susanne was always welcome to visit. Often when Susanne came, Aunt Alice played the banjo and taught her songs. Other times, Aunt Alice read stories to Susanne—and when she began to read herself, Aunt Alice listened while Susanne read the stories aloud. Susanne was so used to seeing her with her calipers, moving around the house, that when she saw her one night without them, crawling to the bathroom, Susanne was "deeply shocked."[3] She recalls that Aunt Alice "was lively and the greatest fun."[4]

Susanne grew up in a religious household, although her family was not strictly observant. They did not follow the laws of *kashrut*, nor did they specifically keep the Sabbath. But she was raised learning all the Bible stories and knows that they did celebrate the festivals—she specifically has memories of one Passover they celebrated in their home. She can still see the table spread out and can feel the excitement of the holiday.

## Memories

Memories of her childhood are extremely specific, yet come in spurts.

*Susanne Schlome*

Her earliest memory is from when she was three. Her mother was carrying a jug of water to the balcony to water the plants. Susanne pleaded for the task and was charged that she must be very careful and not spill any water. She took her job seriously and carried the jug all the way to the door of the balcony without spilling. Taking her time, she carefully set it down on the ground, in front of the door. Then, as she opened the door, the water spilled all over the inside of the sitting room, on its polished wood floor. She was crushed that she had been proved wrong—that indeed her mother should have been the one to carry the jug. Her mother quickly fetched a cloth to mop up the mess and gently chided, "Next time you will understand." Susanne asked, "But what will Vati [father] say?" "Vati does not have to know."[5]

Another memory is of her Aunt Kathe, the one married to Uncle Julian, who had been living in Stettin for a couple of years.

While in Stettin, Susanne had come to visit them. She was about four and a half. At that point, Oscar was only three months old, and Aunt Kathe locked Susanne out of the room when she fed him. In her four-year-old thinking, Susanne was certain that she was forced out because Aunt Kathe was breastfeeding and wanted her privacy. She felt quite proud to have figured this out. Many years later, however, when she found out that her aunt had avoided breastfeeding Oscar altogether, Susanne asked why she had been locked out. To her surprise, she was told, "He was such a poor feeder, if you had been there, chatterbox that you were, he would not have fed at all."[6]

Susanne has another vivid memory of that same trip to her Aunt and Uncle's house. Each night, she slept on a divan at the foot of her Aunt's bed. One night, she wet the bed, something that she never did. Susanne felt quite ashamed of herself, and that shame was magnified when her Aunt pulled away the bedclothes to reveal the blue damask of the divan. There on the damask was a wet patch, and her Aunt scolded, "See what you have done."[7]

Around that same time, Susanne has an altogether different type of memory, and this one is of her mother. In her parents' bedroom, there was a bottle of large, brown, shiny pills. They looked just like chocolate beans, and so they were very tempting to her. She knew that her father took them only occasionally, and she knew that she should not touch them, but one day, she opened the bottle and popped one into her mouth. She indulged in its sweetness, only to be foiled by the fact that within the sweetness was a bitter center.

Not sure what to do with this unwanted portion, Susanne took it from her mouth and dropped it behind a large chest of drawers, where she was sure it would never be found.

Some time later, she broke a plate and did not want to confess to what she had done. Remembering her perfect hiding spot, which had served her well up to this point, Susanne decided that it only made sense to put the plate with the bitter center of that pill.

The hiding place continued to cover her childish deviousness, up until the furniture was rearranged!

At that point, Ruth approached Susanne with pieces of a plate that had gone missing. She was smiling, and stated, "What a very funny place to find these pieces."[8] She then became very serious and explained that in the future, if there were ever an accident, Susanne must tell her. She promised that if Susanne told the truth, she would not get angry with her. Then, reinforcing the lesson, the two of them went out together to buy another plate.

This instance really encapsulates the way in which Susanne remembers her mother: loving, reasonable, and always teaching in a way that Susanne would not resent.

Apparently the bitter center of the pill remained a mystery, despite the fact that the pieces of the plate were found. It was a good hiding place indeed!

The following year, 1936, the Schlome family went on a holiday to the North Coast. Susanne can remember the beautiful sand and watching her mother swim far off from the beach. She was a strong swimmer, and on that holiday, she began to teach Susanne how to swim by holding her under the chin.

Later that year, her father took her to the beach for a day. He too attempted to teach her to swim, but unlike her mother, he did not know how himself. Unfortunately, he held her up by the straps of her swimsuit, which Susanne did not find comfortable at all. Eventually, when the lessons went poorly, he became frustrated and told Susanne that she was not trying. Becoming frustrated in return, Susanne held her tongue, but thought, "How do you expect to teach me when you can not swim yourself?"[9]

**Changes**

Though the German government had already initiated a number of laws regarding Jews, Susanne believes that it was in 1936 that the Schlome family was dealt one of its first major blows by the Nazis. Most of the laws had related to specific professions, none of which had really affected Paul, who was a pharmacist. But in 1936, Paul was forced to leave his position.

This left Paul, Ruth, and Susanne without a main income.

For a while, Paul, along with one of his cousins, owned a few apartment houses in Neukölln, and these helped supply them with some income. At the same time, Susanne's mother started to gather her resources to do what she could to earn a living. She was a trained and highly skilled dressmaker—making a business out of dressmaking from home. Customers would come to the Schlome home with fabric, choose a design, and have Ruth make the dresses. Four or five other women whom she had taught helped her with some of the more routine tasks.

Sometimes Susanne would get dresses made from the extra fabric. Two of her blouses were made from her father's old shirts, and she was specifically fond of these—they were new and exciting because they were like boy's clothes.

Throughout this time, Susanne was not aware of any financial stress—a fact that is quite a testament to the industriousness of her parents and their desire to provide as normal a childhood as they could for their only child.

Around the same time, her mother traveled to London for a week to stay with a friend. When she returned, she did not speak highly of the place. She said that it was cold, wet, and miserable. She could not believe that there was no central heating—only a paraffin stove. At the time, Susanne had not asked why she had gone—but looking back, because some of their friends were already emigrating, it would seem likely that her mother had gone to look into the possibility of earning a living and supporting their family there. Nevertheless, whether that indeed was the purpose, the Schlomes stayed in Germany.

Because her father was at home all day, he could now spend more time with her. Often he took her to visit with his friends, who had also lost their jobs, as all their friends were Jewish. During these visits, Susanne had to sit quietly while the men talked; it was not proper for a little girl to join in their conversation. Susanne tried to sit as quietly as she could, but eventually, she became bored and got into mischief. One time she rocked too hard in the rocking chair. Another time she went outside and stood on her head in the garden. These incidents resulted in a lecture by her father on their walk home.

As time went on, life continued to become increasingly difficult for the Jews in Germany. More restrictions were placed on them, and more people were forced to give up their professions. In an attempt to help alleviate at least some of their suffering, the Jewish community banded together and began to offer welfare and education. Susanne remembers her father taking an English class and a cooking class.

There were so many changes at this time. Not only did her family's economic situation change, but they also brought a new person into their house. Her name was Rita Ganz, she was about 16, came from the country, and worked in their house as an au pair. Susanne loved her. The two of them played together, and Rita taught Susanne new songs. At one point, they went sledding together and fell off the sled, and Rita ended up with a huge graze on her leg. As Ruth cleaned Rita's leg, Susanne could not help but be impressed with Rita's bravery.

Around 1937, Susanne began attending school. It was a Jewish school, part of the synagogue on Princeregenten Street, since on April 9, 1937, the mayor of Berlin had ordered public schools not to admit Jews until further notice.[10] The school no longer exists, as it was destroyed in the events of the following few years.

Susanne's memories of school are quite positive. She loved it and made friends easily. Because a number of the children there would be emigrating, they learned German cursive, English cursive, and the Hebrew *aleph bet*. Susanne remembers that her first Hebrew book was about Dan and Gad.

There was only one time that Susanne got into mischief at school. Thinking that she would play a trick on the school, Susanne noticed that it was possible to climb the wooden dividing wall that separated the stalls in the girls' bathroom. There were five stalls, and after locking the door in the first, she climbed over the dividing wall into the second, and then into the third, until she had locked all the doors. In the fifth stall, she was able to squeeze out under the door. Susanne recalled her teacher's wisdom in handling this situation:

> Soon there was great excitement with girls coming back into the class room to report that all the toilets were locked. Our teacher was very wise! She looked around calmly and asked 'I wonder if there is anyone here clever enough to get these open again?' I volunteered, squeezed in under the first door, opened it, and then climbed over to unlock each one. Halfway along, I began to wonder what would happen to me, but she just looked at me rather hard, said 'Thank you Susanne, now I am sure no one will ever be silly enough to do that again.' I respected her even more after that. I think the others did not realise that I was the culprit. That was the only bad thing I did at school.[11]

Another instance involved a shy boy who had developed a crush on Susanne. He came to her, offering her the hammer out of his tool set. Rather than feeling honored, Susanne told him that he could not ruin his set over her and that he needed to keep the hammer. A second incident happened when that same boy sent Susanne a love letter with money in it. Thinking that money meant that the whole situation had become quite serious, Susanne gave the note and the money to her teacher, knowing that she would deal with this situation judiciously. She apparently did because Susanne never received any more letters.

In the summer of 1938, Susanne was seven. That summer, they did not have a family holiday, but she was sent away for a week to a Jewish Holiday Home in the country. As part of her preparation for this trip, she needed to have all of her clothes labeled. But her family ran out of time to get name tapes printed. Improvising, her mother took a stamp that read *gebucht*, which translates as "booked." She took tape and covered up portions of the stamp—the "ge" at the beginning of the word, and the "t" at the end of the word. They were sure that no one would have the name "buch" at the camp, and so they stamped all of Susanne's clothes with her new and improvised last name.

The year 1938 also brought more restrictions on the Jews. Some shops and parks were closed off to them. In August, every male was forced to take another middle name: Israel. Every female had to add "Sara" as their middle name. This was supposed to help in identifying Jews on documentation, but it was just one more thing that sought to turn them into a collective group rather than individuals. In the same way, in October, all German passports held by Jews were invalidated.[12] Perhaps in lieu of passports, every Jew had to carry an identity card, which was marked with a large "J." The adults had to have a thumbprint on their cards, and Susanne can remember her mother returning home from the police station and saying, "For Nazis, they were quite decent. They offered us water to wash the black off our hands."[13]

Susanne described this time and the way that tensions were rising:

Although my parents still tried to hide their anxieties, I could not help but be aware of what was happening. One day I was playing in the street with other children when a little dog came along to make friends with us. When it was time for us to go in, we tried to send him home, but he would not leave us. He had an address on his collar, so I suggested we should take him to the Police, just around the corner. The two Policemen smiled and promised they would look after him. I went home, to tell my parents how enterprising we had been. They were horrified and said, 'You, a Jewish child, bringing yourself to the notice of the German Police! Never, never do such a thing again.'[14]

Indeed, the atmosphere was becoming trickier to navigate. Susanne can remember two antisemitic incidents:

One day some bigger boys chased me down the street, caught me and chalked a J on my school bag.

Nothing serious! The other was rather more unpleasant. Coming home with Rita one day, we found the caretaker of our house, out in the street, with the door locked, shouting about not letting Jews in the house. I think he might have been drunk, but it felt very nasty. Eventually another family came along and we were able to get in.[15]

Imagine being locked out of your home by the one who was in charge! Not only that, but Susanne used to play with his daughter. But at this point, friends seemed willing to turn upon friends.

### Kristallnacht

Then came *Kristallnacht*—November 9, 1939.

Astonishingly, Susanne witnessed nothing of the events during the night, nor did her parents. When the morning came, they sent her to school at 7:30 as always. She met up with her friend, Lore, and they walked to school together.

When the girls came near the school, located at the synagogue, some women stopped them and said, "Go back home, the Synagogue is on fire."[16]

Lore was extremely upset by the news and began to cry, so Susanne offered to walk home with her. When she arrived at Lore's house, she shared the news with Lore's mother and was further delayed. Thus, Susanne arrived home much later than she would have had she simply turned back and headed home on her own. Her own words paint a vivid picture of the tension that the Nazis had brought upon the Jewish community:

> [I] finally walked home myself. I found my father very upset. 'Why are you not with your mother? She is out looking for you. Did you come straight home?' 'No, I took Lore home first.' He was in the middle of shaving and beat me with the leather razor strap. I lay on my bed and kicked and cried, more at the injustice than the hurt. Eventually my mother came home, very relieved to find me safely there, and all was well again. I hardly like to tell this story. My father was not a violent man. I think it is the only time he ever hit me, which made it seem all the worse. I understand now, and probably understood then, his terrible anxiety. After I had left for school, my mother's pupils had arrived, told what had happened in the night, and she went

straight out to look for me. So, although I did not see any of the terrible events, it was very traumatic for me and it is vivid in my memory.[17]

Many things changed after *Kristallnacht*. The level of violence against the Jews was unprecedented, and thus people began to think that their "civilized" country might proceed in carrying out further unexpected acts of violence.

But for Susanne, life remained relatively normal. Her parents bought her a bicycle, the first one she had ever owned. Susanne loved it. It was heavy, and it was big—so large that the handlebars went up to Susanne's chin. One thing Susanne remembers about it is the adjustable seat: the seat could be moved up and down so that the bicycle could grow throughout the years with her. And it did. She used it until she was 12. For the time being, Rita would run up and down the street with her, steadying the bike, until Susanne was able to ride it on her own.

December brought Chanukah, and Susanne remembers receiving a Bible storybook, which she cherished. She also remembers another present from that December, but the present was not given to her. It was a Christmas present, a pair of woolen gloves, given to the caretaker's daughter—that same caretaker who had locked her family out of their house. It is another testimony of her mother's kindness, considering that Susanne's family did not celebrate Christmas.

Thus, life remained fairly normal for Susanne after *Kristallnacht*. A few things did change however. After the synagogue had been burned, Susanne was not able to return to that school. Instead, she began attending another Jewish school on Joachimsthaler Street. Meanwhile, some of Susanne's friends and family started trying to emigrate. Susanne also remembers her mother sending jewelry and silverware to a cousin in America so the cousin could watch over it for her until all of this had passed. In Germany, these items would be confiscated. Eventually, the Kindertransport movement came together, and Susanne's parents decided to attempt to find a place on one of the trains for their beloved only child.

**Preparing to Leave**

Susanne does not know when her family was told that she had been given a place on the Kindertransport, but she knows that she was not afraid of the journey or the new place. Instead, her parents had been quite positive about all of it with her, so it seemed like an adventure. Her mother taught her a few English words, and her Aunt Alice had a very good friend, Eva Bluth, who was already in England. Eva had sent Aunt Alice a book of children's poems, *Now We Are Six*, by A. A. Milne, and Aunt Alice used to read the poems to Susanne. Though Susanne did not know all the words or understand what they meant, she did learn some of the poems.

Ruth also made more clothes for Susanne's adventure. Susanne described her favorite dress and the story connected to purchasing its buttons:

> One dress was my special favourite, a Dirndl, quite a dark fabric with tiny flowers, and with narrow blue velvet ribbon and white lace around the square neck. We went to buy the buttons (I think at Arnold Muller). The young salesgirl showed us a selection of blue buttons. We both liked a small blue button with a circle of red and yellow flowers painted on it. To encourage us to make a decision, the girl smiled sweetly and said 'They are Adolph Hitler's favourite flowers.' That was the last thing we wanted to know! However, we did like them, so we smiled at each other and decided to buy

them. Of course, we would not have dared to make any comment.[18]

In April 1939, Uncle Julian and Aunt Kathe were forced to give up their apartment. Turning to Susanne's family for help, they moved in with Paul and Ruth. Always trying to keep things positive, Ruth presented this in a cheerful way to Susanne, telling her that it would be fun for her to get to share her bedroom with Oscar, who was now four years old.

Susanne was a bit more cautious about the idea. Though she knew Oscar well, he was a nervous boy and not nearly as outgoing as she was. His mother, Aunt Kathe was unpredictable—sometimes she would be pleasant and cheerful, and other times, she would be like a thunderstorm. You simply never knew what you were going to get. Perhaps it was because of all the events unfolding and everything they had experienced, but because of Aunt Kathe's temperament, poor Oscar always acted with reticence. Nevertheless, Susanne eventually did enjoy sharing a room with him; they took a box and placed it on the end of her dollhouse as a garage for his toy cars.

Uncle Julian was quiet and serious, but he was also kind and willing to talk with Susanne. She can remember asking him what would happen when she learned to speak English. Would she also start thinking in English? He responded that he did not know but if that did happen, she should write to him to tell him. When it finally did happen, it was so subtle that Susanne did not even notice.

Sadly, there was a great deal of tension between Aunt Kathe and Uncle Julian. As noted earlier, Uncle Julian felt fairly secure because of his former career. He once told Aunt Kathe, "The Germans are a civilised people, they respect the Law, they will not harm me."[19] Aunt Kathe, on the other hand, desperately wanted to emigrate.

With so many people in the house, it was necessary to make up some sort of schedule for the washroom. On school days, Rita and Susanne were first, and the men were last. This list was pinned outside the washroom in plain view.

Throughout this time, Susanne's mother was continuing to prepare Susanne for her departure to England. Their latest news was that Susanne would go to a camp in Tunbridge Wells, Kent. Eva Bluth had visited this camp and told them that it was very pleasant but rather cold. Upon hearing that news, Ruth bought Susanne some warmer shorts to make sure she stayed comfortable. These were some of Susanne's only clothes that were not handmade.

In packing for her adventure, Susanne included quite a few things—much more than just a small girl would need. She described the reason for this and also explained the reasons behind a few of the individual items she packed:

> Everything I was to take had to be listed and officially approved. I still have the lists. I was very well equipped and I understood why this was. My parents hoped eventually to get to America or England and I would have clothes to last a long time. For the journey, I wore two sets of underclothes. My foster mother told me later that she wondered why a child was so warmly dressed in July. I knew why, but could not explain.
>
> I took one game, my favourite, Mensch Aergere Dich Nicht [Ludo in England and Parcheesi in the United States]. We had a big discussion about which books I should take, some to be packed now and some to be sent later in a large trunk. The list included my Hebrew

*Oscar, Aunt Kathe, and Susanne, on July 3, 1939, the day before Susanne left Germany.*

prayer book, a German/English dictionary, Till Eulenspiegel, Andersen Merchen, and my mother's song book (I suppose I was allowed six). I wanted to take a small story book which I had recently enjoyed, 'Im Mittelpunkt Renate,' about a girl from a poor family who had won the Lotto. My mother did not agree that it was worth including. Instead, I had to have a large, rather serious book called 'Gut fur unseren Jungen.' This had Jewish religious stories. I did not read it once. My much loved Bible story book was posted to me later.

The day before I left, Aunt Kathe took photographs of me on the Balcony with my parents, with Oscar and with Opa. My hair is newly washed and shining. I have these little pictures but do not remember them being taken.[20]

Susanne also had a doll named Hannelore. She had short hair and a celluloid head, and Susanne's mother had made all the doll's clothes. Susanne states, "Her dress was blue and white with a red belt. Her overcoat was navy blue with brass buttons and matching beret. She looked like a very smart school girl."[21]

Hannelore, however, was not packed. She stayed behind.

## Leaving

It was July 4, 1939, two months before Britain declared war on Germany. Susanne was eight.

Early that morning, Susanne's parents took her to the station. It was full of other families, bustling around, trying to make sure that the children were prepared and that they said a final goodbye. Susanne described her parting:

```
        Dear granddaughter Susanne,


May you always stay as you are now, a good and godfearing child

then the Lord will grant our wishes for you and give you a happy

future.


I hope you will always remember your loving grandparents

                        Hermann and Auguste Schlome

                    Berlin W. 30, the 20.6.39
```

*A translation of the note written in the front of Susanne's Hebrew prayerbook by her grandparents.*

I was not going to cry and was very proud of my mother because she was not crying, unlike my father. I was pleased when I had to get into the train, before it got any more emotional. Of course we did not realise that we were saying goodbye for ever.[22]

Inside the train, Susanne was surrounded by other children; none of the adult chaperones were in her cabin. Each child had a label and some type of small case. They were only allowed to take one Reichsmark with them.

Because none of them knew each other, they barely spoke. From time to time, an adult came to check on them, and eventually, the train stopped and the police walked through. Susanne was incredibly scared—worried that she might be taken and turned back and her adventure would be over. Nevertheless, the men simply looked at papers, said nothing, and passed to the next compartment. They did not do anything untoward. It is likely that this memory was formed at the border between Germany and Holland.

Soon after the visit from the police, the train stopped again. This time they were in Holland; they were allowed to disembark from the train and were greeted by Dutch women who offered them lemonade and currant buns. It had been a long time since Susanne had tasted such white bread.

Back on the train, they eventually stopped at the Hook of Holland, where they boarded a ship bound for England. On the ship, they had a meal and slept for the night. The next day, Susanne walked out on deck and tried out her English—"Good morning"—on anyone "who cared to listen."[23]

## Susanne's Family

The Nazis went on to decimate Susanne's family, as they did with so many others whose children had escaped on the Kindertransport.

The first to be deported were Susanne's grandparents, Hermann and Auguste Schlome—the grandparents who had written the note in Susanne's prayer book. They were deported to Theresienstadt[24] on September 1, 1942. Hermann, who was 85 years old, died 14 days later. Auguste, who was 80, survived longer but eventually perished in the Minsk ghetto.[25] Life in Minsk was brutal, with thousands of Jews being shot or gassed upon arrival. By the fall of 1943, the Minsk ghetto had been destroyed, and all its inhabitants had been either murdered there or sent to the Sobibor killing center.[26]

With her fearful premonitions, Aunt Kathe and Oscar were eventually able to escape Germany. Oscar came on the Kindertransport, and Aunt Kathe was able to follow him a few weeks later—but they found a place in London, and Susanne ended up in the country, so she did not see them for a long time.[27] Tragically, Uncle Julian's confidence was misplaced. Though he was able to stay in Berlin longer than some of the other members of Susanne's family, he too was taken by the Nazis. On May 19, 1943, he was deported to Theresienstadt. After a little over a year in Theresienstadt, he was deported to Auschwitz[28] on September 28, 1944, where he was likely murdered upon arrival.[29] He was 53 years old.

Uncle Adolph, with whom Paul had shared his shop, was deported on March 2, 1943, to Auschwitz, where he was murdered.[30] He was 61 years old. Clara, Adolph's wife, was deported on the same transport and suffered the same fate as that of her husband.[31] She was 50 years old. Eva, their daughter, was taken to Auschwitz on that same day on the same train and was murdered there—two months before her 18th birthday.[32] Walter, their son, was able to immigrate to Argentina around 1938, and so escape the Nazi terror.

Aunt Alice was also killed by the Nazis. Similar to Uncle Julian, she was deported to Theresienstadt, although she was sent there a few months earlier, on October 3, 1942. She survived in Theresienstadt for two years, but on October 23, 1944, she was sent to Auschwitz, where she was murdered upon arrival.[33] She was 52 years old.

Aunt Alice was deported to Theresienstadt with her mother, Therese Türk, or Oma Türk to Susanne. After surviving for two years in Theresienstadt, Oma Türk died on March 7, 1944, in the Theresienstadt ghetto.[34]

Just two weeks after Aunt Alice and Oma Türk were deported to Theresienstadt, on October 19, 1942, Paul Schlome was sent to the Riga ghetto.[35] He was murdered there on October 22, 1942, shortly after his arrival.[36] He was 56 years old.

Susanne's mother, Ruth Schlome, went to Riga on the same transport as her husband. She shared his same fate. On October 22, 1942, in the vicinity of the Riga ghetto, she was killed.[37] She was about to turn 42.

## England

Having left her family back in Germany, Susanne was on a ship bound for England. Eventually, the ship came to Harwich, the port of arrival. Some of the children were picked up there, and the rest were put on another train and taken to Liverpool Street Station in London and from there to Woburn House, the Jewish refugee headquarters. This was the case with Susanne. At Woburn House, the children were taken largely in groups, and Susanne had expected to go with a group to

Tunbridge Wells, the camp where she was to be housed. However, she was quite surprised when that group never materialized. Eventually she was left alone.

Remembering that she had some sandwiches left in her rucksack, she pulled out her little screw-top aluminum sandwich tin, only to discover that it had been bent and that she could not open it.

She was eight years old, in a new country, and all alone.

And now, this little girl who had been so brave and so excited about her new adventure began to cry.

Upon seeing her tears, a woman hurried over to her to explain what had happened. She was not going to Tunbridge Wells after all; instead, she was going to a family that lived out in the country. A family named the Hanslips had heard an appeal on the radio for citizens to house Jewish refugees. The Hanslips responded, and Susanne had been placed with them.

Alfred and Maud Hanslip were Christadelphians.

Though Susanne did not know it at the time, a few surprising changes had taken place, which is what allowed her to go with this family rather than being sent to a camp. The Hanslips had originally volunteered to host a girl from Vienna and had been given her picture and her information. But at the last minute, her father had refused to send her to England. Thus, a spot had opened up for Susanne. The Hanslips were told that instead of the girl they had expected, they would be getting little eight-year-old Susanne.

Susanne's parents were not informed of the changes before she left, but eventually a telegram was sent to them, and they were pleased that Susanne had been sent to live with a family.

Thus, from Woburn House, Susanne was taken back to Liverpool Street Station and put on another train. On that train, she stayed with one of the guards, who watched over her. He eventually took her to the first-class carriage, where he asked a well-dressed woman to watch her:

> She was very kind, tried to talk to me and let herself be entertained by me singing German songs. I found a large needle with a long piece of black thread, stuck in the back of a seat. I got out my little note book, with squared paper, and made cross stitch patterns for her to admire. It was a three hour journey and I think she must have been very patient! By now I was completely cheerful, imagining my new home in the country. There would be other children, perhaps a dog and a cat.[38]

*Susanne with Mr. and Mrs. Hanslip.*

The train arrived at Downham Market in Norfolk. There, Susanne met Mr. and Mrs. Hanslip, who had driven the five miles from their home to meet her at the station. Susanne went with them, and they drove to Susanne's new home in the village of Wereham.

## The Hanslips

When she arrived at the Hanslips' home, Susanne's predictions proved to be partly correct. Just as she had hoped, there was indeed a dog and a cat. However, there were no other children—a situation that suited her well, as she was an only child and was used to being with adults. Susanne described her new home:

> Everything was a complete contrast to my home in Berlin and I felt as if I had stepped into a story-book world. Mr. and Mrs. Hanslip kept the village shop which sold groceries, fruit and vegetables and even some clothes.

*The Hanslips' village shop.*

I had been used to a bathroom, flush toilet and hot and cold water. Here water was pumped up from a well. There was no bathroom. The toilet was in the garden. Once a week a tin bath was taken into the kitchen, rain water from a water barrel was heated in a 'copper' over a fire and carried in buckets. Instead of Central Heating, there were open fireplaces, burning wood and coal. Many people in the village did not yet have electricity but used oil lamps.

There was a walled garden of 1 hectare. Apart from a large lawn, about half of it was orchard, with a great variety of trees, apples, plums and pears. The other half was cultivated with strawberries, potatoes and many other vegetables, which were sold in the shop. There was so much to explore! Of course I did not learn all this on my first day.[39]

Adding to these differences was the fact that Mr. and Mrs. Hanslip knew absolutely no German, and Susanne only knew a few words in English. Moreover, their social status was quite different from that in which Susanne had been raised:

Mrs. Hanslip told me afterwards that she was quite worried when we unpacked my case. She could see from my clothes that I had come from a more prosperous home. What would I think of the different conditions?[40]

Despite these differences, however, Susanne had arrived at a home where she was loved and cherished: "Mr. and Mrs. Hanslip loved children and were very kind to me. . . . She need not have worried at all. I was perfectly happy."[41]

Though everything was new, Susanne was with a family that made her feel comfortable and at home. At times, she would "help" Mr. Hanslip in the garden and, recalling those times, she remembers how patient he was with her and how he enjoyed her company. Mrs. Hanslip "was so kind."[42] In the following months, she repeatedly tried to recreate one of Susanne's favorite puddings—but Susanne only knew the German name. Though Susanne tried to describe it, it took Mrs. Hanslip one attempt after another. Finally, Mrs. Hanslip discovered the cherished dessert—it was semolina pudding.

Mrs. Hanslip was also extremely popular with the other children. Some of them knew her as the shopkeeper, and others knew her as their Sunday school teacher:

> They would quiz me endlessly, 'What is it like living with Mrs Hanslip? Is she nice to you? Does she let you have lots of sweets?' Some of them came from very poor families and would have liked to be in my place.[43]

This was a special family with whom Susanne had come to live, and it was a family to which Susanne would eventually belong. Though she only wanted to call them Mr. and Mrs. Hanslip at first, she eventually warmed to calling them "Mum" and "Dad":

> When I arrived, they said I should call them Aunty and Uncle but I would not do that. What an awkward child! I went on saying Mr. and Mrs. Hanslip to children and village people but after a while I did not call them anything face to face. Once I was sent to the farm with a message. What should I say? They were friends. I thought about it on the way and just said 'She says . . .' It must have been a relief to them, and was certainly a relief to me, when I slipped into saying Mum and Dad like all the other children.[44]

Susanne began to see the Hanslips as another set of loving parents, and they began to see her as their dear child. Susanne summarized her relationship with them in these words:

> I was fortunate to come to loving foster-parents who treated me as their own child. . . . All my family left behind in Berlin perished and I remained with the Hanslips who became 'Mum and Dad' and, eventually, grandparents to our children.[45]

Susanne is indeed quite thankful for the relationship she had with this special family along with the willingness they had, after hearing an appeal on the radio for families to take Jewish children, to bring a new little girl into their family.

## A New Life

On her second day in Wereham, Susanne went to school. This too was an incredibly different experience. Instead of a long walk through the city, as she had taken to school in Berlin, this school was only a few minutes from her house. It was in the center of the village, near a large pond, and was next to the post office and the village church. There were only four classes for ages 5–14, and in the middle of the school day, the students went home for lunch—something no one ever did in Berlin.

Once again, no one spoke German, and in a little village like that, many had never even seen a foreign child. Susanne's dress was different, her hair was different, and the other children were rather intrigued by the new student who had come to their little school.

In school, Susanne's favorite subject was arithmetic. On her first day of school, she was given arithmetic tables to complete, and she did so swiftly. The next day, she was given the same task, which was frustrating because she had proven that she could do these problems the previous day. Thus, she made up her own harder computations to complete.

Susanne also picked up English fairly easily. When she heard words at school she did not understand, she would try to remember them until she came home. Once she was home, she would ask what they meant and have them demonstrated to her. She can remember needing clarification for the difference between "push" and "pull" and "sleeve" and "slide." Occasionally she would come home with swear words, in which case she would be firmly told that she should never repeat those words again.

Once Susanne's parents knew where she was, they began writing her letters. The letters reminded Susanne that she needed to be obedient, thankful, and most importantly, that she needed to write every week. The first letter, which arrived just a few days after Susanne had come to the Hanslips, stressed this point multiple times:

Dear Little Susanne,

Today we have received both your first cards and are very pleased that you have written so promptly, as you had promised. It will stay like that, yes?

Now you are already in England and we hope that you made the rest of the journey as cheerful and enjoyable as the first part. . . . On the typewritten paper is a surprise which I have thought of for you. It is the beginning of a story which will appear in installments, like those in a newspaper.

Every time if you have written to us nicely and diligently and fully, there will come with my letter a new installment. You can collect the sheets and bind

Sonnabend, den 8.7.39.

Liebes Susannchen!

Nun bist Du schon einige Tage in England und es ist gewiss schon sehr schön dort. Dass Du nicht ins Heim gekommen bist, sondern gleich in eine Familie war für Dich wohl eine ebenso grosse Überraschung wie für uns. Aber ich denke, dass es gut so ist. Sonst wärest Du nach 2 oder 3 Wochen Heim erst wieder umgezogen und hättest dich neu eingewöhnen müssen. In 2 oder 3 Wochen aber bist Du in Wareham schon ganz zu Hause und kein bissel mehr fremd. Wir müssen also dankbar sein, dass alles so gekommen ist — der liebe Gott schickt alles so, wie es für seine Kindlein am besten ist.

Wir haben auf Tante Käthes grossem Atlas gleich gefunden, wo Kings Lynn liegt, aber Wareham ist nicht drauf. Nun musst Du mir schreiben, wie es dort aussicht. Liegt es am Wasser? Das Meer ist wohl nicht weit entfernt, nicht wahr? Ist Wareham ein grosser Ort? Und vor allem, schreibe mir von Deinen

*The front page of the letter that Susanne's mother sent to her on July 8, 1939.*

them into a nice book. . . .

Stay loving and good and think of Mutti and Vati as we always think of you.

oxoxoxo (hugs and kisses) Mutti[46]

Both her mother and father wrote her stories. Her mother's story was about Hannelore, in which she and Vati were the doll's grandparents, and Susanne, the doll's mother, had gone off to England.

Her parents yearned for news from her. Perhaps this is best evidenced by the fact that, on July 8, 1939, just one day after sending the above letter, they sent her another:

Dear Little Susanne,

Now you are already several days in England and it is certainly nice there. That you did not go to the Home, but to a family was as much a surprise to you as to us. But I think that it is good so. Otherwise, after 2 or 3

*The Strawberry Tea, the event described in Susanne's unfinished letter. Susanne is on the far right, with her hand shading her face.*

weeks you would have had to move again and get used to new surroundings. We must be thankful that it all happened so—the Dear God gave it all so as it is best for his little child. . . .

You must never forget that Aunt and Uncle Hanslip now act as Mutti and Vati for you. So you must go to them with all your little sorrows and all your little joys. Trust everything to them. When they are so kind and take our beloved Susanne for themselves, then the child must also know always to be thankful and loving to them, as to Mutti and Vati. . . .

Now dear little one, stay good and loving and well and write diligently.

oxoxoxoxo Mutti[47]

Susanne, following her mother's instructions, also wrote letters to her parents, and these letters were always written in German. In one letter, which Susanne still has, as it was never finished, she described a "tea party" that would be held in the Hanslips' garden for children from "another school."[48] Afterward, the letter stated that Susanne and the other children would all play on the farm together. As Susanne found out later, the event described in this letter was actually the Strawberry Tea—an annual event for the local Christadelphian ecclesia's Sunday school students.

The Hanslips' neighbors also happened to be Christadelphians. In another letter, Susanne described their farm and their animals:

The 'Hollies' farm was next to our garden and I was taken to see the animals. There was a herd of cows which were milked by hand. The milk was taken round the village each day and sold from a churn. To my great delight, there were 3 fat sows called Sue, Susi and Susanne. The 3 large cart horses were called Trixy, Pixy and Gipsy. Ducks swam on the pond and chickens ran around the yard. The two fierce guard dogs in a wire run, were rather frightening. It was a real family farm. Now, it would be run by one man with machinery, but then, all the family of 4 sons and 2 daughters were employed. Philip, aged 12 was still at school, but he had his responsibilities. He had his own pony called 'Happy'. Cyril, who was about 19, took great interest in me. When he was collecting hay with a horse and cart, and passed by the shop, he would call for me and let me ride on the horse. How different from life in Berlin![49]

At one point, Susanne's parents wrote that they had heard all about the animals but wanted to hear more about her. Susanne remembers thinking, "I have told them that I am alright and happy, why do I have to write so much?"[50]

After two weeks, Eva Bluth, Aunt Alice's friend, came to see Susanne for three days. It was such a joy for Susanne to be able to speak freely with someone—and someone who could also speak German. It was also a treat for Paul and Ruth to have someone who could see Susanne with the Hanslips and could report on her progress, happiness, and safety.

There was, however, one problem that Eva conveyed in her report: Susanne, fairly typical of an eight year old, refused to have her hair washed.

Back in Berlin, Susanne's hair would be washed in a bath and then rinsed under the shower. When the time came to wash her hair in England, an enamel bowl would be put on the kitchen table so the whole process could be done in the kitchen. Susanne simply could not fathom this, and so she protested, "You have not the things." She explained:

> I had long, wavy hair and my mother would twist it around with a comb, while it was still wet, so that it formed sausage curls, one each side and three at the back. I was afraid that it would not go right. Eva spoke to me very firmly and washed it for me. She must have told my mother about this, because I had a letter saying that now I was out in the fields, my hair would get more dusty. I must let Mrs. Hanslip wash it whenever she wanted.[51]

During the summer of 1939, Susanne received a large shipment from her parents. This shipment was quite expansive, containing many more clothes and books, along with ice skates, a set of cutlery, small silver dishes, a camera, and two more exciting items: Hannelore and Susanne's bicycle. Ruth sent Mrs. Hanslip a few requests about the bicycle: "Dear Mrs. Hanslip, Susanne will say that she can ride, but she has only learned for a little while and now she has to ride on the other side. Please do not let her ride in the street by herself."[52]

This was not a problem, as the Hanslips had such a large yard, and Susanne could ride around in it. Many of the children in the village were impressed with Susanne's bike and its back-pedal brake.

At the end of November, in anticipation of her birthday the following month, Susanne's father sent her a very touching letter. She had been gone for six months:

November 24, 1939

My Dear Little Susanne,

It is about time I wrote you a few lines.

It is the first time that we are not celebrating your birthday together and also you will not be receiving a birthday present from us. If it were possible we would love to be with you. We speak every day of your birthday and think of last year and how lovely it was to be together. We shall trust in the dear God and hope that you are healthy and that from now on, you may have a happy life and carefree youth that it may be granted to us to be reunited with you soon.

Dear Susanne, 9 years old! You are indeed almost a young lady, and must fully understand why we allowed you to leave the family home. You will know that this decision was not taken lightly. It is the highest achievement and the greatest happiness for parents to raise their children and help them to develop into decent people. Unfortunately, at the moment, we are unable to fulfill that role. Thank God, we know you are in good hands, being taken care of by those taking over the parental role.

As you are now living in the country, you have a lot to do with animals, which I know you enjoy, and so you will have noticed that the animals, chickens, ducks, pigs, cows, geese etc look after their offspring for only as long as they cannot feed themselves, however, as soon as the time is right, they do not look after the little one any longer, and let them go their own way. Therein lies the difference between humans and animals. We parents take care of the development and education of our children, until they are fully grown, but our care and love lasts as long as we live, yes, we live for our children and are, therefore, only happy and contented when our children are happy.

Think of dear Opa, he is 83 years old and comes to see his children every day, and most of all he loved to see his six grandchildren around him.

And also with Oma Turk, Tante Ita [Aunt Alice] and darling Mutti, you could see how they depend on each other. So you will understand that every day we receive a letter from you, it is a feast day, and today we even received two! Dear Opa was especially pleased that you sent him your best wishes.

Now we celebrate Chanukah, in memory of difficult times and in the hope of a better future, and we will imagine you with us, as you sang along with us in past years with your little squeaky voice.

Perhaps there will be some Birthday surprises and you will write to us about them.

Stay well and all good wishes to you from Vati, who is always thinking of you.

Greet Mr. and Mrs. Hanslip from us.[53]

**The War Years**

When war broke out in September 1939, Susanne experienced a bit of animosity. At school, some of the boys began to call her "Bosch," a derogatory name for the Germans derived from the French word translated as "head"—and used to imply that the Germans had thick heads, or were slow to comprehend. The headmaster of the school quickly put a stop to that. On another occasion, Susanne remembers that the Hanslips were asked why they chose to take in a little German girl, as the Germans were the enemies. Mrs. Hanslip patiently explained that although Susanne was German, she was also Jewish and that the Nazis were enemies with the Jews so, therefore, Susanne had actually fled from the Nazis.

It must have been terrifying to be a child whose home country had gone to war with her adopted country.

At the same time, her parents could no longer write directly to the Hanslips—instead, letters had to first be sent to Holland because it was a neutral country. When that was no longer possible after Germany had overtaken Holland in May 1940, the letters came through the United States. Eventually, communication had to come via the Red Cross, and messages were limited to 25 words. Susanne's responses were also limited to the same number.

Three months after the war had broken out, in December 1939, Eva Bluth again came to visit. It was Chanukah and also Susanne's ninth birthday: "It was a wonderful surprise for me. This time I only wanted to speak English with her. She could see that I was very settled in my new life. I was speaking English fluently and reading English books."[54]

Susanne recalls skating on the frozen pond in January of that year, after the headmaster of her school walked to the middle of the pond and jumped up and down on the ice, testing its strength. In the spring of that year, Susanne was given her own garden plot where she grew radishes and sweet peas. This young girl from Berlin eventually became a country girl who very much enjoyed the outdoor life.

Throughout this period, there was rationing, conscription, and forced blackouts for all the homes. Because they were in the country, there were never any bombings, but that brought about the new challenge of evacuees from London who had temporarily resettled to escape the bombing in the cities.

Even though there was rationing, living in a farming village meant that, as Susanne recalls, there was always plenty to eat. This location also brought a unique opportunity to the Christadelphians in the village, as Christadelphians are conscientious objectors. During conscription, many of the Christadelphians in the area were able to retain their jobs rather than serve in the military because their farming was essential to the war effort.

## The Christadelphians

It was not easy for the Hanslips to add another member to their family. They were country folk who ran a small shop in a village. But before a family could bring a Jewish refugee into their home, they had to pledge £50, which would fund the child's return to his or her parents when things settled down on the European mainland. Regardless, the Hanslips made this pledge, not entirely sure where they would find the £50 if it were eventually necessary but believing that somehow God would provide it:

> The Hanslips, although they seemed financially OK, having a village shop and land, did not have any spare money. Every penny was ploughed back into the business. So they pledged in the spirit of 'God will provide.'[55]

This was the type of thinking that motivated the Hanslips. Their beliefs, as Christadelphians, pushed them into taking action. In fact, as is the case in so many of these stories, Susanne found out the specific reason that the Hanslips had been so moved to help her. One day, Mrs. Hanslip explained,

"True Christians love Jews and try to help them. That was why she had wanted to give a home to a Jewish child."[56]

It was because of their fervent belief in what was taught in the Bible that Mr. and Mrs. Hanslip responded to the radio broadcast, as was true for so many Christadelphians. Their beliefs influenced their actions.

At the same time, it was an adjustment for Susanne to move from a Jewish family to a Christadelphian family. As part of the Hanslip's family, she attended Sunday school. Both of the Hanslips were Sunday school teachers, so there was not much of an option—she could not stay at home by herself. But she remembers that she enjoyed going, specifically because they were learning the stories of the Old Testament: "As it was [Old Testament] at the time, I enjoyed it very much. I would not have reacted well if I had been faced with Jesus straight away."[57]

Though she enjoyed Sunday school, she felt animosity toward Jesus.

Throughout her childhood, Susanne had known of two groups of people—*Juden* and *Christen*. To her, *Christen* were simply those who were not Jewish, or gentiles—and these *Christen* were those who had persecuted her and her family. When she came to England, Mrs. Hanslip had to explain to her what Biblical Christianity meant. Though "Christian" and "*Christen*" sounded similar, one was a religion, and one was a term used to describe everyone who was non-Jewish. Eventually, Mrs. Hanslip taught Susanne that Biblical Christianity, unlike the *Christen* Susanne had known in Berlin, does not teach hatred for the Jews. What Susanne had experienced in Germany was completely the opposite of Biblical Christianity. In fact, Mrs. Hanslip told Susanne that

Jesus himself was a Jew, so it was contradictory for any Christians to hate Jews.

But at the beginning, Christianity and its focus on Christ was not something Susanne appreciated. After Sunday school, she sat through the Christadelphian adult lectures where she occupied her time with her own activities. But she half-listened to the preaching:

> From time to time, I would hear the word Jesus and would mutter, under my breath, 'Zat man' (I could not manage the English 'th' yet). I don't remember saying this, but was told about it later. But I remember the feeling.[58]

Susanne described these feelings toward Jesus, before she had learned more about Biblical Christianity, as "antagonistic."[59] In another recollection, she remembered wanting to somehow prevent Jesus from coming into their meeting hall:

> On the wall at the front of the Meeting Room there was a semi-circle of words 'Christ is coming and will reign on Earth.' Overhead there was a large ventilation grill which was propped open in Summer. I think I understood just the first three words. When every one stood up for prayers, with their eyes shut, I thought 'I suppose they think he will come through there while they have their eyes shut. I am going to keep mine open so he won't be able to come.'[60]

Susanne did not think that she could stop Christ's coming to the earth; she only understood the first three words: "Christ is coming." With the ventilation panel overhead being propped open, Susanne had the idea that Jesus was going to come straight through the opening. Somehow, she thought, if she kept her eyes open, Jesus would not come through that opening! She could prevent him from coming there. Eventually, however, these feelings softened.

> As I got older I listened critically and absorbed the teaching at the meetings. When travel restrictions were lifted, after the War, we had outstanding visiting speakers (they were pleased to come to a country village). Often they stayed with us and influenced me a lot. By the time I was 15+, I was accepting Christadelphian teaching, influenced also by the godliness of my foster parents. . . . When I was 16 we had a local Bible Campaign, with enthusiastic visiting members. I was moved to want to be baptised by an emotional public talk on 'The Cross of Christ.'[61]

Thus, about a year later, in January of 1948, moved by the teaching of the Christian scriptures, aligned with the teaching of the Jewish scriptures, Susanne chose to join the Christadelphians. No one forced her to do it, and she was free to make her own decisions. This was something that she wanted to do and she has continued as a practicing Christadelphian throughout her life.

**After the War**

After the war, Susanne went away to college at Leicester and there attended a large Christadelphian ecclesia. For a few years, she moved around the country as a teacher, but Wereham was always home for her, until 1959, when she married Charles Woodin, who was also a Christadelphian. Together they made their home in Kent and raised a family.

Susanne, along with other family members, has returned to Berlin a number of times since the war, once as part of the reconciliation program and a few times to place memorial stones for her family members.

*Susanne and Charles's wedding, 1959. Front row: Alfred and Maud Hanslip. Back row (from left to right): Edward Woodin (Charles Woodin's father), Susanne Woodin, and Charles Woodin.*

Even though many decades have passed, the Hanslips and their kindness made an impression on Susanne that will never fade. Eventually, Mr. and Mrs. Hanslip became Mum and Dad. When Susanne had children, the Hanslips became grandparents to her children. They were a family, all because the Hanslips had been compelled by their beliefs to act for the sake of the Jews.

Therefore, when the Hanslips passed away, though it had been over 30 years since they had first met Susanne, she indeed was still their daughter. In 1972, after the death of Mr. Hanslip, *The Christadelphian* magazine reported:

> With a deep sense of loss we report the falling asleep of Bro. Alfred Edward Hanslip. Baptised at Lincoln in 1923, he had been for 39 years a faithful servant of this ecclesia. Bro. Hanslip was a living example to us all of the 'Man of God'. He did justly, loved mercy, and

walked humbly with his God. Now he awaits his Master's call. Our sympathy is with Sis. Hanslip and daughter, Sis. Susanne Woodin, and family.[62]

Five years later, in 1977, similar words were written about the death of Mrs. Hanslip:

Our sympathies are with Sis. Sue Woodin and family in the loss of her mother, Sis. Maud Hanslip of Wereham, who had been living in the area for the last two years. Her cheerfulness under pain and disability was an example to us all.[63]

Alfred Hanslip became Susanne's father, and Maud Hanslip became Susanne's mother. And all three of them were grateful to have one another.

---

[1] Susanne Woodin, "My Childhood Memories," Typescript, February 2010, 3.

[2] Ibid., 1.

[3] Ibid., 4.

[4] Ibid., 3.

[5] Ibid., 1.

[6] Ibid., 2.

[7] Ibid.

[8] Ruth Schlome, quoted in Susanne Woodin, "My Childhood Memories," Typescript, February 2010, 2.

[9] Ibid., 4.

[10] "Antisemitic Legislation 1933-1939," *United States Holocaust Memorial Museum*, last modified January 29, 2016, https://www.ushmm.org/wlc/en/article.php?ModuleId=10007901.

[11] Susanne Woodin, "My Childhood Memories," Typescript, February 2010, 8.

[12] "Examples of Antisemitic Legislation 1933-1939," *United States Holocaust Memorial Museum,* last modified January 29, 2016, https://www.ushmm.org/wlc/en/article.php?ModuleId=10007459.

[13] Susanne Woodin, "My Childhood Memories," Typescript, February 2010, 10.

[14] Ibid.

[15] Ibid.

[16] Ibid., 11.

[17] Ibid.

[18] Ibid., 13.

[19] Ibid., 14.

[20] Ibid., 15.

[21] Ibid., 14.

[22] Ibid., 15-16.

[23] Ibid., 16.

[24] More details about this ghetto in Hana Holman's biography and the glossary.

[25] Susanne Woodin, e-mail message to author, April 1, 2016.

[26] "Minsk," *United States Holocaust Memorial Museum,* last modified January 29, 2016, https://www.ushmm.org/wlc/en/article.php?ModuleId=10005187.

[27] Susanne Woodin, "My Childhood Memories," Typescript, February 2010, 22.

[28] More details about this extermination camp in Charles Ohlenberg's biography and the glossary.

[29] "Julius Schlome," *Stolpersteine in Berlin,* accessed April 22, 2016, http://neu.stolpersteine-berlin.de/en/biografie/1094.

[30] "Adolf Cohn," *Stolpersteine in Berlin,* accessed April 22, 2016, http://neu.stolpersteine-berlin.de/en/biografie/978.

[31] "Clara Cohn," *Stolpersteine in Berlin,* accessed April 22, 2016, https://www.stolpersteine-berlin.de/en/biografie/977.

[32] "Eva Cohn," *Stolpersteine in Berlin,* accessed April 22, 2016, https://www.stolpersteine-berlin.de/en/biografie/979.

33 "Alice Türk," *Stolpersteine in Berlin,* accessed April 22, 2016, http://neu.stolpersteine-berlin.de/en/biografie/3221.

34 "Therese Türk (geb. Kantorowicz)," *Stolpersteine in Berlin,* accessed April 22, 2016, http://www.stolpersteine-berlin.de/de/biografie/3222.

35 See description of this ghetto in Ursula Meyer's biography.

36 "Paul Schlome," *Stolpersteine in Berlin,* accessed April 22, 2016, http://neu.stolpersteine-berlin.de/en/biografie/1095.

37 "Ruth Schlome (geb. Türk)," *Stolpersteine in Berlin,* accessed April 22, 2016, http://neu.stolpersteine-berlin.de/en/biografie/1096.

38 Susanne Woodin, "My Childhood Memories," Typescript, February 2010, 17.

39 Ibid., 18.

40 Ibid.

41 Ibid.

42 Ibid., 22.

43 Ibid., 24.

44 Ibid.

45 Susanne Woodin, e-mail message to author, February 9, 2016.

46 Ruth Schlome, letter to Susanne Schlome, July 7, 1939. In possession of Susanne Woodin. Translated into English in the United Kingdom.

47 Ruth Schlome, letter to Susanne Schlome, July 8, 1939. In possession of Susanne Woodin. Translated into English in the United Kingdom.

48 Susanne Woodin, "My Childhood Memories," Typescript, February 2010, 19.

49 Ibid., 20.

50 Ibid.

51 Ibid.

52 Ibid.

53 Paul Schlome, letter to Susanne Schlome, November 24, 1939. In possession of Susanne Woodin. Translated into English in the United Kingdom.

54 Ibid., 24.

[55] Susanne Woodin, e-mail message to author, February 29, 2016.

[56] Susanne Woodin, "My Childhood Memories," Typescript, February 2010, 23.

[57] Susanne Woodin, e-mail message to author, February 17, 2016.

[58] Susanne Woodin, "My Childhood Memories," Typescript, February 2010, 22.

[59] Susanne Woodin, e-mail message to author, April 1, 2016.

[60] Susanne Woodin, "My Childhood Memories," Typescript, February 2010, 22.

[61] Susanne Woodin, e-mail message to author, February 17, 2016.

[62] Raymond Carter, "The Brotherhood Near and Far," *The Christadelphian,* March 1972, 140.

[63] Paul Ford, "The Brotherhood Near and Far," *The Christadelphian,* November 1977, 431.

# SUSE ROSENSTOCK

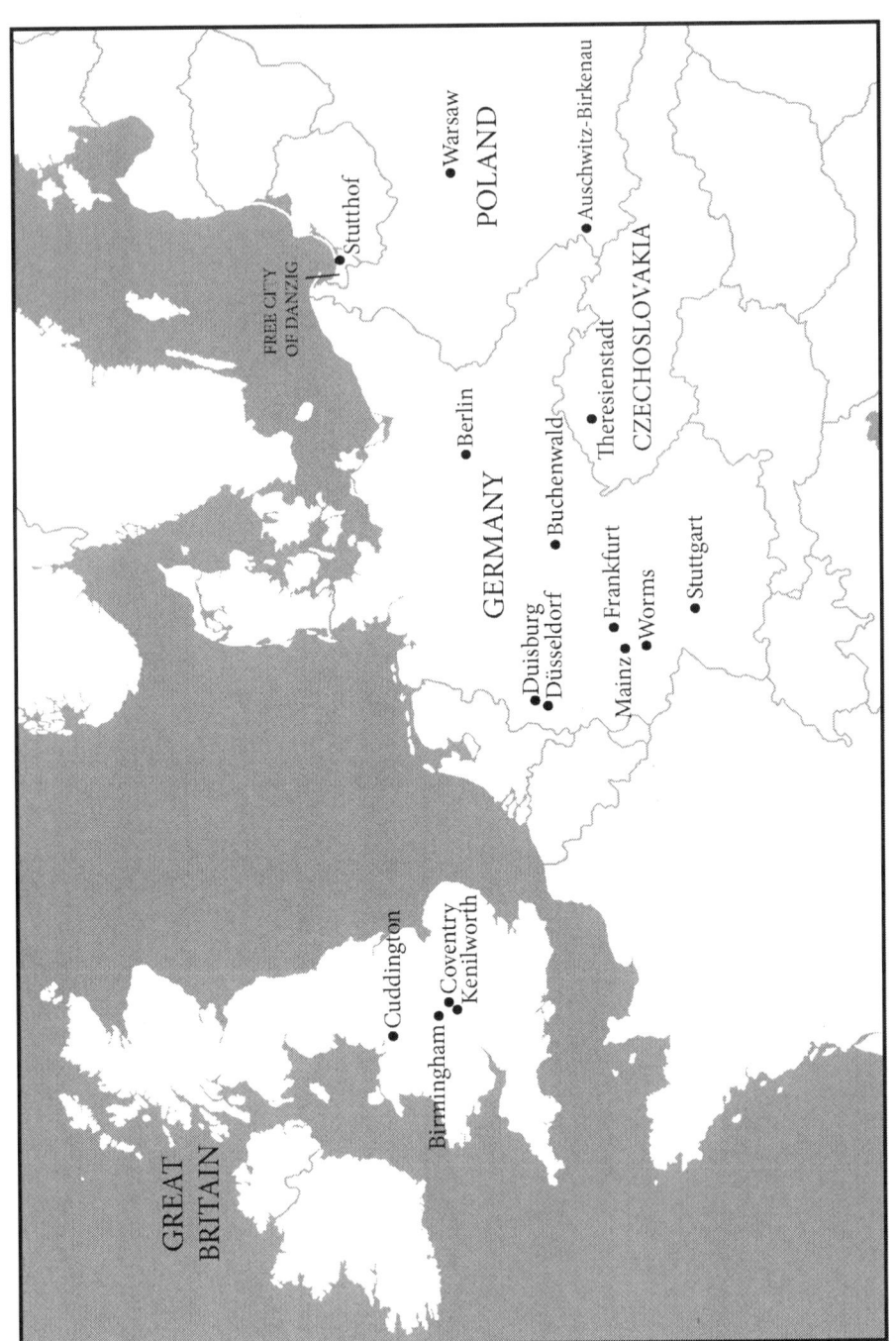

# 9

---

# SUSE ROSENSTOCK, NÉE HERZ

History has marked October 24, 1929, as "Black Thursday." Throughout the summer of 1929, the United States experienced a typical recession—sales slowed, and unsold goods began to pile up. However, stock prices continued to rise. In the fall of that year, it was recognized that projected corporate earnings simply could not justify the high stock prices. Eventually, the bubble burst, and the stock market crashed, beginning on Black Thursday.

A record was set that day: 12.9 million shares of stock were traded. The previous record was set on March 12, 1928, when more than 3.9 million trades were made. At noon on Black Thursday, bankers set up a $50 million rescue fund in hopes of continuing to prop up falling stock prices. Through their efforts, the industrial average only fell 12 points that day. The small investors who had been speculating—purchasing stocks with borrowed money, in hopes that the prices would quickly rise, as they had for the last few years, lost nearly everything in the drops from this week, but the market had not yet collapsed.

The following Monday, the market opened with a selling frenzy, and the industrial average fell 38 points. It was an enormous drop and a devastating hit for those who had speculated. This time, the banks did not rescue the markets—stating that their goal was to maintain order in the market rather than protect prices or investor profits.

Tuesday, October 29, 1929, was deemed "Black Tuesday." This was when the millionaires panicked. The small investors had been hit the previous week, and now the millionaires wanted out before they too lost everything. Within the first half-hour of the markets' opening, 3.5 million shares were traded. The bottom fell out of the market. Brenda Lange, in her book *The Stock Market Crash of 1929: The End of Prosperity*, described the tragedy:

> Investors and their brokers were reduced to tears . . . By 3 P.M., the industrial average had dropped to 230, down an additional 43 points from the day before. This represented a loss of about 12 percent for the day—a total of nearly 40 percent from its high of September 3, less than two months before . . . More than $14 billion was lost in the 16,410,030 shares that had been traded—a new record. The entire budget of the U.S. federal government in 1929 was just $3 billion.[1]

The next day, investors continued to sell their shares even though this meant losing money. An additional 16 million shares were sold. The financial system in the United States had collapsed, and many investors lost everything.

Unfortunately, this crash had terrible ripple effects in Germany.

In 1924, Germany had accepted the Dawes Plan, which stipulated that Germany would pay reparations in a payment plan that would rise over the years—peaking in 1929. Additionally, a massive loan was made to Germany, with half of the funds being raised in the United States.

This payment rescheduling, along with the loan, gave Germany temporary relief. Before this, it was feared that the

German economy could again collapse and that the hyperinflation that struck the nation between 1920 and 1923 would strike again. This payment plan helped stabilize the economy, and the loan helped pave the way for foreign investors, particularly investors from the United States, to loan money to Germany. From 1924 to 1928, Americans were lending approximately $500 million a year to Europe, with a large portion of that going to Germany. The result was tremendous: "The German economy made a remarkable recovery. . . . By the late 1920s the average German was much better off economically than before World War I."[2]

By 1928, as the stock markets in the United States began to swell, many American investors began to invest their money in U.S. stocks. The foreign investing in Germany slowed, and by 1929, it was down to a fraction of what it had been in previous years. Yet 1929 was the year in which Germany, according to the Dawes plan, owed the greatest amount in reparations.[3]

In the beginning of 1929, a revision was made to the Dawes Plan, known as the Young Plan. Its requirements were finalized in June 1929 and went into effect on September 1, 1930. It set up 59 annuities,[4] in which Germany would ultimately repay its debt in 1988. Adolf Hitler vehemently opposed this plan, encouraging a referendum that threw in prison any Cabinet member who continued to allow Germany to pay reparations.[5]

When the stock market in the United States crashed, American investors pulled much of their remaining capital out of Germany. Additionally, a lack of American demand led to a slump in world prices and, eventually, a standstill in international trade. Between 1929 and 1932, German industrial production dropped by 39 percent, and the registered number of unemployed reached 6 million. As the German economy fell apart once again, any confidence that middle-class Germans felt in "economic and political liberalism" continued to erode.[6] For some, it seemed as though the only way to get out of the economic crisis was by some radical means.

In May 1931, the *Oesterreichische Creditanstalt,* Austria's largest bank, collapsed. This event was felt in Germany too, because, as the bank collapsed, it withdrew 288 million Reichsmarks as loans from German banks.[7] By the middle of June, many banks in Germany were forced to close. This was exacerbated by the fact that a few days earlier, on June 5, German Chancellor Heinrich Bruning had announced that Germany would no longer pay reparations on the Young Plan. With all this uncertainty in Germany, more foreign money that had been invested in the country was also withdrawn.[8] Consequently, more banks collapsed.

On July 13, 1931, *Danat,* a large German bank, closed its doors, and many attempted to withdraw their money from all German banks.[9] The German government then intervened and ordered all banks to close for two days; during those two days, another large German bank, *Dresdner,* declared bankruptcy.[10]

These bank failures further destroyed any confidence that Germans had in their government and the economy and were used by Adolf Hitler to demonstrate that a change in government and policy was essential. On July 31, 1931, *The New York Times* reported Hitler's reaction to the crisis, which he had published in his newspaper, *Voelkischer Beobachter*:

> 'Never in my life,' he wrote, 'have I been in such high spirits and inwardly so thoroughly at peace, so entirely satisfied, as in these days. . . . The broad masses of the public have seen for themselves, perhaps for the first time, who was right—the Young Plan swindlers of the

Social Democratic, Centrist and affiliated parties, or the men of the Young Plan referendum.[11]

While the German economic world collapsed, Adolf Hitler could see that the pieces were slowly coming together to enable his rise to power.

## Beginnings

Suse Margot Herz was born on May 6, 1931, in Worms, Germany—directly in the midst of this financial crisis. Yet she knew nothing of it. Her childhood was comfortable, carefree, and surrounded by family members who loved her.

The Herz family was middle-class and owned a hardware store in Worms, named "The Herz Brothers," where both of Suse's parents worked. Albert Herz and his brother, Ferdinand, opened the store in 1919. The store and the Herz apartment

*Albert and Flora Herz with Edith.*

were connected; the apartment stood on the opposite end of the courtyard. They were a family of four: Albert Herz and

*Suse Herz, 1932.*

Flora Herz were Suse's parents, and Edith Herz, four years older than Suse, was her sister.

Life for Suse was very good. Though the economy in Germany was collapsing when she was born, her family's standard of living remained high. Although both her parents were quite strict—especially when it came to education—Suse felt well loved. Albert Herz held strong values and beliefs, one of which was his certainty that because he had fought in the First World War for Germany and had received the Iron Cross, he would be spared from any radical persecution against the Jewish people. Flora Herz was an extremely strong woman with a character and opinions to match. If something needed to be done, even if she had no interest in doing it, she would see that it got done. Both Albert and Flora kept a welcoming home, propping the door open on Sundays so that anyone could drop by. There was always lively conversation and laughter filling the house.

Suse's family celebrated all of the Jewish holidays together, typically at her maternal grandparents' house. She remembered her parents, aunts, uncles, and grandparents all being there. At Passover, there were stacks and stacks of matzah; for Rosh Hashanah, there were huge plum cakes and crumb cakes—and it was all prepared and made before she had awakened that morning! She remembered simply being astonished and wondering where it all had come from.

For the Herz family, the festivals were not just a time for family, but also a time to remember their religion. Albert Herz belonged to the synagogue at Worms, the oldest synagogue in Germany, and well-known in Judaism because of its connections to Rashi, the famous Jewish scholar—and the Herz family were active synagogue members. Every Friday and Saturday, they attended Sabbath services there, and Edith belonged to the children's choir. At her Jewish school, Suse was taught her prayers and how to host a Passover Seder.

Education was extremely important for the Herz family. Suse remembered being berated when she did not bring home the best marks. Edith, in her autobiography, wrote similarly:

> My parents wanted Suse and me to become broadly educated, so that if and when we immigrated to another country—America, Palestine or wherever we could be safe—we would be prepared for anything that might come our way. In addition to Hebrew, Chumash, Talmud, and English, we were taught the basic subjects.[12]

> My parents firmly believed in education. I can still hear them saying, 'Whatever you know up here,' (in your brain) 'it's very easy to carry.' When I graduated from this school . . . my father insisted that I go on to the equivalent of high school. With no such school available in Duisburg, I traveled one hour by train to the Javne Jewish School in Cologne. This was the best time of my life then. I loved learning, and we were taught a variety of subjects from some of the finest teachers.[13]

Edith relished her studies and did well in school, both of which pleased her parents. Suse wanted to be just like Edith but not just in school; being four years younger than Edith, Suse always saw Edith as the one she should emulate:

> [I] want[ed] to always do what my older sister did; she's four-and-a-half years older than I. Of course in those years, that was a lot of difference. She had a lot of different privileges than I did, and I didn't like that. I wanted to be just like her.[14]

*Edith and Suse at a wedding.*

Despite the squabbles that sometimes arise between siblings, Suse and Edith had a strong relationship all throughout their lives. In her autobiography, Edith lovingly described Suse and showed that although Suse longed so much to be like her older sister, Suse had a character all of her own.

> What haven't I told you about my dear sister Suse? . . . We were as different as night and day, as two sisters born to the same parents can often be. When I came home from school, I looked neat as a pin. When Suse walked in the door, her backpack was off the shoulder, her stockings were sagging, and her shoelaces were untied. Her homework was always messy. I would erase it from the slate before my mother had a chance to check it, because I knew she would get angry if it looked the way it did.[15]

> She had a wonderful sense of humor and a dry wit, even at a young age. Back in Worms, a heavy lady came

*Suse Herz with classmates at the beginning of the school year. Suse is the third from the right.*

into our hardware store looking to buy a chamber pot. Suse asked her, with a little twinkle in her eye, 'What size?' She couldn't have been older than 7![16]

In another instance, Edith told two other stories about Suse's humor: both taking place when Suse was six. Edith remembered their grandmother shaking her head at Suse and asking: "How come you always fall on your knees?" Suse responded, "Let me fall how I'm used to it." In the second instance, Suse and her grandfather were getting ready to go to the synagogue. Grandpa tried to hurry Suse along: "Hurry up. Let's go, child. I'm sitting on hot coals." Suse, not understanding the problem, simply said to her grandfather: "Well, sit on another chair."[17]

Suse Herz was a dear child, one with a strong imagination, a fun sense of humor, and a loving family. She played cards with her friends, was taught how to sing by her mother because her father could not carry a tune and was afraid that she would not be able to do so either, and went to pick white cherries on Sunday mornings when it was the season.

She was a typical child with a happy childhood.

**Antisemitism**

But then, in Suse's own words, "Childhood melted away."[18]

At school, Suse remembered being prevented from playing with the non-Jewish children. She simply did not understand what was happening. Suddenly, students at school were no longer allowed to associate with her. Parents snatched their children away in hopes that they had prevented them from interacting with Suse. Multiple times, she was chased home from school by children who were throwing stones at her and yelling, "Dirty Jew!" and "We don't want you here!"[19]

Edith had similar experiences. After Hitler was elected, she, along with the other Jewish students, was placed in the back of the classroom. She received tardy notices even though she came to class on time. For the first time in her life, she came home with Ds on her report card despite the fact that she had done all of her work well. Albert and Flora, who placed such a strong emphasis on education, were in shock that their daughter was receiving terrible marks simply because she was Jewish.

For Suse, life had changed: "Things were serious; it wasn't all fun and games anymore."[20] She was still a child who had a jolly and amiable personality, but her childhood was disappearing. And she was no longer carefree.

In 1935, Suse and Edith were prohibited from attending public school, so they went to the Jewish school in Worms. Edith wrote about how life became progressively harder:

> Things began to get worse for the Jewish citizens of Worms. The Jewish School was denied tax exemption, mass arrests of Jews occurred, Jewish doctors lost their professional status, and Jewish lawyers were disbarred. Special identity cards were issued, all Jewish passports had to be stamped with a large red letter 'J' and, as a further measure, an ordinance was enacted which required all Jews to adopt Sarah or Israel as an additional name to clearly identify them as Jews.[21]

The law regarding the name change was issued in August 1938, and all the Jewish passports were stamped with a "J" in the autumn of that year.[22] Albert Herz brazenly refused to change his name: he was a man of values and religion. He had a Hebrew name, he claimed: Albert Zadok Herz, *zadok* being the Hebrew word that translates to "righteous" in English.

For the whole family, shopping became extremely difficult. When they walked into stores, they could feel the atmosphere change. Shopkeepers did not want to sell to them. And the converse was true, too: the hardware store was boycotted. Repeatedly, the Herz family woke up to find red swastikas or slogans painted all over the sidewalk in front of the shop, saying things such as "Dirty Jew" and "Don't buy here."[23] And repeatedly, Albert Herz woke up in the middle of the night and went out to the front of the store to scrub away the paint, attempting to rid his business of its stigma. At times, Flora, Edith, and Suse joined Albert in the scrubbing once the morning had come.

Eventually, the hardware store was moved from Main Street to a back street in hopes that the Nazis would leave the business alone. Albert and Flora also made the difficult decision to attempt to immigrate. Flora's parents still lived in Germany, and she struggled to fathom leaving the country without them. But life in Germany had changed so dramatically, and this was not a way to raise children.

To apply for a visa, Albert made the journey from Worms to Stuttgart, a city about an hour and a half south. After applying, he was given the disheartening information that he was number 49,000 on the waiting list for a visa.

Then, November 9–10, 1938 was *Kristallnacht*. Life changed inalterably.

### Kristallnacht

On *Kristallnacht,* the synagogue in Worms was reduced to rubble, Jewish shops were destroyed, and 87 Jewish men from Worms were arrested. Suse described that night as follows:

*[Kristallnacht]* is something that is etched in my memory, and of course will be forever. My father had been saying *Kaddish* for my grandparents, my mother's parents who had died, and ran home quickly to tell us that there would be no school that morning . . . that the synagogue was on fire. And my mother was in the store with my father at the time, and she ran upstairs and gathered my sister and me, and we went to hide in the attic: a terrifying experience because it was the shattering of glass; it was the terror of not knowing what was going to happen to us. We were all crouching together, the three of us, not being able to move . . . and seven-and-a-half years old—things like going to the bathroom, you know, just trying to keep still. My mother wanted to go and save what she could and here she was with two little girls; what was she going to do? She stayed with us. Cold, basically hungry, and then after a long time, coming downstairs and viewing what had been done to our house by other people. . . . A cupboard in the kitchen was completely smashed . . . I can still remember it . . . seeing all the glass, all your belongings on the street, having to gather them up. And then of course watching my father being taken away, not knowing where, and there we were, in this mess, my mother with two little girls.[24]

Edith described the terror and gave a few more details regarding what had happened with their father. Just before *Kristallnacht*, the son of Flora's vegetable vendor gave their family a tip: "Go away. Go away. You will all be imprisoned and everything will happen to you."[25] He was a Nazi stormtrooper, knew about what was going to happen, and was absolutely forbidden from conveying that information to their family.

Nevertheless, because he had done so, their family was able to develop a plan. Because it was more likely that the men would be arrested, Albert would leave his family and go into hiding temporarily, returning to them once the danger had passed. After learning that the synagogue was on fire, Albert warned his family and then fled. The rest of the family, meanwhile, hid in the attic. When the violence was over, they left their hiding place, surveyed the damage, and wondered what had happened to their beloved husband and father:

> Where was my father? Somewhere in the forest . . . cold, hungry and fearful for us. After a while, my father returned to the apartment; but, unfortunately, a little too early. Moments later, two SA men burst through the door, pushed me aside, and arrested my father. No crime had been committed. He was Jewish, that's all. So there we were, Mother and Suse and I, just standing there in the wreckage of our home. Not a window left. Not a lock on the door. The furniture was smashed, upside down, and strewn all over the apartment and in the street. The trolley car that came down our street couldn't help but run over our bedding, and hundreds of feathers slowly drifted upward into the sky. I can still see the crooked keys on the busted cash registers. Utter devastation. We had no way to contact anyone. It was now just the three of us, bewildered and fearful of the unknown: a young woman not knowing whether she would ever see her husband again, and her two juvenile daughters not knowing if they would ever again see their father. Somehow we were able to board up the windows and clean up the entire store and apartment. I can't recall any friends or neighbors helping.[26]

After attempting to pick up the pieces of their shattered business, home, and family, Flora, Edith, and seven-year-old Suse tried to make the best of the tragedy. Each day, Flora summoned up her courage and went to the police station in an attempt to free her husband. But it was to no avail. November 12 was Albert's 50th birthday, and he spent it in jail.

One day, when Flora came to the police station, she found that he was no longer there—but neither had he been set free. Instead, like so many of those innocent Jewish men who had been arrested on *Kristallnacht,* Albert Zadok Herz was taken to Buchenwald concentration camp.[27]

At this point, Suse cried daily—for her father and for their ruined home and because of the unpredictability and the fear. To allow Suse some space away from the destruction, in hopes that she would be able to recover, Flora sent Suse to Frankfurt, about an hour north of Worms. There, for a couple of weeks while she recovered, Suse lived with Herta and Toni, Flora's sisters, whose apartment had not sustained any damage during *Kristallnacht.* She returned home before Albert was released from Buchenwald.

After a number of weeks, many of the men who were taken during *Kristallnacht* were released, Albert Herz being one of them. Suse remembered clearly the day that he returned:

> By the time he came back . . . he didn't even look like our father . . . the weight he had lost, the stress and the strain, the dirt. . . . Word had gotten to us that he was coming home; we had this big gate that . . . the car was driven into next to the store, and we waited for his familiar knock that night that he came home . . . the middle of the night. . . . I remember standing behind that gate with my mother and my sister.[28]

Edith described her father's return home in a similar way. Albert Herz was a different man when he came home from the terror of Buchenwald:

But when he came home, I hardly recognized him—he had aged 10 years. My father came back a broken man, but never talked about it, at least not to me. He saw things . . . he knew the worst was yet to come, and he knew in his heart that he would never make it through.[29]

## The Kindertransport

Eventually, it became clear that the four of them could no longer stay in Worms. Albert and Flora were now prohibited from owning a business, so they sold what they could of the hardware store and lived off the money. While Albert and Edith stayed in Worms dissolving the business, Flora and Suse moved to Duisburg, about three hours north of Worms, where Flora's aunt and uncle lived.

After all these experiences, Flora and Albert Herz contacted organizers in Berlin, working with World Jewish Relief, to seek places for both their girls on the Kindertransport. Albert Herz, though he had lived through Buchenwald, did not feel very comfortable with this prospect—the idea that his daughters would go to live with non-Jews was not an idea that he favored. However, when he argued against it, Flora reminded him that he had not registered them at the American Embassy to see whether they could somehow get out, because he had mistakenly thought that his World War I record would keep them safe. Flora, with her iron will, pushed hard for immigration, saying that they needed to save whom they could from their family. Eventually, Albert agreed.

Within a couple of weeks, it was time to leave for England.

It was July 25, 1939. There was approximately one month left before Great Britain declared war on Nazi Germany, so Suse was on one of the last transports out of the country.

Because their family was currently living in two separate locations, Suse and Flora took a train from Duisburg to meet with Albert and Edith in Worms. There, Suse said goodbye to her father. She would never see him again.

One parent was allowed to go with her as far as Mainz, and it was decided that it would be Flora. Once they arrived in Mainz and waited for the train bound for Holland, Suse saw another side of her tenacious and determined mother. She described the parting:

> The train pulled in, and that's the first time that I saw my mother flinch. The first two cars of my train were babies in hammocks . . . my mother saw that, and that

*The suitcase that Suse took with her to England.*

was the first time in all those horrible months that I saw her flinch . . . and she was going to put her daughter onto that train. . . . The last thing that she said to me was 'Be a good girl. Whoever you're going to go to, help in the household and just be a good girl' . . . this is the way that I was brought up. You do the proper thing all the time.[30]

As they parted, Suse's mother was most concerned that Suse grow up to be a respectable woman: a woman who did what was right, regardless of the cost. In those parting words, Flora conveyed what was most important to their family.

Suse sat on the train alone. It was not that she had chosen to sit apart from Edith; it was that Edith was not there. Although her parents had sought a place for both of their daughters on the Kindertransport, only Suse was able to escape to England. On that train bound for Holland, Suse could no longer follow the older sister she adored. This time, she was given a privilege that was not allotted to Edith. Edith and Suse had said their goodbyes in Worms.

Suse's only companion was her suitcase. It had been packed with clothes her family had salvaged from a store owned by Flora's aunt and uncle, before it had been taken over by the Nazis.

She was eight years old.

### The Journey

On the train, Suse sat in a compartment with nine other children. Five of them sat on one side, and five of them sat on the other. She sat there, throughout the entire journey, terrified.

After arriving in Holland, Suse was meant to meet one of her aunts, her mother's sister. Flora had given Suse a few pieces of jewelry she was supposed to pass on to her aunt—in hopes that the aunt would be able to trade the jewelry for whatever supplies she might need.

Suddenly, after riding all day without seeing any chaperones, Suse heard her name called out. They were almost to Holland, and as part of the check to make sure that none of the children were smuggling any valuables, Suse's suitcase was going to be searched.

She was petrified: she knew that she had two pieces of jewelry that had not been declared and that she was not supposed to have with her. What would happen if she were caught? Would she be detained at the German border and sent back?

Thinking quickly about what she might be able to do, Suse thought of places where she could hide the jewelry:

> My mother had bought me [a] pen . . . I took out the pen and I dropped the necklace into the little case and put the pen back in neatly. I found another hiding place . . . I put two other necklaces down my hosiery, down my stockings, and so it would land in the instep of my shoes, and so when they turned my suitcases upside down, and they searched them, there was nothing there but clothing. And the couple of things that my father had given me, such as my personal pictures; he had given me an alarm clock . . . but they found nothing else. And we finally reached the border of Holland.[31]

It was a near disaster, but by thinking quickly, at eight years old, Suse stayed on the train and entered Holland. There she met up with her aunt, delivered the jewelry, and around midnight, she boarded a boat bound for England.

On the boat, two children were assigned to each cabin. Suse's partner was a six year old, so Suse was in charge. On the journey, this poor little girl became terribly seasick, and Suse began to feel the same. Trying to think of what she could do, as the elder in the cabin, Suse remembered that whenever she was ill, Flora would dab a small bit of 4711 cologne on her forehead. Suse's mother just so happened to have packed a bottle of this cologne. Suse recalled her attempt at mothering this little girl: "Well, if a little is good, then a lot has to be better, and I must tell you that that cabin reeked from 4711 cologne. But nothing helped."[32]

Suse knew that she needed real medicine to help her cabin-mate and herself. In Germany, Suse and Flora had sought to buy Dramamine for the sea journey but had not been able to purchase any—not because they could not find it but because they could not find someone willing to sell it to Jews. Nevertheless, Suse remembered that there were a couple of older girls on the boat, about 12 or 13 years old, who had mentioned that they had some.

In a desperate attempt to find the girls with the medicine, Suse exited her cabin. Unfortunately, her timing happened to be bad—when she stepped out, it was just as a steward was walking round the boat to make sure that all of the children were in their rooms. In English, he told her to go back to sleep. She did not speak English. Finally, in frustration, he grabbed her arm, shoved her back into the cabin, and closed the door.

> My mother said everything was going to be fine. Nothing had been fine. My mother was left on the platform . . . I'm on the train with people I don't know,

and all these 'wonderful things' are happening. . . . I finally snuck out and found the girls.[33]

The next morning, after the little girl had been able to sleep, the children were all fed an English breakfast: white toast and tea. Suse had never seen white bread. Suspicious, after that night's incident with the steward, Suse warned the children around her: "Maybe you shouldn't eat this because I think they're trying to poison us."[34]

Sadly, Suse's trip was off to a difficult start.

## Suse's Family

Flora Herz had hoped that she would be able to send both of her girls away to safety—and in fact, at one point, that is what the whole family had thought was going to happen. Suse was to be sent on the Kindertransport, and Edith was going to be sent on a similar type of movement, albeit much smaller, to the United States. It was thought that this U.S. movement would accept 1,000 children. Edith packed up her suitcase, a family was found to sponsor her, and all of the Herz family was certain that she was going to leave for Cincinnati, Ohio.

But she never left.

Albert and Flora never heard back from the family in the United States, and Edith's suitcase was given to Suse.

Instead, Edith stayed in Germany, in Worms, with her father.

Eventually, Albert and Edith were able to move to Duisburg to be with Flora. Edith attended a Jewish school in Duisburg, which she loved. Other than her schooling, however, life was not pleasant:

We had to make do with what little money we had from the sale of the scrap of our hardware store in Worms. My mother seemed to make the best of it. My father, a medaled German military veteran forced to do slave labor in a burlap factory, was in a constant state of depression. By April 1940, the Jewish population of Duisburg was dwindling. Those who remained were forced to live communally in one section of the city. We lived in a small, cramped apartment with two other families. It was not unusual for bombs to burst through the air.[35]

In 1941, trains began to leave Duisburg for "the East." Edith was 14 and wanted to go with the first transport—not knowing where they were bound. Many of her friends were placed on it, and so was her boyfriend; yet Albert refused. Only later did Edith find out that the trains were bound for the nightmare that came to be known as the Holocaust.

After the second train departed in December 1941, all the remaining Jews in Duisburg were forced to live in a department store attic. Flora managed the cooking: the few provisions that some of the women were able to collect—along with the food that she and Edith were able to gather when they visited the baker, the fish shop, and some others during the cover of night. The owners of the shops all refused payment.

On July 26, 1942, Albert, Flora, and Edith were deported from Duisburg. They were among the last Jews in the town. They knew that their future looked grim, but they had no idea what awaited them when they stepped on the train.

The train took them to Dusseldorf, where they were corralled into an animal slaughterhouse, which reeked of death. They stayed there overnight, waiting to be joined by Jews from other transports. The next day, when their group numbered about

1,000, they boarded another train. This train took them to Theresienstadt.[36]

In Theresienstadt, Albert, Flora, and Edith were given numbers—not tattoos. Albert was VII/2-500, Flora was VII/2-501, and Edith was VII/2-502. They no longer had names, only numbers.

After a few months of life in Theresienstadt, Albert contracted a bladder infection and was taken to the infirmary there. He had no access to medication or doctors. On October 2, 1942, Albert Zadok Herz perished. He was 53 years old. Suse said the following about her father's death:

> My father died in Terezin (the Czech name for Theresienstadt) in October of 1942. He had been taken there . . . in July of 1942, and he died in . . . October. I thank God that he didn't have to suffer anymore. He had already suffered once in Buchenwald, and God was good to him.[37]

Flora and Edith continued to live in Theresienstadt for nearly two more years. Then, in mid-1944, they were selected for another transport. This time, the trains were made up of cattle cars.

After what seemed like a couple of days, the train stopped, and the door swung open. It was the middle of the night. Edith saw lights, barbed wire, SS guards with dogs, towers with weapons, machine guns and rifles, and a large sign that read *Arbeit Macht Frei*—"Work Makes You Free."

They were at Auschwitz.[38]

Edith was 17, and Flora was 42.

They were given tattoos with their numbers. Flora's was A-2674 and Edith's was A-2676.

At one point, the two of them were forced, along with a number of other female Jews, into a large room where they were told to take a shower:

> There were probably 100 women in our group, all ushered into a large room with tiered benches, like a modern day sauna, and multiple 'shower' heads. We looked around—no soap, no towels, no water. My mother looked puzzled and said to me, 'I thought we'd have a shower.' The window was locked, the airtight steel doors were bolted shut and there we sat in the dark.[39]

Somehow, astonishingly, when it was their time to die, the machinery of death malfunctioned:

> But nothing happened. Maybe 10-15 minutes later, the SS opened the doors and angrily said, 'Get your stuff and get dressed'. . . By some miracle, the gas chamber had malfunctioned and we were all saved. I think this was one of the only times in Auschwitz that this happened. A few years ago, I watched a documentary on television about Auschwitz. The gassing of the Jews in Birkenau and Auschwitz took place in two old farmhouses described as 'the little white house' and 'the little red brick house.' There it was as plain as day. My mother and I had been in that red brick house.[40]

In July 1944, Flora and Edith were sent to Stutthof.[41] In Stutthof, they were able to join a group of women that was leaving the camp to dig ditches. They were put on another cattle car and taken to the "middle of nowhere"[42] where they were woken up while it was still dark, given spades and

*Flora Herz, 1946. Note the number on her forearm.*

shovels, and forced to dig ditches for telephone cables. There were about 1,000 women. They began digging ditches in September 1944 and continued to dig until January 1945—into the middle of winter.

One bitterly cold day, they were called to stand in roll call. They got up, stood, and were told to start walking. When they were thirsty, they ate the snow that was on the side of the road.

At one point in this march, they reached a farmhouse and were told to go inside. Both Flora and Edith were ill. Flora had eczema all over her body; Edith's feet were frozen, and she could not remove her shoes. Some of the women there told her to urinate on her feet because they had heard that urine had the ability to heal. At that point, nothing was too repulsive.

Exhausted and aching, they eventually collapsed and fell asleep.

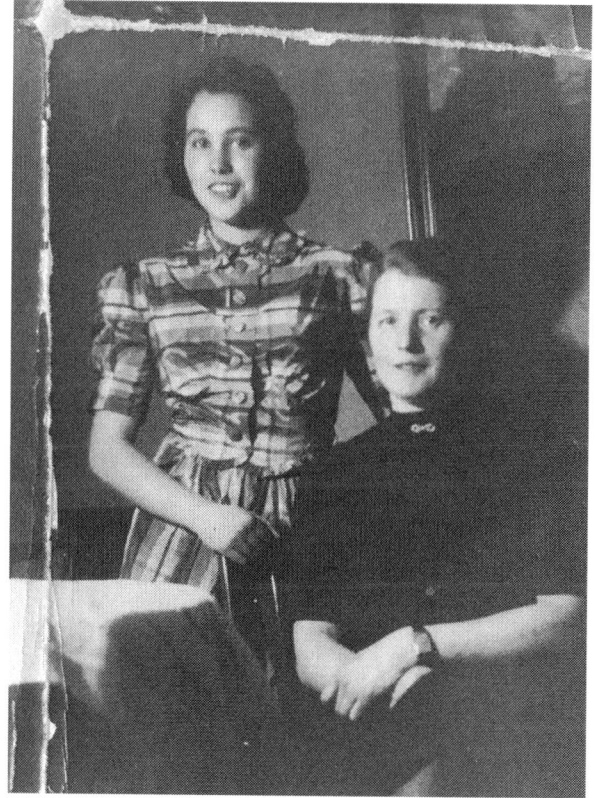

*Edith and Flora Herz, 1946.*

Flora and Edith Herz were awakened by voices—by cries of joy. The SS had gone. There were no more guards. The SS had herded them into the farmhouse and had left. Unbeknownst to the women, the Russian army had made steady headway into German territory and had liberated that region from the Germans. Flora and Edith were free.

It was January 1945.

For a few months after liberation, Flora and Edith struggled to survive. They were on their own in a strange land. Finally, by March, they made their way to Warsaw. From Warsaw, they went to Berlin. After living in Berlin as displaced persons for over six months, Edith and Flora were finally able to get on a transport back to Duisburg. It was November 1945.

In Duisburg, aside from survival, Flora and Edith had one major goal: to get in touch with Suse and see if she had survived the war.

Meanwhile, Suse was safely living in England.

**Arrival**

Suse Herz arrived in England on July 26, 1939. When she disembarked from the boat, she was led to a huge room where she was told, in German, to get her luggage and wait for her name to be called. Children around her were crying so, following her mother's reminder to be a good and helpful girl, Suse told those children to sit on her own suitcase while she helped them find theirs.

Hours passed. Suse continued to wait. Finally, she, along with three others, were told that it was their turn.

The four of them were met by two men, Mr. Laxon and Mr. Overton. All six of them boarded another train, which was bound for Kenilworth, a town near Coventry. On the train, Suse was the oldest, and she recalled, once again because she was supposed to behave, telling the younger children to settle down.

*Suse Herz in the Laxon's garden, Kenilworth, 1939.*

Once they arrived, they were all taken to the Laxons' house. Suse described that experience:

> One of the gentlemen's name was Sydney Laxon, who was a member of the Christadelphian ecclesia in Coventry. Christadelphians are a sect of people, very fundamental, 'brothers in Christ.' It turns out that they established hostels for refugees, and they took us into their homes. Sydney Laxon was particularly benevolent. . . . He had a lovely estate in Kenilworth, and there was sort of the first glimmer that things were not going to be bad, that they were okay. He already had a refugee from Prague. She had been with him, a couple of months, spoke some English, translated for us, and said in essence, 'It's okay guys; you're now fine.'[43]

The terror had been left behind in Germany. Now they were with friends. Now they were safe. Now they were with people who would treat them as their own family.

Suse and the three others stayed in Kenilworth for a few days and were then taken by Mr. Laxon to the respective Christadelphian homes that had agreed to house them. Suse was the first to be dropped off. Mr. Laxon drove to the house of George and Florrie Parry, a Christadelphian family in Coventry:

> They were a young couple, about 28 years old; they had a little boy who was 13 months old. . . . They knew nothing about me. These people knew nothing about us. They volunteered to take us in. I was chosen purely by my name. Their little boy was named David; had [he] been a girl [he], would have been Susie. The other three were taken in by three other families. . . . The

Coventry ecclesia, or congregation, was about 100 families I think. Out of that 100, there were 6 of us that lived with Christadelphians in Coventry—a big percentage, when you think about it.[44]

Apart from their beliefs, the Christadelphians had no connection with the Jews from Europe. But they volunteered to have them come to live with them because they believed in the promises made to Abraham.

Suse lived with the Parrys for the next five years. During that time, George and Florrie had another son, John, and a daughter—Suse.

## The Christadelphians

As so many of these stories go, Suse became part of the family. One of Suse's daughters, Deborah Rosenstock, wrote about the time her mother spent with the Parrys: "My mother's stay with the Parrys was wonderful from what my mother shared with me. They took care of her, loved her like a daughter, provided the best they could and made her feel a part of the family."[45]

As part of the family, Suse went to the meeting with George, Florrie, David, and eventually John. Nevertheless, this was not until the Parrys had received permission from Suse's parents to do so. As soon as Suse came to live with them, George and Florrie wrote a letter to Albert and Flora, letting them know where Suse was and asking how they felt about Suse attending Sunday school:

> My foster father outlined to my father what would be taught to me as part of their religion—going through Sunday school, or going with them to their services. Of course my father demurred, you know, what was he

going to do? He wasn't going to agree; this wasn't anything Jewish.[46]

Flora agreed, but Albert, being so religious, was not happy with the idea of his daughter attending a non-Jewish service. He raised objections, but the two families eventually decided that Suse would attend the meeting with the Parrys. Deborah Rosenstock explained why it was so important for her mother to attend:

> They never attempted to change her religion, and Auntie Florrie even asked my grandparents in a letter if they would be ok if my mom attended Church with them so she could fit in and be family. . . .They treated her like family.[47]

The Parrys all went to the meeting on Sundays. They did not want Suse to feel different or excluded. To this end, when Suse arrived in England, all of her clothes were German clothes— they were not the types of things that English schoolgirls wore. George and Florrie, though they were not people of great means, bought her English clothes so that she would fit in with all of the young girls around her.

But in a difficult balance, the Parrys wanted to make sure that Suse did not forget her heritage. She came with them to the Christadelphian functions, and she started to acclimate to English culture, but they always wanted her to remember that she was Jewish. Again, Deborah Rosenstock said:

> They were concerned that she fit in . . . never trying to convert her in any way, but to maintain her Judaism. When they could get together with other Jewish children, they did get together with them. My Auntie Florrie was really quite remarkable.[48]

In fact, Suse explained further just how hard George and Florrie tried to keep her bonded with her heritage. George Parry sought out opportunities for her to connect with Judaism:

> My foster father was the one who found out that the . . . liberal synagogue in London was doing correspondence courses in Jewish history and registered me for that. It had nothing to do with anybody else. They tried to get ahold of anybody . . . any Jewish people in Coventry—nobody came forward unfortunately. My foster parents had tried.[49]

For the first few months of her stay with the Parrys, Suse was able to correspond with her parents. But when war broke out between Britain and Germany, on September 3, 1939, the letters stopped. Adding to that trauma, Suse was a German living in England:

*A birthday party that the Parrys threw for Suse. Suse is the second from the right.*

319

And that's also when the neighbors—and my foster parents had to deal with this—the neighbors came to them and said 'Get rid of what you've got there in your house, she's a Nazi and we don't want Nazis here.' And they had to explain that I was not a Nazi; they had rescued me from the Nazis. But of course when I heard all this, I retreated to the house and refused to go out until it was cleared up . . . it took a couple of weeks until they convinced me.[50]

Not only did the Parrys open their house to a refugee—when they already had a small child!—but they also had to manage the stigma of having a German living with them. However, regardless of what people thought, Suse was family; even David and John's grandparents became "Gran" and "Gramps" to Suse.[51]

Around the time that the war began, the summer ended, and school started. Suse attended the local school and did quite well, although she remembered that she was much more serious than all of the other children. She had more to think about.

She picked up English easily, although words with multiple meanings were a bit tricky:

My first day in school, it was a new term, and the teacher is reviewing and asking about times tables. . . . I didn't know it was 'times tables' at the time; it was 'tables.' . . . after eight, I became completely perplexed and very upset . . . well to me a table was a table that you eat from, and I figured that a table could be extended eight times, two leaves from each end, but not to twelve.[52]

There were far more serious concerns, however, than mastering words with multiple meanings and times tables. Coventry was one of Germany's major bombing targets. Suse had to carry a gas mask to school and with her wherever she went. Some children were evacuated from their homes, and Suse was one of them. In November 1940, she was evacuated to the home of another Christadelphian couple in Cuddington, who became her second set of foster parents. They were older, and they had an older son, but they lived out in the country. Suse loved the country and from that point always hoped that she someday would have her own house in the countryside.

A few months after being evacuated, Suse returned to live with the Parrys. Life was difficult because it was wartime. Food was rationed:

> We had severe rationing in England. Food was at a premium . . . there was very little of it; bread was a big mainstay. Other things were gone . . . there were no eggs, there was no fruit, except apples and pears in the summer time; vegetables in the winter were cabbage and carrots. . . . All the parks in England had no more flowers—they had vegetable beds.[53]

Despite the hardships, the Parrys had a lovely house, and Suse was given her own bedroom. She helped take care of David and John, and one of her favorite activities was reading. *Anne of Green Gables* was one of her favorite books —because she could relate with Anne.

June 6, 1944, was D-Day, the day the Allies landed on the banks of Normandy. Suse became more anxious after this:

> After June 6 . . . it became more poignant because of it reaching Europe. Now, what was going to happen? Was I going to see my parents again—was I going to

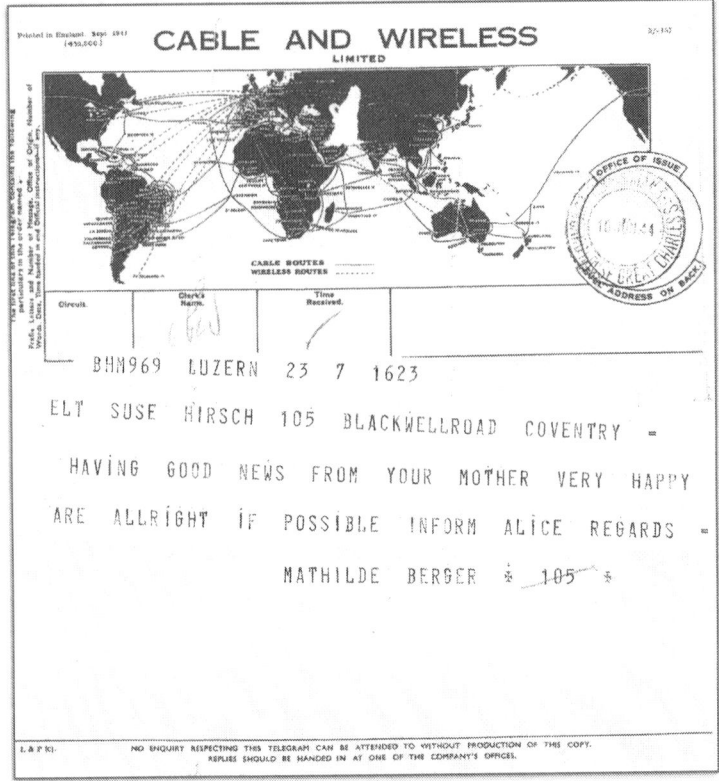

*The telegram that Suse received in 1944, telling her that her mother, and at least one other member of the family, was still alive.*

have parents? How quickly were they going to get into Germany, and were we going to win this war?[54]

Suse did not have long to wait. Four days later, on June 10, 1944, she received a very short telegram. Somehow, while living in the camps, her mother had been able to communicate with Suse's great aunt in Switzerland, and this aunt sent Suse a brief bit of news: "Having good news from your mother very happy are alright if possible inform Alice."

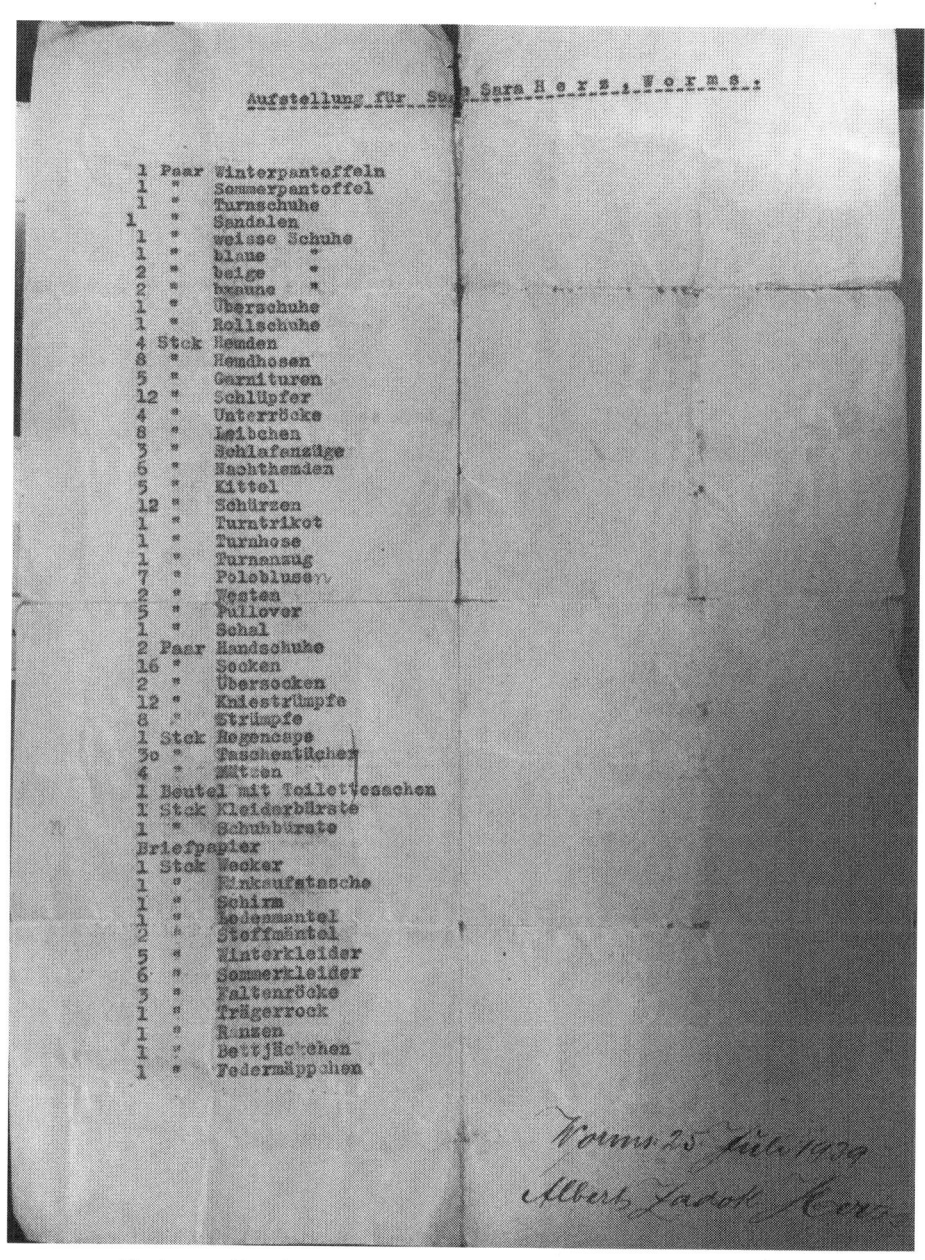

*The itemized list that Suse brought with her to England, and which Florrie Parry kept close to her, in her purse, until the day of her death.*

*The family portrait that was taken just before Suse left the Parry's house, 1944.*

Alice was Flora's sister—the only one of Flora's three siblings who had escaped Europe before war had broken out. She had emigrated from Germany to New York.

Upon receiving this news, Suse was overjoyed. Her family was alive. But what did the telegram mean when it said "your mother"? What about her father?

## The End of the War

At the end of 1944, Suse was contacted by a refugee committee at Bloomsbury House, a hotel in London that had become a central meeting place for refugee committees. She was told that she was going to be moved to a Jewish hostel.

She was not pleased about this; leaving the Parrys was not something that Suse wanted to do. The Parrys were also not pleased. Shortly before Suse left, they paid for a professional to

Top: *The bank box that the Parrys kept when Suse left their home.*
Bottom: *The bottom of the bank box, etched with Suse's name and the date of her arrival.*

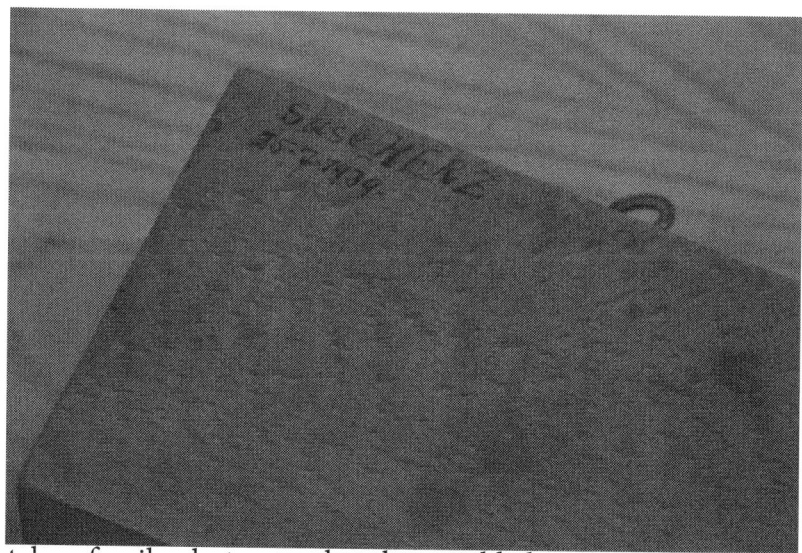

take a family photo—so that they could always remember their daughter. Deborah Rosenstock explained:

> [A] family portrait was taken just before she left the Parry's. My mom was definitely considered a daughter as much as their biological sons. They loved her so much—which is why they went to take this formal photo before they had to say goodbye to her.[55]

It was time to say goodbye to another set of parents.

When Suse was moved from the Parrys' house, the Parrys held onto two things that Suse had originally brought with her to England—a little bank box, etched on the bottom with the date of Suse's arrival, and the itemized list of what Suse had brought with her on her journey to England. These two items would help them remember the dear girl who had lived with them for so many years. For decades, until the day of her death, Florrie Parry kept the itemized list close to her, folded up in her purse.

Suse was moved to a Jewish hostel where she lived with a number of other refugees:

> In November 1944, I was taken from my foster family and put into a Jewish hostel in Birmingham where there were 27 other Kindertransport kinder. We lived together; we had a house mother and father. I did finish school because you have to go to school until you're 14 in England. I did not sit for the secondary school exam because that costs money, and there wasn't any. And then I went to work for the social service department of Singer's Hill synagogue in Birmingham. It was a terrible experience. . . . The woman who was my boss was a mean person. The hostel . . . I was on my own. The hostel took some of the money that I made, and I kept very little. . . . I was

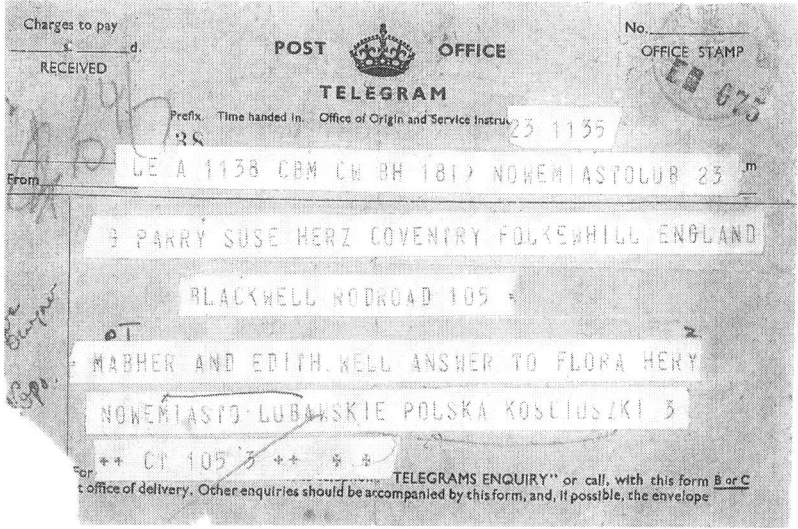

*The telegram that told Suse that her mother and her sister had survived.*

supposed to take care of myself, but it was barely enough.[56]

Suse did enjoy, however, appreciate being surrounded by other Jews. Though they all had diverse religious backgrounds, they celebrated the holidays together, and Suse began attending the synagogue again. She felt quite a camaraderie with a number of the young women who lived there—they were all in the same circumstances and all waiting for news about their families. When one of them received good news, everyone rejoiced together. When one of them received terrible news, everyone mourned together.

Then, Suse's day for news came:

> By that time, lists were coming out of Europe of survivors and of those who did not survive. . . . Every day when we came home from work, we would pore over these lists . . . one day it was my turn to rejoice. A

telegram found me from Poland that my mother and my sister indeed had survived hell.[57]

Suse wanted to respond to their telegram immediately, but she did not have the money to do so:

> I went to the office of the hostel, the secretary, and she refused me money, which of course, needless to say, upset me terribly. But my foster father and mother followed up and telephoned me and said, 'Did you answer the telegram?' And I lied: 'Yes.' But my foster father saw through it, and they came running to Birmingham that Saturday afternoon. . . . They took me to the main post office to answer the telegram.[58]

Though she had not lived with them for months, George and Florrie had not forgotten about their foster daughter. They knew that this telegram had been sent to her because it had originally arrived at their house: Edith had remembered the Parrys' address, through Theresienstadt, Auschwitz, and Stutthof, from that first letter that the Parrys wrote to Albert and Flora about Suse's whereabouts. The telegram arrived at George and Florrie's and was forwarded to the hostel in Birmingham. Because they knew about the telegram and its importance, they wanted to rejoice with Suse and make sure that she was able to respond.

## Reconnecting with Family

With the Parrys' help, Suse was able to send a response to Flora and Edith. But it was too late. Her mother and her sister had already left Poland.

Eventually, Flora and Edith contacted Suse again with a letter from Berlin. The letter was from both Flora and Edith. In it, they sent their love to the Parrys—still not knowing that she no longer lived with them. Because of the debacle with the telegram, they still had not yet heard from her. The following is a translation from the German:

Berlin . . . October 45

My dear Suse-Child,

Most of all, I hope this letter reaches you in good health. After an absence of 3 years, Edith & I landed back in Germany. But with what disappointment. We cannot go to Duisburg and are waiting for an opportunity to go. Our health is good.

We anxiously await a sign of life from you, my dear, good child. We sent you a telegram . . . but did not receive a response. When and how will we get together? Do you have contact with dear Aunt Alice? We don't have her address.

How is the Parry family? We owe them a great debt of gratitude. Please give them our heartfelt regards.

Please, dear child, write as soon as possible, to this address and maybe to Duisburg.

My greatest wish is to be together with you again; that will be a joy. It is a great miracle that Edith and I are still alive after having been in the Auschwitz concentration camp. So write or telegraph right away.

You are greeted and kissed by your mommy.[59]

Just below Flora's letter was a letter from Edith:

> My dear Suse,
> You will certainly be very surprised to finally receive a
> sign of life from us. I hope you are doing well and that
> you are healthy. You have grown to be a big girl, and
> maybe we will barely recognize you . . . Please write to
> us right away about everything. We eagerly await news
> from you. It would be even more beautiful if we could
> all see each other again soon.
>
> Many heartfelt regards and kisses
> Yours, Edith
>
> Special greetings to the Parry family![60]

Eventually, through the British Army, which was stationed in
Duisburg, Suse was able to respond and then maintain contact
with her mother and sister.

In 1946, before seeing her mother and her sister again, Suse
was granted a visa to move to the United States to live with her
Aunt Alice. Suse came to New York on May 14 of that year.
Throughout all of those months, Aunt Alice spoke German to
Suse, believing that Suse still somehow knew it, somewhere in
the back of her mind. Each time, however, Suse could not
understand, and she never spoke German back to her aunt. All
of the conversations had to take place in English.

Nine months later, her mother and sister came to join her—
permanently. The separation was over. After eight years apart,
they were reunited on February 11, 1947, at the New York
Harbor. Suse described the reunion:

> It was an incredible moment. I jumped over a barrier
> on the pier . . . I have no idea how I did, and I ran

down the pier to greet them . . . My sister and I are extremely close. My mother lived to see my grandson, her great grandson before she died . . . She did what she could to save her family, and she deserves an awful lot of credit for that. It's not easy to send away a child. I've looked at each of my children as they've reached the age of eight. I have three . . . I looked at each one of them and wondered if I could have that strength to do what she did.[61]

Edith also described the thrill of that day:

Naturally, a stack of paperwork had to be completed before they would allow the passengers to disembark. We were very anxious to see Suse and my aunt, who we assumed would be meeting us at the pier, but the minutes turned into hours. Impatiently, we stood on deck and looked at all the people waiting to greet the passengers, hoping to pick Suse out from the crowd . . . At one point, we noticed a ship steward getting ready to go ashore. My mother gave him her last dollar and a picture of Suse taken in 1946 after coming to America. She said, 'Maybe you'll see her and let me know.' And lo and behold, he came back aboard the ship and told us, 'I saw her in the luncheonette. I told her you are onboard waiting to disembark.' How lucky could one be? The miracles were continuing. All of a sudden, a booming voice on the ship's loudspeaker announced, 'There's a mother and a daughter who haven't seen each other in eight years.' My sister, now almost sixteen years old, but never an athlete, leaped over the barrier when she caught a glimpse of us. This was our sweet reunion.[62]

When Suse was reunited with her sister and her mother, she immediately spoke with them—in German.

*Top: Alan Rosenstock on a visit with the Parry family, 1970.*
*Bottom: Elaine and Deborah visiting with the Parrys on their way back from Israel, 1973.*

## Conclusion

After their reunion, Suse, Edith, and Flora lived in New York. There, Suse met Walter Rosenstock, whom she married in 1950. They were happily married, for over 50 years, until her death in 2002. They had three children: Elaine, Alan, and Deborah, and four grandchildren.

Suse Rosenstock never forgot her past. She also never considered herself a survivor, but eventually, decades after moving to the United States, she began to go to schools, churches, and synagogues telling her story. At a reunion of the Kindertransport refugees, Suse stood up and thanked the Christadelphians for "being so generous with us refugees."[63]

For years, Suse stayed in contact with George and Florrie Parry. Suse's children grew up knowing them. Her kids called them "Uncle George" and "Auntie Florrie," and the Parrys were like grandparents to them. Every year, for every birthday, the Parrys sent a card, not just to Suse but to her children, too. John Parry, Suse's foster brother, described the contact that their families maintained:

> In the early years after the war ended and when Suse was in the States we, from time to time, received what I can only describe as food parcels . . . The parcels were very welcome, not because we were in desperate need of food, we were well supplied, but more important, it showed the love and concern that Suse had for us.[64]

Over the years, the Parrys and the Rosenstocks visited each other on a number of occasions. At one point, Suse actually flew George and Florrie out to New Jersey so that she could see them once again. Suse's eldest daughter, Elaine, visited the Parrys on her travels back from Israel, as did her youngest daughter, Deborah, who also stayed with them and was able to sleep in the very bed in which her mother had slept. David and his wife visited Suse and her family twice—once when she was in New Jersey and once when she was in California. John and his wife also met up with Suse in the United States:

> I . . . was able to go and meet with Suse. While there it happened to be the Bible class evening at the Echo Lake ecclesia and Suse thought we would like to go. She had previously found out the time and place and came with us to the Bible Class. The subject happened to be, 'The Passover.' After the brother had given his talk and at the end of the meeting, Suse asked whether she could say a few words. She narrated to the brothers and sisters there the experiences of her early life and how she came to know the Christadelphians in the UK and expressed her gratitude. She then went on to talk about the Passover, which as a practicing Jew I suspect she knew rather more than most of us![65]

When George and Florrie first welcomed Suse Herz to their family, they began a relationship that would stand the test of time. Suse would never forget their compassion and their kindness—their willingness to make her part of the family. Nor would the Parrys forget her.

Elaine believes it is a testament to the love and care her mother received from the Parrys that Suse was able to live her life with optimism in spite of all the hardships she endured as a child. Her generous spirit was evident in all she did for her family, friends, and community.[66]

When Suse Rosenstock passed away, 400 people attended her funeral. She was certainly well-loved. Many remembered her as a "mother" who was always willing to help, and who gave whatever she had to offer. She never complained. Her life was the synagogue, and she devoted her time in service to others.

Such was the life saved when, on a day in 1939, a Christadelphian family in Coventry opened their home to a little eight-year-old girl, a girl who became their daughter for the next five years. Perhaps it could be said that it was in fact for the following 62 years, as she always thought of them as her foster parents, and they remembered her as one of their children.

---

[1] Brenda Lange, *The Stock Market Crash of 1929: The End of Prosperity* (New York: Chelsea House, 2007), 32.

[2] Thomas Hall and J. David Ferguson, *Great Depression: An International Disaster of Perverse Economic Policies* (Michigan: University of Michigan Press, 1998), 57.

[3] Ibid.

[4] "Young Plan," *Encyclopedia Britannica Online,* accessed April 22, 2016, http://www.britannica.com/event/Young-Plan.

[5] "Adolf Hitler Is Satisfied by German Troubles; Writes He has Never Been in Such High Spirits," *The New York Times* (New York, NY), July 31, 1931.

[6] Roderick Stackelberg, *Hitler's Germany: Origins, Interpretations, Legacies* (London: Routledge, 1999), 82-83.

[7] Caroline Fohlin, *Finance Capitalism and Germany's Rise to Industrial Power* (Cambridge: Cambridge University Press, 2007), 295.

[8] Thomas Hall and J. David Ferguson, *The Great Depression: An International Disaster of Perverse Economic Policies* (Michigan: University of Michigan Press, 1998), 95.

[9] Marcus Nadler and Jules Bogen, *The Banking Crisis: The End of an Epoch* (New York: Dodd, Mead &, 1933), 66.

[10] Youssef Cassis and Jacqueline Collier, *Capitals of Capital: The Rise and Fall of International Finance Centres 1780-2009* (Cambridge: Cambridge University Press, 2010), 183.

[11] "Adolf Hitler Is Satisfied by German Troubles; Writes He has Never Been in Such High Spirits," *The New York Times* (New York, NY), July 31, 1931.

[12] Edith Lucas Pagelson, *Against All Odds: A Miracle of Holocaust Survival* (Rockland: Maine Authors Publishing, 2012. Kindle), 143–145.

[13] Ibid., 235–238.

[14] Suse Rosenstock, *USC Foundation Institute Testimony of Suse Rosenstock,* USC Shoah Foundation Interview, January 19, 1996.

[15] Edith Lucas Pagelson, *Against All Odds: A Miracle of Holocaust Survival* (Rockland: Maine Authors Publishing, 2012. Kindle), 1532–1536.

[16] Ibid., 1541–1543.

[17] Ibid., 1415–1419.

[18] Suse Rosenstock, *USC Foundation Institute Testimony of Suse Rosenstock,* USC Shoah Foundation Interview, January 19, 1996.

[19] Ibid.

[20] Ibid.

[21] Edith Lucas Pagelson, *Against All Odds: A Miracle of Holocaust Survival* (Rockland: Maine Authors Publishing, 2012. Kindle), 147–150.

[22] "German Jews' Passports Declared Invalid," *United States Holocaust Memorial Museum,* accessed May 3, 2016, https://www.ushmm.org/learn/timeline-of-events/1933-1938/reich-ministry-of-the -interior-invalidates-all-german-passports-held-by-jew.

[23] Suse Rosenstock, *USC Foundation Institute Testimony of Suse Rosenstock,* USC Shoah Foundation Interview, January 19, 1996.

Edith Lucas Pagelson, *Against All Odds: A Miracle of Holocaust Survival* (Rockland: Maine Authors Publishing, 2012. Kindle), 152–153.

[24] Suse Rosenstock, *USC Foundation Institute Testimony of Suse Rosenstock,* USC Shoah Foundation Interview, January 19, 1996.

[25] Edith Lucas Pagelson, *Against All Odds: A Miracle of Holocaust Survival* (Rockland: Maine Authors Publishing, 2012. Kindle), 162-163.

[26] Ibid., 177-186.

[27] More details this concentration camp in Ingrid Wuga's biography and the glossary.

[28] Suse Rosenstock, *USC Foundation Institute Testimony of Suse Rosenstock,* USC Shoah Foundation Interview, January 19, 1996.

[29] Edith Lucas Pagelson, *Against All Odds: A Miracle of Holocaust Survival* (Rockland: Maine Authors Publishing, 2012. Kindle), 143-145.

30 Suse Rosenstock, *USC Foundation Institute Testimony of Suse Rosenstock,* USC Shoah Foundation Interview, January 19, 1996.

31 Ibid.

32 Ibid.

33 Ibid.

34 Ibid.

35 Edith Lucas Pagelson, *Against All Odds: A Miracle of Holocaust Survival* (Rockland: Maine Authors Publishing, 2012. Kindle), 255-258.

36 More details about this ghetto in Hana Holman's biography and the glossary.

37 Suse Rosenstock, *USC Foundation Institute Testimony of Suse Rosenstock,* USC Shoah Foundation Interview, January 19, 1996.

38 More details about this extermination camp in Charles Ohlenberg's biography and the glossary.

39 Edith Lucas Pagelson, *Against All Odds: A Miracle of Holocaust Survival* (Rockland: Maine Authors Publishing, 2012. Kindle), 555-558.

40 Ibid., 558, 563-566.

41 See description of this concentration camp in Ursula Meyer's biography.

42 Edith Lucas Pagelson, *Against All Odds: A Miracle of Holocaust Survival* (Rockland: Maine Authors Publishing, 2012. Kindle), 623-624.

43 Suse Rosenstock, *USC Foundation Institute Testimony of Suse Rosenstock,* USC Shoah Foundation Interview, January 19, 1996.

44 Ibid.

45 Deborah Rosenstock, e-mail message to author, February 24, 2016.

46 Suse Rosenstock, *USC Foundation Institute Testimony of Suse Rosenstock,* USC Shoah Foundation Interview, January 19, 1996.

47 Deborah Rosenstock, e-mail message to author, February 24, 2016.

48 Deborah Rosenstock, in discussion with the author, February 17, 2016.

49 Suse Rosenstock, *USC Foundation Institute Testimony of Suse Rosenstock,* USC Shoah Foundation Interview, January 19, 1996.

50 Ibid.

[51] Ibid.

[52] Ibid.

[53] Ibid.

[54] Ibid.

[55] Deborah Rosenstock, e-mail message to author, March 3, 2016.

[56] Suse Rosenstock, *USC Foundation Institute Testimony of Suse Rosenstock,* USC Shoah Foundation Interview, January 19, 1996.

[57] Ibid.

[58] Ibid.

[59] Flora Herz, letter to Suse Herz, October 3, 1945. Copy of original and translation in possession of the author. Original in possession of Deborah Rosenstock. Likely translated into English the United States.

[60] Ibid.

[61] Suse Rosenstock, *USC Foundation Institute Testimony of Suse Rosenstock,* USC Shoah Foundation Interview, January 19, 1996.

[62] Edith Lucas Pagelson, *Against All Odds: A Miracle of Holocaust Survival* (Rockland: Maine Authors Publishing, 2012. Kindle), 827-836.

[63] Suse Rosenstock, letter to Bruce Overton, 1999.

[64] John Parry, e-mail message to author, March 6, 2016.

[65] Ibid.

[66] Elaine Peizer, e-mail message to author, April 18, 2016.

# RELLA ADLER

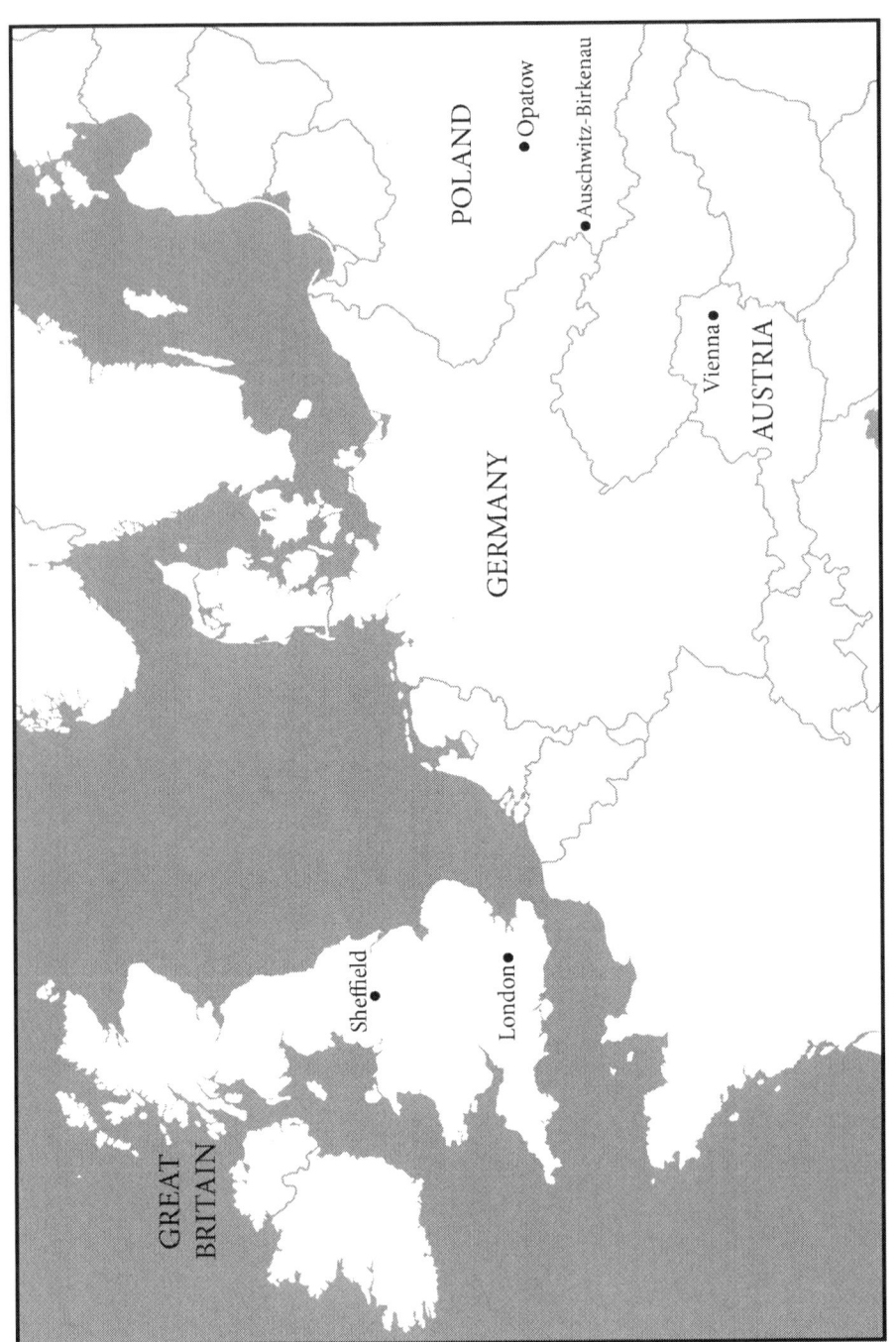

# 10

RELLA ADLER, NÉE HUDES

"**B**ottom line to everything I would ever have to say: there is nothing negative I can say about the Christadelphians, only positive things, and that comes from seven-and-a-half years of living with a family."[1]

These were the words that began my interview with Mrs. Rella Adler, an Austrian refugee, who was taken in by a Christadelphian family during World War II. Her statement was unequivocal and unabashed. After elaborating on it multiple times, it was abundantly clear that Rella's experiences with the Christadelphians, from June 1939 to October 1946, were extremely positive.

**Beginnings**

Rella was born to Isak and Klara Hudes in September 1931. It was just six months before the 1932 German presidential elections, in which Adolf Hitler was defeated by the incumbent, Paul von Hindenburg, but earned a shockingly large portion of the votes. Just one year after the elections, Hindenburg was persuaded to appoint Hitler as chancellor of Germany. The stage was set for Hitler to unleash terror upon the Jews of Europe.

Rella was born in Vienna, Austria, only two years before Hitler came to power. She grew up speaking German, but was largely sheltered from the antisemitism that was sweeping through

Germany during her childhood—until the *Anschluss*, the annexation of Austria by Germany in March 1938.

When Rella was an infant, Isak Hudes, Rella's father, was determined to move his family to Palestine. Immigration to the British-controlled land was very difficult in the 1930s, especially for an entire family. Isak went alone and illegally. As an adult, Rella was told that Isak intended to establish himself in Palestine and then would send for Klara, Rella and her older brother Sigmund. Isak came to the Holy Land but the rest of the family never did follow him. To this day Rella does not know why.

Rella grew up in a home with her mother, Klara, her brother, Sigmund, her grandmother, Mirjam, and her aunts, Ida and Josefine. Somehow, unknown to Rella, her family supported themselves without any adult males in the house.

Rella remembers only bits and pieces of that time. She remembers that they all lived in one unit in a multistory apartment building, that the apartment had several rooms, and that she slept in a room with her mother. The apartment was located in a Jewish neighborhood, and the street they lived on was lined with shops. Occasionally, her grandmother would give her money for her to run down to the shops to buy groceries.

Rella attended a Jewish day school, and though the Hudes family did not attend the local synagogue, they fervently observed the Sabbath within the confines of their apartment. They did not turn on any lights, or even light the stove—having a friend come and light it for them instead. The only fire they would ever kindle was that of the Shabbat candles.

## After the *Anschluss*

Austria changed dramatically following the annexation of 1938. Even at age seven Rella could sense the tension in her household. She watched the Nazi motorcades drive past the apartment windows, and before long curfews were enacted, and signs were posted declaring "No Jews" in the places she had once frequented.

She described the change as "night and day."[2] One day she was a happy and carefree child, and then the next day, there were so many restrictions she had to observe—without any explanation why. When she and her mother would walk down the street, she could no longer walk freely by her mother's side; now her mother held her hand tightly, ensuring that Rella did not accidentally walk onto a forbidden patch of grass or mistakenly venture into a section of the city in which Jews were no longer permitted. Recalling these memories, Rella said that her mother held her hand so tightly that she thought that her "knuckles would crack."[3]

Curfews were initiated. She remembers men being picked up in the streets and taken away. As her brother was eight years older than she was and in his early to mid-teens, there was great nervousness regarding his fate. If he went out and took his time returning home, Rella could feel the tension and anxiety in the house.

Rella remembers hearing banging on their front door one day—it was the Gestapo. Without a clear understanding of the sociopolitical climate, this was a terrifying experience for Rella. The new regulations, the disappearing men, the sudden hatred that the Nazis felt towards her, and the banging on the door— it was all new and unexplained.

Yet those memories are just the broad way in which antisemitism affected both Rella and her family. Nevertheless, Rella was not simply targeted as part of a group—there are specific instances of antisemitism that have been emblazoned in her memory for nearly 80 years, and it is in part due to these traumatic experiences that Rella can recall the memories of their first apartment at all. One instance was when Rella was six years old and had been asked by her grandmother to pick an item up from a store. On her journey home, she was stopped by a group of Hitler Youth that confronted and shoved her, then forced her to give them the change from her purchase. After this altercation, for the remaining few months that the Hudes family lived in that area, Rella did not go shopping alone.

Rella and her family were forced to move from their apartment in 1939. Their next apartment was newer, had shops close by and was likely in a Jewish neighborhood, but unlike the first, this neighborhood was not very busy. Rella experienced the antisemitism of the Hitler Youth here as well.

Just as the last attack, Rella was on her way back from the store when she encountered the Hitler Youth. They took her, placed her against a lamp pole, and tied her hands behind her back. Then they stood and laughed at her helplessness.

And helpless she was—minute after minute elapsed, turning into hours. Adults walked past her, looked at her, and continued unfazed. This was unfathomable for Rella. Clearly she needed their help, and yet just as clearly, no one lifted a finger.

Finally, after she did not return home, Sigmund was sent to find her. He released her from her bonds and brought her home.

She never ventured out alone again in Austria.

In one other extremely troubling memory, Rella recalls looking out the apartment window at the street. Swastikas had been painted on the street. Older women, including Rella's grandmother, had been rounded up and forced to kneel down on the ground and scrub the graffiti.

Rella remembers watching this and being concerned for her grandmother, still unaware of the reason behind this blatant act of humiliation.

At last, Rella asked her mother why her grandmother was being forced to do this. The scrubbing was clearly not removing the paint, and yet the women continued to scrub the streets. Why?

Klara did not answer her daughter's question. Perhaps at that moment, overcome by what she was witnessing, she could not.

## Preparations

Klara Hudes knew that the situation was desperate. Hearing that families in other countries were willing to take Jewish refugee children, Klara sought to find a place for Sigmund. But after all of her efforts had been exhausted, it seemed that there would be no way out for her son. Thus, she refocused her energy on securing an escape for Rella, who was only seven years old.

After sending out picture after picture and tirelessly writing letters, Klara found a family in Holland that was willing to take Rella into their home. But the offer was too good to be true.

One day, a letter arrived at the Hudes household from this Dutch family. The family was staunchly Catholic and proud of its Catholic roots and values; and thus, the letter explained that the family would take Rella into their home under the condition that she must accept Catholic rites and practices.

But Rella had been raised a Jew. Sending their daughter away to be immersed in Catholicism, a denomination that had promoted such animosity toward the Jews for so many centuries, was not a thought Rella's anxious family could countenance. Upon reading this letter, Rella's grandmother took it and tore it up in front of the rest of the family.

Though this moment was quite dramatic and would seem to have completely dashed Rella's hopes for survival, it was perhaps an act of Providence; in May 1940, the Nazis overtook Holland.

After this setback, Klara remained steadfast in finding a safe place for her daughter. Finally, another home was found—this time a family in England. The couple's names were Philip and Lilian Adams. They were Christadelphians.

*Philip and Lilian Adams, 1937.*

Just two months before Rella arrived, in April 1939, in a time when so many were turning against the Jewish people, Philip Adams, an associate editor of *The Testimony* magazine, made his feelings for the Jews clear in an article in *The Testimony*:

> Great though their nation had been in the spacious days of David and Solomon, God had a still greater purpose with His people. Israel's true destiny had not yet been reached. They were God's chosen nation; they were His 'anointed ones,' His 'prophets' to mankind. [God] intended to restore the kingdom to Israel, and Israel would then fulfil her Divine mission to the world. . . . The nation of Israel, as the seed of Abraham, was destined to be the medium through which all the families of the earth would be blessed.[4]

## Leaving

Finally, the day came for Rella to leave her family, her home, and Austria behind. It was June 8, 1939—only three months before World War II was officially declared and Kindertransports out of Germany ceased. Rella does not remember any of the preparations her family made, she can only remember her departure.

Just one adult was allowed to come to the train, so Rella walked with her mother one last time. While the farewell was devastating for her mother, at age seven Rella was relieved and giddy when she approached the train. Seeing the other children made her feel carefree again, as she had felt before the Nazis came into Austria. She saw before her an exciting journey which she had the privilege of joining. Alone on the train, Rella felt excitement about this new adventure.

She would never see Klara or Sigmund, or Mirjam, or Josefine again.

## Rella's Family

Isak Hudes died of natural causes in Palestine in 1942. He was 50 years old. After his death, Rella's uncle in Palestine sent a letter to the Adams family, notifying them of his death. The following are excerpts from the letter—which was likely translated into English in Palestine. It was the last news that Rella ever had of her father:

> 5th March 1942
>
> Dear Mssrs. Adam,
>
> I received your letter from September 41 together with the enclosed letter from Rella and I thank you very much for it. I beg to apology for the delay in answer, but I received this letter only recently.
>
> I regret to inform you, that the father of little Rella died a few month ago, and if you find it advisable you could tell his daughter about it in some way. I leave it to you about how to deal in this matter. . . .
>
> Now I beg to thank you very much, that you are so good for little Rella and that you take so much care of the child. Lets hope she will once be in a position to repay you all this kindness. We have been very glad about the letter she wrote us, she has done it indeed very nice. . . .[5]

Of the six members of Rella's family who had lived together in Vienna, only Rella and one of her aunts, Aunt Ida, survived.

Aunt Ida immigrated to the United States in July 1939, before Great Britain declared war on Germany. Ida was able to enter the United States by meeting a man who had come from America, marrying him, moving to the United States as his wife, and then divorcing him promptly upon arrival. The entire marriage was simply a ruse—on both their parts.

When the war was over, although most of Rella's family had perished, Aunt Ida was alive and well in Brooklyn, New York and her survival would ultimately have a profound effect on Rella's future.

Her grandmother Mirjam and Aunt Josefine were deported from Vienna to the Opatow ghetto, a small ghetto in southeastern Poland, on March 12, 1941, where they both perished. Mirjam was 69 and Josefine was 52.[6]

On March 31, 1943, Klara and Sigmund were called to the police station in Vienna. That very day, they were put onto "Transport 47b," which took them to the infamous Auschwitz-Birkenau extermination camp.[7] Klara was 44 and Sigmund was only 20.

## Arrival

Rella cannot remember very much of the train trip or the boat ride across the channel. However, she does remember that she enjoyed it, still feeling as though she were on her great adventure.

When she arrived at Liverpool Street Station in London, Rella was taken to a huge hall with a large glass ceiling and rows and rows of folding chairs. Each child took a seat and waited. At the front of the room there a large table piled with papers. Men sat behind the table who called out the names of each child—when a child's name was called, he or she rose from their chair and walked over to the families or individuals who had come to pick them up.

The minutes passed. The names were called. And Rella sat and sat. After a while, she began to feel anxious and nervous. What if she had left her family in Austria and no one would come to collect her?

Finally, a man from the front called her name. The Adams family had arrived. And this is when Rella realized that she was not simply on an adventure. This was real. Her aunts were gone. Her brother was gone. And her mother was gone too. She was now completely alone, in a foreign country, and walking toward an older man and woman, complete strangers, whom she would call "auntie" and "uncle" and eventually "mum" and "father."

Rella describes this time as the "worst period" of her life.[8] The customs and traditions of the country were so different from what she had known in Vienna. She feared for her family, and

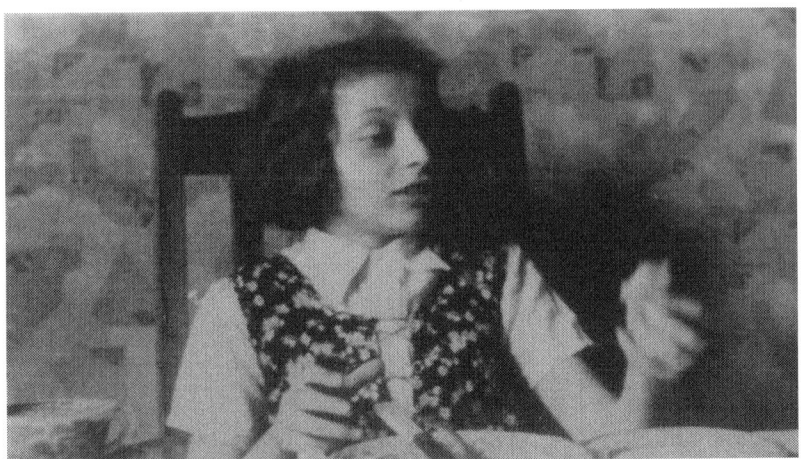

*Rella in England, 1939.*

*Top: Rella in the Adams' garden, the day after she arrived in England, 1939.*
*Bottom: Philip and Lilian Adams.*

she only knew about 10 words of English.

While Rella struggled with grief and internal turmoil, her relationship with the Adams family grew to be one of love and acceptance. This family took Rella in during this most agonizing period of her life and sympathized with her, tried to comfort her, and did all they could to provide her with a stable home and good values. And for that, Rella is immensely grateful.

## The Adams Family

Philip and Lilian Adams were older than most parents who would have a seven year old living in their house. They had six children, five of whom had already moved out of the house, and one daughter, Phyllis, who was 15 and still living with them. Sybil Dawson, Lilian's eldest surviving grandchild, described her grandmother as "a loving and caring person" and stated, "I remember her with great affection."[9]

Similarly Rella could feel their compassion and understanding for her unfortunate circumstance. Lilian and Philip Adams brought her into their family, and although they could not legally adopt her, she became much like a daughter to them. Rella fondly remembers their reaction when she would grieve for her mother, aunts, and brother: "At the beginning, I was a very, very sad child. I was so sad; I just cried all the time. And they cried too. We used to sit at the table at tea, and I would look up, and I would see them crying because I was crying."[10]

Rella had come into a home where she would be respected and cherished. This caring environment was also remembered by Sybil Dawson, who wrote:

> As a couple . . . [they] were very suited, they seemed always to be respectful of each other and I never heard

of any discord in their home. It was a very settled daily routine with prayers before meals and I am sure that I learned a basic moral code from them . . . I remember going to the meeting [Christadelphian Church services] when I was staying with them but not at any other time. We three children always went to Sunday school . . .[11]

Philip and Lilian were always respectful of each other, and their morals stemmed from their dedication to the Christadelphian faith. The ecclesia was a large part of the Adams' life. Sybil went on to explain the importance of religion for their family:

Grandpa was much respected for his leadership in the church. He had lots of theology books . . . Nanny had put together a book of daily readings in 1913 . . . consisting of extracts from scripture and poetry. . . . My husband (who is a Church of England priest) has some of Grandpa's books and was very impressed with his breadth of theology.[12]

Philip and Lilian Adams were dedicated Christadelphians and dedicated Bible readers. Another grandchild, Andrew Coleman, had similar memories of his grandparents' dedication:

[Grandpa] was much appreciated as a preacher (speaker) and used to be away speaking on alternate Sundays. He was also Recording Brother (church secretary) for Sheffield Meeting for many years. In the 1930s he edited part of *The Testimony* magazine.[13]

Philip Adams's faith was not something he simply kept to himself. He shared it through speaking and writing and by supporting the Sheffield Christadelphian ecclesia. As their faith was such a prominent part of their lives, Rella also elaborated on this, and explained the family's strong relationship with the Christadelphian ecclesia:

> They belonged to a sect called Christadelphians . . . they are very pro-Jewish. And many of them took children . . . they read portions of the Bible every day, every night . . . later, when I got to be a little older, I would stay [at the ecclesia] all day. I would go in the morning and stay through lunch. There were always people there for lunch, and I would stay all night.[14]

As their daughter, she would join Philip and Lilian in their worship and in their daily Bible readings.

> Everything they did themselves was expected of me. Yes. And I did it all. And I became an A1 student, and I always was first in my religious school class—always— from as soon as I could master the English language,

*The garden at the Adams' house, along with the back house, where chickens were kept during the war.*

and took lessons, that's how I was. I just immersed myself in this whole environment, all the while knowing that I was Jewish.[15]

Rella was not bothered by being Jewish and growing up in this Christadelphian environment. The Christadelphians focus heavily on the Jewish scriptures, and so much of what she learned at Sunday school was about the history and stories of her people.

But being part of the Adams family also meant learning the family's values and high standards. Although her friends (also Christadelphians) may have been allowed to go to the cinema, Rella was not. In fact, Rella recalled that the only movie she was ever allowed to see was *Fantasia*—the movie without any words! Nevertheless, though she felt they were strict, she was clear that they did not have a double standard. They expected certain behavior from her, but they were not hypocrites, and that made quite an impression on her:

> I was never made to do something that the adults . . . didn't do . . . if I wasn't allowed to do it, they didn't do it. There was never any phoniness there. . . . they didn't do these things either! They didn't say, 'Rella, you can't go to the movies' and then they went to them. There was nothing like that! . . . This was a wonderful family.[16]

She acknowledged that they were strict and strongly guided by their religion, but Rella could not say enough good about them. In her interview with the Shoah Foundation from 1998, she explained how thankful she was to them for their values and how helpful she found them to be. Perhaps it is best to have her explain her relationship with them in her own words:

They were very, very nice people. I really was very lucky. . . . They came to the station, they brought a doll—a beautiful little china doll with clear blue eyes, gorgeous. And we rode back. They were a very, very, moral . . . they were very religious people, very religious Christians, basically fundamentalist Christians.

I have to tell you, fundamentalism is bad most of the time because it's so extreme. But I saw it, living with it, growing up, and it was not bad. For me, living in that, it was not bad. They were very tolerant of other people, and they really just kept their religion in the way that it was supposedly meant to be kept for them. That's how they lived their lives, daily! It was really . . . a good thing to have as a child, especially at that particular time, when I had lost, you know, any family unity was not there, so I did go into another family environment, just an extremely different one. And they were really very lovely.[17]

Almost 20 years later, in an interview for this book, Rella continued to express the same sentiments:

I didn't think of myself as lucky then, but after I became an adult, I realized how fortunate I was. I had lost all connections to my own family. I went to another family environment that was just an extremely different one, but it worked out very well for all of us.[18]

I had such a good upbringing, I am so thankful for that, you have no idea. . . . I was so well respected. It was just a wonderful upbringing. I had to look at it back as an adult, and it served a great purpose for my children. . . . It was a great upbringing.[19]

The values that she learned in Philip and Lilian Adams' house are ones that have stayed with her throughout her life, even affecting the way she raised her own children. A good moral code had been established, and Rella can look back as an adult to see how that moral code has helped her throughout her life.

Hence, "There is nothing negative I can say about the Christadelphians, only positive things."[20]

**The War Years**

Rella lived with the Adams family for seven and a half years, from 1939 to 1946. Philip and Lilian had a large three-story house in a suburban neighborhood of the Sheffield area. Within that house was a beautiful banister—and it was polished, which made it perfect for sliding. This was a pleasure in which Rella indulged frequently. Upon arrival, Rella was given her own room in the house, and she would often spend her time outside in the lovely British garden—a luxury which she did not have in either of her family's apartments in Vienna. She had grown up in the city, so this type of environment was all new to her.

And there was much more that was new to her, too.

When Rella arrived, she only knew a few words of English. It was summer, so there was no school, and the children of the neighborhood played ball outside. Rella watched them from the curb—not joining in because she was not able to talk with them. Somehow though, they must have been told about her because they knew her name. As they played, they sang songs about her, chanting her name and rhyming it with words like "umbrella" and "sarsaparilla."

Rella had no idea what these things were. However, she could understand the tone—and the tone was not a friendly one, but one that was mocking. She knew that somehow, with these words, these children playing ball were making fun of her.

Finally, after repeated instances of this, Rella became so frustrated that she charged into the group of children and started swinging. She hit anything that was in front of her. She could not believe what she was doing—it was not in her nature to act that way—all of the pent up frustration and anger of leaving her family and coming to a new place simply came out on these children. Rella was incredibly frustrated with her situation. What seven year old would not be? Nevertheless, after this, the children showed her respect and never chanted her name again.

Thus, the environment was new, the language and the children were new, and soon, Rella would have an entirely new set of experiences—those of wartime. Approximately a year after Rella's arrival, the bombings began. Sheffield was a major target, so the bombing preparation began immediately. There were shelters in their schools and drills were regularly held. All the children were given gas masks, which had to be worn on the side of their bodies in a little box at all times. They had a buddy system in which each child's partner would check the other's mask to make sure the masks were secure. At night, there were blackout regulations, so all of the lights had to be turned off, and blackout shades had to be installed in the homes.

Rella can remember the whistle of the bombs as they were being dropped. When she heard the whistle, she tried to guess where the bombs were going to hit. She was so afraid—she had run from the Germans by fleeing all the way to England, and here they were dropping bombs on her! There seemed to be no escape.

During those bombing raids, she would find herself, driven by fear, making promises to God. She would pray to Him, stating that if she survived the night, she would do one thing or another. But then, as the noises of the bombing became louder and louder, her prayers would become more and more frantic—and she would simply assume that their house would be hit. Then her prayers changed from "please do not let us be hit" to "if we are going to be hit, please don't let us be buried."[21]

And then, as suddenly as it had started, the raid would be over. The all-clear signal would sound. Even though there were only a few hours before school, she would return to her room, sleep for a little longer, and then go to school the next day. Life went on. The bombs were just one more challenge.

But there was another challenge, and this one was much more emotional than physical.

When Rella first came to live with Philip and Lilian, they expressed that they would do whatever they could to bring her family to England. This hope, however, was crushed when the war began just three months later. Yet, it was not only that Rella's family would not be able to come over, but also as the war began, the Red Cross contacted the Adams family to say that Rella could no longer communicate with her family in Austria, as doing so would put them in jeopardy:

> I knew the reality of it. I mean I knew the logic of it. They did tell me there, 'Rella you can't write because it won't, it won't be good.' I mean they were very good. They were so upset at my crying all the time that they told me, I don't know how they managed to get it across to me, that they were going to start some paperwork, going to see if they could bring my mother and my brother over . . . and then that perked me up a

little bit, and then the war broke out . . . so, that was that.[22]

Despite the fact that Rella could not write to her family in Austria, she did have Aunt Ida, who had moved to the United States before the war began, and Philip and Lilian were insistent that Rella stay in contact with her. The entire time she lived with them, though she went to all of their Christadelphian functions, it was extremely important to both Philip and Lilian that Rella not lose contact with her family and her roots:

> The family never allowed me . . . to forget what was in Austria . . . one of these aunts that lived with us, came to the United States, and she was in touch with me the whole time, and they used to make me—I didn't want to after a long time—write. 'You have to write; you have to write.' They made me write, and she sent packages, and there was a constant communication over the years. So it wasn't that they were trying to separate me from that . . . I did it myself.[23]

With all the pain of separation, the trauma of coming to a new environment, and the task of learning a new language and making new friends, Rella found it difficult to want to stay in touch. Although she did continue to remain in contact with Aunt Ida, it was done somewhat reluctantly, in a desire to start a new life and actually be able to plant roots in England. She longed for some form of stability, so while she yearned for her Jewish family, she found herself consciously focusing solely on the people and places that were directly in front of her eyes.

## The United States

By the summer of 1946, Rella had lived with Philip and Lilian for seven-and-a-half years. She was 15 and planned on joining the Christadelphian community through baptism that October.

Shortly after Rella found out what had happened to her mother and her brother she was contacted by Aunt Ida, who lived in Brooklyn, New York. Ida told Rella that she wanted Rella to come live with her in the States. They no longer had any family left—they only had each other.

This was news that Rella did not want to hear.

She had spent so many years trying to acclimate to everything that was new in England, and she had focused so hard on what was specifically in front of her, that she did not want to start all over again. She was a Christadelphian, she was part of Philip and Lilian's family, and she did not want to leave:

> I didn't decide to leave. I would have stayed. And they would have loved me to stay. I was . . . a few months away from being baptized. But I had this aunt here . . . my aunts were like my mother . . . they were all equal in my mind. . . . It wasn't your normal usual family. . . . She was a favorite aunt of mine . . . she wanted me here; that was it . . . she had never had any children.[24]

Philip and Lilian could not legally adopt Rella because she had living relatives—Ida, her aunt who lived in the United States, and Shlomo, her uncle who lived in Palestine—who claimed her. In October 1946, after a year of planning, Rella moved to the United States to be with Ida. She said goodbye to the life she had created in England with the Adams family, and prepared herself to adapt, yet again, to a new culture.

This time, she would be enveloped by the Jewish American community.

Aunt Ida was extremely unhappy about the Christadelphian upbringing that Rella had received while living with Philip and Lilian. Rella was used to doing her daily readings, so when she came to New York, she brought her Bible with her and read two portions from the Old Testament and one portion from the New Testament. Moreover, she read these frequently. Aunt Ida was unimpressed:

> My aunt was so upset that I was reading the Bible—I didn't do anything else but that, you know, and then she would talk about my family, and this, 'Remember,' and 'Nobody is here anymore.' Such a feeling of guilt came over me that I was alive and they were dead, and only because they were Jews, for no other reason . . . I couldn't pursue this other religion that I knew so well.[25]

When Rella prepared to leave England, Philip and Lilian gave her the address of the nearest Christadelphian meeting hall in New York. They told her that it was her choice whether or not she wished to follow the Christadelphian religion. Upon arriving in New York, having these conversations with her aunt, and realizing that nearly all the rest of her family had perished simply because they were Jewish, Rella decided that she would return to Judaism.

The years with Aunt Ida were tumultuous. Ida remembered Rella as a seven year old. She was now 15. In and of itself, that presented issues. Moreover, Rella had grown up in a family where consistency was emphasized so strongly, so she expected her aunt to be consistent about her own religion. The fact that Ida was so insistent about Judaism and yet owned a store that she kept open on Saturdays was a sore spot for Rella. She "had no tolerance for this," because she believed that it was essential to practice what was preached.[26]

Though Ida had been Rella's favorite aunt growing up, they never really bonded again as they had during Rella's childhood. In 1973, Ida moved to Israel. Years later, when Rella heard that her aunt was dying, Rella went to be with her in Israel. Being with Aunt Ida when she died brought comfort to Rella, and seeing her aunt pass away peacefully, in a way that the rest of her immediate family did not, brought her closure.

## The Later Years

As the years passed, Rella began to feel more at home in the United States. She married Harold Adler, a Jewish man from the Bronx, New York. She became a bookkeeper and returned to her Jewish roots. She and Harold have three children together: Nancy, Hilary and Debra. They also have four grandchildren—Rachel, Jordan, Noah, and Lara.

Nancy and Hilary knew they were Jewish, but because Rella still felt somewhat estranged from Jewish customs and traditions, Harold and Rella did not send them to Hebrew school. Only boys were required to go to Hebrew school. Girls had a choice; however, by the time Debra was six years old, Rella had become comfortable in her Jewish identity and wanted Debra to have a Jewish education. Debra loved her Jewish upbringing just as Rella had loved her Christadelphian upbringing in England, and went on to teach in Hebrew school in addition to her teaching job at a secular school.

Nevertheless, the kindness of the Christadelphians, and specifically of the Adams family, has not been forgotten in Rella's household. Harold would sing the praises of the Christadelphians to anyone he thought might know about them. So their legacy lives on through Rella's family:

Look, if I wasn't taken, I wouldn't be alive. There's no question about it. . . . If it wasn't for this, I wouldn't be here. . . .

I have a granddaughter. . . . My daughter told her . . . 'there's no family on my side.' . . . She was seven, almost eight. 'I feel so bad for Grammy that she had to go through this . . . but, if she wasn't saved and didn't go to England, then you wouldn't be here, and if you weren't here, then I wouldn't be here, and Noah wouldn't be here. Daddy would be here, but . . .'[27]

Rella's family has been indelibly changed by the act of kindness shown to her by Philip and Lilian Adams—who were compelled by their beliefs to act on behalf of the Jewish people. But at the same time, it was not just Rella's family that was

*Philip and Lilian Adams, just a year or two before Philip passed away in 1967.*

*Rella Adler at a luncheon for the Kindertransport Association, 2016.*

changed. When Lilian Adams passed away, her obituary in *The Christadelphian* magazine made it very clear that her family too had been powerfully touched by those seven and a half years that Rella lived in their house:

> It is with sadness that we learn of the death of Sis. L. Adams, of the Plymouth ecclesia. Sis. Adams, the wife of our late Bro. P. H. Adams, was for many years a member of the Sheffield ecclesia and was well loved for her untiring labours in this ecclesia. She came to Sheffield in 1928 from Liverpool and took over the duties of mother and homemaker for our late Bro. Adams, who had a family of four girls when his first wife died; and with her own two sons performed a noble task in caring for them and at a later stage took on the further responsibility of a Jewish refugee during the war years. In her quiet way she contributed much spiritual guidance in the sisters' class and also as a co-worker with our Bro. Adams as co-editor in the

work of the *Testimony Magazine.* Latterly as the wife of the recording brother she worked behind the scenes with good effect. Bro. and Sis. Adams moved to Plymouth in 1961 where they spent their declining years. Our dear sister now sleeps in Jesus awaiting his return.[28]

Lilian Adams passed away in 1971. It had been 25 years since Rella had lived with Philip and Lilian, yet she was not forgotten. Although many things had happened in those 25 years, Rella's story was mentioned alongside those of Philip and Lilian's children. Rella had indeed become part of the family.

---

[1] Rella Adler, in discussion with the author, January 29, 2016.

[2] Rella Adler, *USC Shoah Foundation Institute Testimony of Rella Adler,* USC Shoah Foundation Interview, August 24, 1998.

[3] Ibid.

[4] P. H. Adams, "Messiah in the Prophets," *The Testimony,* April 1939, 151-152.

[5] Shlomo Landwehr, letter to Philip and Lilian Adams, March 5, 1942. Copy in possession of the author. Original in possession of Rella Adler. Likely translated into English in Palestine.

[6] "The Central Database of Shoah Victims' Names - Mirjam Hodes," *Yad Vashem,* accessed April 22, 2016, http://yvng.yadvashem.org/nameDetails.html?language=en&s_lastName=hudes&s_firstName=miriam&s_place=&itemId=722841&ind=3&winId=-5564477282211710703.

"The Central Database of Shoah Victims' Names - Josefine Hodes," *Yad Vashem,* accessed April 22, 2016, http://yvng.yadvashem.org/nameDetails.html?language=en&s_lastName=hudes&s_firstName=josephine&s_place=&itemId=4921261&ind=1&winId=-7234554289528559526.

[7] Head archivist at the State Museum Auschwitz-Birkenau, e-mail message to author, February 25, 2016.

[8] Rella Adler, *USC Shoah Foundation Institute Testimony of Rella Adler*, USC Shoah Foundation Interview, August 24, 1998.

[9] Sybil Dawson, e-mail message to author, February 9, 2016.

[10] Rella Adler, *USC Shoah Foundation Institute Testimony of Rella Adler*, USC Shoah Foundation Interview, August 24, 1998.

[11] Sybil Dawson, e-mail message to author, February 9, 2016.

[12] Ibid.

[13] Andrew Coleman in an email to Sybil Dawson. Permission granted to the author to quote Andrew's words.

[14] Rella Adler, *USC Shoah Foundation Institute Testimony of Rella Adler*, USC Shoah Foundation Interview, August 24, 1998.

[15] Ibid.

[16] Rella Adler, in discussion with the author, January 29, 2016.

[17] Rella Adler, *USC Shoah Foundation Institute Testimony of Rella Adler*, USC Shoah Foundation Interview, August 24, 1998.

[18] Rella Adler, in discussion with the author, April 13, 2016.

[19] Rella Adler, in discussion with the author, January 29, 2016.

[20] Ibid.

[21] Rella Adler, *USC Shoah Foundation Institute Testimony of Rella Adler*, USC Shoah Foundation Interview, August 24, 1998.

[22] Ibid.

[23] Ibid.

[24] Ibid.

[25] Rella Adler, in discussion with the author, January 29, 2016.

[26] Rella Adler, *USC Shoah Foundation Institute Testimony of Rella Adler*, USC Shoah Foundation Interview, August 24, 1998.

[27] Rella Adler, in discussion with the author, February 18, 2016.

[28] Walter Hardy, "The Brotherhood Near and Far," *The Christadelphian,* May 1971, 233.

# GLOSSARY

*The definitions below were taken, with permission, from the Echoes and Reflections glossary of terms. For the full glossary, see http://echoesandreflections.org/the-lessons/glossary.*

**antisemitism**
Prejudice or discrimination against Jews. Antisemitism can be based on hatred against Jews because of their religious beliefs or their group membership (ethnicity), but also on the erroneous belief that Jews are a race. Nazi antisemitism was racial in nature; Jews were viewed as racially inferior to Aryans and destructive of the world order. —**antisemitic** *adj.*

**Aryan**
A rather ambiguous term the Nazis primarily applied to people of Northern European racial background. Although never defined, in April 1933, the Nazis defined "non-Aryans" as individuals who had a parent or grandparent who was Jewish.

**Auschwitz** (ow sch vits), Auschwitz camp complex (Auschwitz I, Auschwitz II-Birkenau, Auschwitz III-Monowitz)

Auschwitz I was the first and main camp of the Auschwitz camp complex. Established near the town of Oswiecim in Polish Upper Silesia, it was 37 miles west of Cracow and located in a former Polish military compound. On April 27, 1940, Heinrich Himmler ordered the establishment of a concentration camp at the site. Construction began in May 1940 and the officially reported date of the camp's opening was May 20, 1940. The first prisoners were Germans and Poles, sent from Sachsenhausen and Tarnow. By March 1941, prisoner ranks had swelled to 11,000. Primarily a concentration camp serving penal functions, Auschwitz I included a crematorium and, in late summer 1941, the camp briefly operated an experimental gas chamber. From 1940 to 1942, prisoners were primarily Polish political, civic, and spiritual leaders, the intelligentsia, and members of the resistance. Beginning in 1942, some of the Jews deported to Auschwitz were admitted to this main camp. Auschwitz I was also a testing ground for SS physicians carrying out inhumane and pseudoscientific medical experiments in the camp "hospital" (Block 10). Near the hospital was the Death Wall (a.k.a. "Black Wall") where thousands of prisoners were shot. Auschwitz I expanded rapidly and by late 1941 held 18,000 prisoners; by 1943 it held approximately 30,000 inmates. The evacuation from the camp started on January 18, 1945. On January 27, 1945, Soviet troops liberated 1,200 prisoners at Auschwitz I.

During his March 1, 1941 visit to Auschwitz I, Heinrich Himmler ordered an expansion of the camp. In October 1941, 10,000 Soviet POWs began the construction of Auschwitz II-Birkenau. The site of the camp was near the Polish village of Brzezinka which was emptied of its Polish population for the project. Overcrowding in Auschwitz I, caused by the arrival of Soviet prisoners of war in late 1941, forced the acceleration of the camp's construction. The first sections of Auschwitz II-Birkenau were completed in 1942. When construction was complete, the camp had nine sections separated by electrified barbed-wire fences. Originally intended as a camp for 100,000 Soviet POWs, Auschwitz II-Birkenau's main function became the murder of European Jews. The insecticide Zyklon B was used in the camp's gas chambers. The first provisional gas chambers were judged inadequate for the scale of gassing planned. Four large gas chamber and crematoria facilities became operational between March and June 1943. When all four were operational, Auschwitz II-Birkenau possessed an unsurpassed capacity for mass murder and body disposal. Gassing operations continued until November 1944. The pace of deportations increased in the spring of 1944 after the German occupation of Hungary. The Hungarian Jewish community was by then the largest remaining Jewish community in German-controlled Europe. Between April and November 1944 Auschwitz received more Jewish deportees than it had in the previous two years. During the initial selection, newly arrived prisoners were declared fit or unfit for forced labor by SS physicians or other camp officials. Most were sent immediately to the gas chambers. On January 27, 1945, the Auschwitz camp complex was liberated by Soviet forces; at Auschwitz II-Birkenau 5,800 prisoners remained alive. During the course of its existence, prisoners in the camp represented many categories including political prisoners, Poles, criminals, Jews, Soviet POWs, and Sinti-Roma. It is estimated that between 1.1 and 1.6 million predominantly Jewish men, women, and children were murdered at Auschwitz, nearly all of them in the gas chambers at Auschwitz II-Birkenau.

Auschwitz III-Monowitz, also called Buna, was located near the Polish town of Monowice and was the last of three Auschwitz camps established in the vicinity of Oswiecim. Construction began in late 1941 and the camp opened in 1942. Auschwitz III-Monowitz was a massive slave-labor camp that supplied workers for the large chemical and synthetic-rubber works of IG Farbenindustrie's Buna Werke. By summer 1944, the prisoner population rose to over 10,000 not including the prisoners of its forty subcamps. Due to conditions in the camp, the average life span of prisoners was three to four months and even less in the subcamps. Over 30,000 prisoners died in Auschwitz III-Monowitz during its existence. The evacuation of Auschwitz III-Monowitz and its subsidiary camps began on January 18, 1945, and the prisoners were sent to the camp at Gleiwitz. On January 27, 1945, when Soviet forces liberated Auschwitz, there were only 600 remaining prisoners at Auschwitz III-Monowitz.

**boycott**
To abstain from using, buying, or dealing with a business as an expression of protest or disfavor or as a means of coercion.

**Brownshirts (SA, Sturmabteilung** <shturm ap tile ung>, **Storm Troopers)**
The Nazi militia created in 1921 that helped the Nazi Party come to power but was eclipsed by the SS in 1934; known as "Brownshirts" because of the color of the uniform.

**Buchenwald** (boo khen vald)
A concentration camp established in 1937 near Weimar, Germany. While it was primarily a labor camp in the German concentration camp system and not an extermination center, thousands died there from exposure, over-work, and execution. Many Jews from other camps were forcibly marched there by the Nazis in early 1945.

**cantor**
A role (traditionally held by a man) within formal Jewish religious worship which employs elaborate musical chanting while leading a congregation in prayer.

**Chanukah** *or* **Hanukkah**
An eight-day holiday that celebrates the unlikely victory of the Israelites, led by the Maccabees, against Greek Assyrian persecution and religious oppression in the Land of Israel in the second century B.C.E. In addition to marking a military victory against religious oppression and the subsequent rededication of the Temple in Jerusalem, Chanukah recognizes a miracle in that a single flask of oil used to light the Temple menorah lasted for eight days.

**Christianity**
A monotheistic system of beliefs and practices based on the Old Testament and the teachings of Jesus as embodied in the New Testament and emphasizing the role of Jesus as savior.

**concentration camp**
Camps established by the Nazi regime, which eventually became a major instrument of terror, control, punishment, and killing performed through both deliberate means as well as attrition by hunger and/or disease.

**D-Day (Invasion of Normandy)**
The name associated with June 6, 1944 when some 160,000 American, British, and Canadian forces landed on five beaches along a 50-mile stretch of the heavily fortified coast of France's Normandy region. The invasion was one of the largest amphibious military assaults in history.

**Dachau** (dak how)
Dachau was a concentration camp located near Munich, Bavaria. The opening of Dachau was announced at a press conference by Heinrich Himmler on March 20, 1933. The first group of prisoners, consisting mainly of Communists and Social Democrats, were brought to Dachau on March 22, 1933. During the camp's 12-year existence, the prisoner population included, among others, political opponents, criminals, Sinti and Roma, Jews, homosexuals, Jehovah's Witnesses, and members of the Catholic clergy. During World War II, Dachau and its system of subcamps was principally responsible for furnishing slave labor to the armament industries. Over 200,000 prisoners were incarcerated at Dachau during its existence. American forces liberated Dachau on April 29, 1945. They found box cars near the camp filled with bodies in an advanced state of decomposition. These were prisoners who were brought to Dachau from other camps towards the end of the war. In the main camp, American forces liberated approximately 30,000 prisoners.

**deportation**
Removal of people from their areas of residency for purposes of resettlement elsewhere. With regard to the Jews of Europe during the Holocaust, deportation by the Nazis meant removal to another city, ghetto, concentration camp, or extermination center.

**Euthanasia Program**
Referring to the Nazi order for the deliberate extermination of German people institutionalized with physical, mental, and emotional disabilities, carried out as a measure to prevent contamination of the Nazi-defined Aryan race. The Euthanasia Program began in 1939, with German non-Jews as the first victims.

**extermination camp** *also called* **death camp**
A Nazi facility where victims were killed on a mass industrialized scale and their bodies burned or buried in mass graves. The Nazis operated six extermination camps: Auschwitz-Birkenau, Belzec, Chelmno, Majdanek, Sobibor, and Treblinka.

**"Final Solution of the Jewish Question" ("Final Solution")**
A Nazi code phrase referring to their systematic plan to murder every Jewish man, woman, and child in Europe.

**Gentile**
Someone who is not of the Jewish faith; most often referring to a Christian.

**Gestapo** (gesh tah poh)
The Nazi Secret State Police who were directly involved in implementing the murder of Jews and other Nazi victims during the Holocaust.

**ghetto**
Sections of towns and cities that the German occupation authorities and their allies used to concentrate, exploit, and starve regional Jewish populations.

**Great Depression**
The economic crisis beginning with the stock market crash in the United States in 1929 and continuing through the 1930s; a worldwide economic downturn resulted.

**Hitler Youth (Hitlerjugend <hit ler yoo gent>)**
The Nazi Party's compulsory (after 1939) youth movement, which emphasized physical training, Nazi ideology, and absolute obedience to Hitler and the Nazi Party. Youth were subject to intensive propaganda regarding racial and national superiority.

**Holocaust**
The murder of approximately six million Jews by the Nazis and their collaborators. Sinti-Roma, Poles, people with physical and mental disabilities, homosexuals, Jehovah's Witnesses, Soviet prisoners of war, and political dissidents were also targeted by the Nazis.

**Jewish Badge**
Symbol that Jews were forced to wear during the Holocaust so they could be identified as Jews. The Germans used the Jewish Badge, often in the

form of a yellow Star of David, to harass and isolate the Jews, thereby creating a wide rift between Jews and the rest of the population.

## Judaism

A religion developed among the ancient Hebrews and characterized by belief in one God who has revealed himself to Abraham, Moses, and the Hebrew prophets and by a religious life in accordance with Scriptures and rabbinic traditions.

## Kindertransport

A rescue operation carried out primarily by British organizations for Jewish children from Greater Germany, following the *Kristallnacht Pogrom*. The British government allowed 10,000 children to enter Great Britain.

## kosher

Food that is permissible to eat under Jewish dietary laws; can also describe any other ritual object that is fit for use according to Jewish law.

## Kristallnacht (kris tahl nakht) Pogrom

An organized pogrom against Jews in Germany and Austria on November 9–10, 1938. *Kristallnacht* is also known as the "Night of Broken Glass," or "Crystal Night." Orchestrated by the Nazis in retaliation for the assassination of a German embassy official in Paris by a seventeen-year-old Jewish youth named Herchel Grynzspan, 1,400 synagogues and 7,000 businesses were destroyed, almost 100 Jews were killed, and 30,000 were arrested and sent to concentration camps. German Jews were subsequently held financially responsible for the destruction wrought upon their property during this *pogrom*. (See also **pogram.**)

## League of Nations

An intergovernmental organization founded as a result of the Paris Peace Conference that ended World War I. It was the first international organization whose principal mission was to maintain world peace.

## Nazi

Short for Nationalsozialistische deutsche Arbeiter-Partei (N.S.D.A.P.), the German national socialist political party that emerged in Munich after World War I. The party was taken over by Adolf Hitler in the early 1920s. The swastika was the party symbol.

**Nazi ideology** *or* **Nazi racial ideology**
The Nazi system of beliefs, based on a racial view of the world. According to Nazi ideology, the Nordic Aryan Germans were the "master race." Other races were inferior to them and the Jews were considered to be the "anti-race," the exact opposite of the Germans, and an evil and destructive race. Germans were said to be the natural rulers of the world and, in order to achieve that position, influence of the Jews needed to be ended. Thus, racial antisemitism and solving the so-called "Jewish Question" lay at the heart of Nazi ideology, as did the desire for more territory or *Lebensraum* (living space).

**Palestine**
The Roman term for what is now Israel; the name used by the British during World War II to denote the area they held under a League of Nations mandate.

**Passover**
The celebration of the Jewish people's freedom from Egyptian bondage that took place approximately 3,500 years ago, as told in the first fifteen chapters of the biblical Book of Exodus. The celebration is organized into a feast called the Passover *Seder*. The word *"seder"* means "order" or "procedure" in Hebrew and refers to the order of historical events recalled in the Passover meal as well as the meal itself.

**pogrom**
Originally a Russian word meaning "devastation" used to describe organized, large-scale acts of violence against Jewish communities, especially the kind instigated by the authorities in Czarist Russia.

**refugee**
One who flees or is deported in search of safety, as in times of war, political oppression, or religious persecution.

**Reich** (rye ch), **Third Reich**
The official name of the Nazi regime; ruled from 1933 to 1945 under the command of Adolf Hitler. Historically, the First Reich was the medieval Holy Roman Empire, which lasted until 1806. The Second Reich included the German Empire from 1871–1918.

**SA** (See **Brownshirts.**)

**SS, Schutzstaffel** (shoe ts shtah fel)
Originally organized as Hitler's personal bodyguard, the SS was transformed into a giant organization under Heinrich Himmler. Although various SS units were assigned to the battlefield, the organization is best known for carrying out the destruction of European Jewry.

**Shoah** (sho ah)
A Hebrew word meaning "catastrophe," referring to the Holocaust.

**survivor**
Within the context of the Holocaust, a survivor is someone who escaped death at the hands of the Nazis and their collaborators.

**swastika**
An ancient Eastern symbol appropriated by the Nazis as their emblem.

**Theresienstadt**
A ghetto in Theresienstadt (Terezin), a town in Northwestern Czechoslovakia, where the Jews of Bohemia and Moravia, elderly Jews and persons of "special merit" in the Reich, and several thousand Jews from the Netherlands and Denmark were interned. Although in practice the ghetto, run by the SS, served as a transit camp for Jews en route to extermination camps, it was also presented as a "model Jewish settlement" for propaganda purposes.

**Treaty of Versailles** (ver sigh)
A peace treaty that was signed at the end of World War I in Versailles, France.

**Treblinka** (tre blink a)
The Treblinka death camp was built in a thinly populated area four kilometers from the village and train station of Treblinka, Poland. The camp was established as a part of Aktion Reinhard in 1942. The first transports arrived from the Warsaw ghetto in July 1942. Between July 23 and September 21, 1942, 254,000 Jews from Warsaw and 112,000 from other places in the Warsaw district were murdered at Treblinka II. From mid-November 1942 until January 1943, transports to Treblinka II came primarily from Bialystok. Some transports of Jews from the Warsaw ghetto were sent to Treblinka II in the second half of January 1943. It is estimated that around 900,000 Jews were murdered in Treblinka between July 1942 and March 1943.

In March 1943, an operation was launched to burn the bodies of the victims in order to obliterate traces of the killing. An uprising in the camp took place on August 2, 1943. About 850 inmates were at the camp during the uprising. A number of prisoners managed to escape, but only about 150-200 evaded capture but many of them did not survive the war. It is estimated that around 70 prisoners from Treblinka were alive at the end of World War II. The last transports to Treblinka II came from the Bialystok ghetto on August 18 and 19, 1943. In November 1943 about thirty Jewish prisoners remained in Treblinka II. They were all shot before the German and Ukrainian staff left the site of the dismantled camp.

**Warsaw ghetto**
The Warsaw ghetto was officially established on October 2, 1940 and sealed on November 16, 1940. At one point, the ghetto held over 500,000 Jews. The first wave of mass deportations took place between July 22, 1942 and September 12, 1942. A second wave of deportations, meant to clear the ghetto, began January 18, 1943 but was suspended after four days due to armed resistance. The Warsaw Ghetto Uprising began on April 19, 1943, in response to renewed efforts to deport the remaining Jews and was led by the commander of the Zydowska Organizacja Bojowa (Z.O.B.), Mordecai Anielewicz. The Germans declared the ghetto liquidated on May 16, 1943, although fighting continued after that date and some Jews remained in bunkers within the razed ghetto area until at least January 1944.

**Weimar** (vi mahr) **Republic**
The period of German history from 1919 to 1933; named after the city of Weimar, where a national assembly convened to produce a new constitution after the German monarchy was abolished following the nation's defeat in World War I. The first attempt at establishing a democracy in Germany was a time of great tension and conflict, and it ultimately failed with the ascent of Adolf Hitler and the Nazi Party in 1933.

**Yad Vashem**
The Holocaust Martyrs' and Heroes' Remembrance Authority in Jerusalem. The name Yad Vashem is taken from an Old Testament passage: *"I will build for them a name and a memorial."* (Isaiah 56:5).

# BIBLIOGRAPHY

*The following are the sources that were consulted for each section of the book.*

## Part I

### Christadelphians and the Jews

Andrew, J. J. "Editorial." *The Christadelphian,* March 1882.

Amit, Thomas. "Laurence Oliphant: Financial Sources for His Activities in Palestine in the 1880s." *Palestine Exploration Quarterly* 139, no. 3 (2007): 205–212, accessed April 22, 2016, doi:10.1179/003103207x227328.

Anonymous. "Copy of Letter addressed to Sir Moses Montefiore." *Herald of the Kingdom and Age to Come*, March 1855.

Arnold, C. H. "Prayer Changes Things." *The Testimony,* December 1938.

Baumel-Schwartz, Judith Tydor. *Never Look Back: The Jewish Refugee Children in Great Britain, 1938–1945 (Shofar Supplements in Jewish Studies).* West Lafayette: Purdue University Press, 2012. Electronic.

"[Bill 7.] Second Reading." *Hansard, 17 March 1875.* Accessed April 15, 2016. http://hansard.millbanksystems.com/commons/1875/mar/17/bill-7-second-reading#S3V0222P0_18750317_HOC_8.

Burkitt, Nicholas, "British Society and the Jews: A Study into the Impact of the Second World War Era and the Establishment of Israel, *1938–1948."* doctoral thesis, University of Exeter, 2011.

Cameron, James. "Letter from certain Friends of Judah to the Chief Rabbi in London." *Herald of the Kingdom and Age to Come*, September 1854.

Carroll, James. *Constantine's Sword.* New York: First Mariner Books, 2002.

Carter, John. "Jewish Refugee Fund." *The Christadelphian,* March 1939.

377

Carter, John. "Jewish Refugee Fund." *The Christadelphian,* June 1939.

Carter, John. "Relief for Jewish Refugees." *The Christadelphian,* January 1939.

"Christadelphians." *BBC.co.uk.* last modified June 25, 2009. http://www.bbc.co.uk/religion/religions/christianity/subdivisions/christadelphians_1.shtml

"City and Metropolitan Police." *Hansard, 31 May 1916.* Accessed April 15, 2016. http://hansard.millbanksystems.com/written_answers/1916/may/31/city-and-metropolitan-police#S5CV0082P0_19160531_CWA_59.

Cymet, David. *History vs. Apologetics: The Holocaust, the Third Reich, and the Catholic Church.* Lanham: Lexington Books, 2010.

Davies, T. L. "Events of the Month." *The Fraternal Visitor,* May 1933.

Davies, T. L. "Events of the Month." *The Fraternal Visitor,* August 1934.

Davis, A. E. "Affairs in Jerusalem." *The Christadelphian,* April 1893.

Davis, A. E. "From Jerusalem." *The Christadelphian,* August 1893.

Davis, A. E. "Letter from Jerusalem." *The Christadelphian,* October 1895.

Davis, A. E. "Letter from Jerusalem." *The Christadelphian,* September 1900.

Davis, A. E. "Letter from Jerusalem." *The Christadelphian,* October 1900.

Davis, A. E. "Letters from Jerusalem." *The Christadelphian,* January 1904.

Davis, A. E. "Letter from Jerusalem." *The Christadelphian,* February 1904.

Davis, A. E. "Letters from Jerusalem." *The Christadelphian,* July 1904.

Davis, A. E. "Letters from the Holy Land." *The Christadelphian,* July 1903.

"Debate on the Address." *Hansard, 29 November 1939.* Accessed April 15, 2016.

http://hansard.millbanksystems.com/commons/1939/nov/29/debate-on-the-address#S5CV0355P0_19391129_HOC_55.

Dinnerstein, Leonard. *Anti-Semitism in America*. New York: Oxford University Press, 1994.

Harris, Mark Jonathan, and Deborah Oppenheimer. *Into the Arms of Strangers: Stories of the Kindertransport*. New York: Bloomsbury Pub., 2000.

Hitler, Adolf. Mein Kampf. Boston: Houghton Mifflin Company, 1943.

Holden, Herbert. "Herbert Holden." In *I Came Alone*, edited by Bertha Leverton and Shmuel Lowensohn, 149–150. Sussex: The Book Guild Ltd., 1990.

Huehns, Ernst. *The Luckiest Boy In Germany*. CreateSpace Independent Publishing Platform, 2015.

Kotzin, Chana Revell, "Christian Responses in Britain to Jewish Refugees in Europe: 1933–1939." doctoral thesis, University of Southampton, 2000.

Kovarik, Bill. *Revolutions in Communication: Media History from Gutenberg to the Digital Age*. New York: Continuum, 2011.

Ladson, C. A. "The Jews and Zionism." *The Christadelphian*, April 1933.

Ladson, C. A. "The Jews and Zionism." *The Christadelphian*, January 1936.

Ladson, C. A. "The Jews and Zionism." *The Christadelphian*, June 1936.

Ladson, C. A. "The Jews and Zionism." *The Christadelphian*, April 1938.

Ladson, C. A. "The Jews and Zionism." *The Christadelphian*, December 1938.

Laqueur, Walter. *Generation Exodus: The Fate of Young Jewish Refugees from Nazi Germany*. Hanover: Brandeis University Press, University Press of New England, 2001.

Levy Green, Aaron. "Letter from certain Friends of Judah to the Chief Rabbi in London." *Herald of the Kingdom and Age to Come,* September 1854.

Luther, Martin. "The Jews and Their Lies." *Jewish Virtual Library.* Accessed March 21, 2014. http://www.jewishvirtuallibrary.org/jsource/anti-semitism/Luther_on_Jews.html.

Montefiore, Moses. "Letters Received in Reply to the Foregoing." *Herald of the Kingdom and Age to Come,* March 1855.

"National Average Wages." *Hansard, 29 November 1960.* Accessed April 15, 2016. http://hansard.millbanksystems.com/written_answers/1960/nov/29/national-average-wages.

"Notes" *The Christadelphian,* December 1905.

Oliphant, Laurence. "The Christadelphian Contribution to Palestine Colonization." *The Christadelphian,* August 1883.

Phayer, Michael. *The Catholic Church and the Holocaust: 1930–1965.* Bloomington: Indiana University Press, 2000.

Roberts, Robert. "Editorial." *The Christadelphian,* August 1875.

Roberts, Robert. "Editorial." *The Christadelphian,* May 1882.

Roberts, Robert. "Editorial." *The Christadelphian,* January 1884.

Roberts, Robert. "Editorial." *The Christadelphian,* March 1884.

Roberts, Robert. "Interviews with Mr. Oliphant." *The Christadelphian,* January 1887.

Roberts, Robert. "The Jewish Contribution." *The Christadelphian,* February 1885.

Roberts, Robert. "The Jews and Their Affairs." *The Christadelphian,* June 1875.

"Rosh-Pina." *Www.goisrael.com.* Accessed April 15, 2016.http://www.goisrael.com/Tourism_Eng/TouristInformation/Discover Israel/Cities/Pages/Rosh-pina.aspx.

R. T. W. S. "Current Events." *The Fraternal Visitor,* December 1937.

R. T. W. S. "Events of the Month." *The Fraternal Visitor,* December 1938.

Rudin, A. James. *Christians & Jews Faith to Faith: Tragic History, Promising Present, Fragile Future.* Woodstock: Jewish Lights Pub., 2011.

"Second Reading." *Hansard, 21 February 1870.* Accessed April 15, 2016. http://hansard.millbanksystems.com/commons/1870/feb/21/second-reading#S3V0199P0_18700221_HOC_48.

Sterns, Emerson. "Dr. D'Arbela and Mrs. Davis, of Jerusalem: Who They Are." *The Christadelphian,* February 1893.

"Table 3. - Population(1) of Localities Numbering Above 2,000 Residents." *Cbs.gov.il.* Accessed April 15, 2016. http://www.cbs.gov.il/population/new_2010/table3.pdf.

Taylor, Edgar. "Back to the Mandate." *The Testimony,* December 1938.

Taylor, Edgar "In the Footsteps of Haman." *The Testimony,* April 1933.

Taylor, Edgar. "Ye Shall Be an Execration." *The Testimony,* September 1936.

Thomas, John. *Elpis Israel: Being an Exposition of the Kingdom of God ; with Reference to the Time of the End, and the Age to Come.* New York: Fowlers and Wells., 1851.

Turner, Barry. . . . *And the Policeman Smiled.* London: Bloomsbury, 1990.

Walker, C. C. "Joseph." *The Christadelphian,* March 1939.

Walker, C. C. "Birmingham Miscellanies." *The Christadelphian,* January 1906.

Walker, C. C. "Jewish Relief Fund." *The Christadelphian,* May 1916.

Walker, C. C. "Jewish Relief Fund." *The Christadelphian,* July 1916.

Walker, C. C. "Jewish Relief Fund." *The Christadelphian,* September 1916.

Walker, C. C. "Jewish Relief Fund." *The Christadelphian,* April 1918.

Walker, C. C. "The 'Elpis Israel' Bed." *The Christadelphian,* October 1912.

Walker, C. C. "The Jewish Refugees." *The Christadelphian,* July 1917.

Walker, C. C. "The Jewish Relief Fund." *The Christadelphian,* June 1918.

Walker, C. C. "The Jewish Relief Fund." *The Christadelphian,* August 1918.

"War Service for Women." *Hansard, 11 May 1916.* Accessed April 15, 2016. http://hansard.millbanksystems.com/commons/1916/may/11/war-service-for-women#S5CV0082P0_19160511_HOC_226.

White, W. J. "Signs of the Times," *The Berean,* May 1935.

Woodin, Susanne. "My Childhood Memories." Typescript. February 2010.

Zuccotti, Susan. *Under His Very Windows: The Vatican and the Holocaust in Italy.* New Haven: Yale University Press, 2000.

**Part II**

**Introduction**

Baldwin, Stanley. "An Appeal for the Jewish and Non-Aryan and Christian Refugees." *BBC,* (December 1938).

Baumel-Schwartz, Judith Tydor. *Never Look Back: The Jewish Refugee Children in Great Britain, 1938–1945 (Shofar Supplements in Jewish Studies).* West Lafayette, In.: Purdue University Press, 2012. Electronic.

Fast, Vera. *Children's Exodus: A History of the Kindertransport.* London: I. B. Tauris & Co. Ltd., 2011.

Gilbert, Martin. *The Holocaust: A History of the Jews of Europe during the Second World War.* New York: Henry Holt and Company, 1985.

"Kindertransport, 1938–1940." *United States Holocaust Memorial Museum.* Last modified January 29, 2016. https://www.ushmm.org/wlc/en/article.php?ModuleId=10005260.

"Kristallnacht." *United States Holocaust Memorial Museum.* Last modified January 29, 2016. https://www.ushmm.org/wlc/en/article.php?ModuleId=10005201.

Ladson, C. A. "The Jews and Zionism." *The Christadelphian,* December 1939.

Turner, Barry. . . . *And the Policeman Smiled.* London: Bloomsbury, 1990.

**Charles Ohlenberg's Biography**

"Auschwitz." United States Holocaust Memorial Museum. Last modified January 29, 2016. https://www.ushmm.org/wlc/en/article.php?ModuleId=10005189.

Brown, Cyril. "New Popular Idol Rises in Bavaria." *The New York Times* (New York, NY), November 21, 1922.

C. R. "Germany's Hyperinflation-phobia." *The Economist.* Last modified November 15, 2013. http://www.economist.com/blogs/freeexchange/2013/11/economic-history-1.

Feigenbaum, Susan K., and R. W. Hafer. *Principles of Macroeconomics: The Way We Live.* New York: Worth Publishers, First Edition, 2011.

Hall, Robert E. *Inflation: Causes and Effects.* Chicago: University of Chicago Press, 1982.

"Memorial Book - Victims of the Persecution of Jews under the National Socialist Tyranny in Germany 1933–1945." *Das Bundesarchiv.* Last modified January 14, 2016. https://www.bundesarchiv.de/gedenkbuch/zwangsausweisung.html.en.

Ohlenberg, Charles. *USC Shoah Foundation Institute Testimony of Charles Ohlenberg*. USC Shoah Foundation Institute, May 13, 1996.

"The Central Database of Shoah Victims' Names - Paul Oehlenberg." *Yad Vashem*. Accessed April 15, 2016.
http://yvng.yadvashem.org/nameDetails.html?language=en&s_lastNa me=ohlenberg&s_firstName=&s_place=&itemId=7856036&ind=37& winId=-5466662086370935376.

### Ingrid Wuga's Biography

"Buchenwald." *United States Holocaust Memorial Museum*. Last modified January 29, 2016.
http://www.ushmm.org/wlc/en/article.php?ModuleId=10005198.

Greenaway, Heather. "Couple Who Found Love in Scotland after Fleeing Nazis Tell Why We Must Never Forget." *Daily Record*, January 22, 2012.
http://www.dailyrecord.co.uk/news/real-life/couple-who-found-love-in-scotland-1114615#jj8q5iqb6uS9iCj5.97.

"Ingrid Wuga - Life Before The War." *Gathering The Voices*. Accessed April 15, 2016.
http://www.gatheringthevoices.com/testimonies/ingrid-wuga1.

"Making It Home: How One Couple Found Happiness against All Odds." *Scotsman*, June 20, 2011.
http://www.scotsman.com/lifestyle/making-it-home-how-one-couple -found-happiness-against-all-odds-1-1701165.

Wuga, Ingrid, and Henry Wuga. "Ingrid's Story." Typescript. July 2002.

Wuga, Ingrid, and Henry Wuga. "Wednesday 23rd January Fettes College Historical Society." Typescript. January 2013.

### Ursula Meyer's Biography

Carroll, John M. "American Diplomacy in the 1920s." In *Modern American Diplomacy,* ed. John Martin Carroll and George C. Herring. Lanham: SR Books, 2004.

Clapper, Susan. *USC Shoah Foundation Institute Testimony of Susan Clapper*. USC Shoah Foundation Institute, November 23, 1995.

"Dawes Plan." *Encyclopedia Britannica Online*. Accessed May 6, 2016. http://www.britannica.com/event/Dawes-Plan.

Grosz, Hanus, Kristen Grosz, and Anita Grosz. *Kindertransport Memory Quilt*. Kindertransport Association of North America, 2000.

"Riga." *United States Holocaust Memorial Museum*. Last modified January 29, 2016. http://www.ushmm.org/wlc/en/article.php?ModuleId=10005463.

"Stolpersteine in Schötmar." *Stolpersteine in Schötmar*. Accessed April 15, 2016. http://www.schoetmar.net/index.php?id=63.

"Stutthof." *United States Holocaust Memorial Museum*. Last modified January 29, 2016. http://www.ushmm.org/wlc/en/article.php?ModuleId=10005197.

"Gedenkbuch - Opfer Der Verfolgung Der Juden Unter Der Nationalsozialistischen Gewaltherrscha in Deutschland 1933–1945." *Das Bundesarchiv*. Accessed April 15, 2016. http://www.bundesarchiv.de/gedenkbuch/de854544.

"Gedenkbuch - Opfer Der Verfolgung Der Juden Unter Der Nationalsozialistischen Gewaltherrscha in Deutschland 1933–1945." *Das Bundesarchiv*. accessed April 15, 2016. http://www.bundesarchiv.de/gedenkbuch/de854556.

"Gedenkbuch - Opfer Der Verfolgung Der Juden Unter Der Nationalsozialistischen Gewaltherrscha in Deutschland 1933–1945." *Das Bundesarchiv*. Accessed April 15, 2016. http://www.bundesarchiv.de/gedenkbuch/de854559.

Sawyer, Mark. "My Big Sister Ursula." *Christadelphiansisters.org*. Accessed April 15, 2016. http://www.christadelphiansisters.org/URSULA.HTM.

"The Dawes Plan, the Young Plan, German Reparations, and Inter-allied War Debts." *Office of the Historian, Bureau of Public Affairs, United*

*States Department of State.* Accessed May 6, 2016.
https://history.state.gov/milestones/1921-1936/dawes.

Turner, Barry. . . . *And the Policeman Smiled.* London: Bloomsbury, 1990.

**Hana Holman's Biography**

Cull, Nicholas J., David Holbrook Culbert, and David Welch. "Mein
Kampf," in *Propaganda and Mass Persuasion: A Historical
Encyclopedia, 1500 to the Present.* Santa Barbara: ABC-CLIO, 2003.

Mühlberger, Detlef. *Hitler's Voice: Organisation and Development of the
Nazi Party.* Oxford: Lang, 2004.

Owen, F. G. "Intelligence." *The Christadelphian.* February 1943.

Ryback, Timothy. *Hitler's Private Library.* New York: Alfred A. Knopf,
2008.

"Sudetenland." *Encyclopedia Britannica Online.* Accessed April 16, 2016.
http://www.britannica.com/place/Sudetenland.

"The Great Synagogue." *Municipality of the City of Pilsen.* Accessed May 3,
2016.
http://www.pilsen.eu/tourist/visit/top-tourist-destinations/the-great-
synagogue/the-great-synagogue.aspx.

"Theresienstadt." *United States Holocaust Memorial Museum.* Last
modified January 29, 2016.
https://www.ushmm.org/wlc/en/article.php?ModuleId=10005424.

Waite, Susan. "How My Mother, Sis. Hana Holman, Learnt the Truth."
*Christadelphiansisters.org.* Accessed February 14, 2016.
http://www.christadelphiansisters.org/HANA.HTM.

**Charles Borger's Biography**

"Czechoslovakia." *United States Holocaust Memorial Museum.* Last
modified January 29, 2016.
https://www.ushmm.org/wlc/en/article.php?ModuleId=10005688.

Khanna, V. N. *International Relations, 4E.* Vikas Publishing House, 2009.

Kotzin, Chana Revell, "Christian Responses in Britain to Jewish Refugees in Europe: 1933–1939." doctoral thesis, University of Southampton, 2000.

"Pact of Locarno."*Encyclopedia Britannica Online.* Accessed April 22, 2016. http://www.britannica.com/event/Pact-of-Locarno.

"The Central Database of Shoah Victims' Names - Alfred Borger." *Yad Vashem.* Accessed April 22, 2016. http://yvng.yadvashem.org/nameDetails.html? language=en&s_lastName=&s_rstName=&s_place=&itemId=670589 4&ind=1&wi nId=-4962800414323544064.

"The Central Database of Shoah Victims' Names - Alfred Geduldig." *Yad Vashem.* Accessed April 22, 2016. http://yvng.yadvashem.org/nameDetails.html?language=en&s_lastNa me=&s_place=&itemId=6705899&ind=7&winId=3173333848311561 6866.

"The Central Database of Shoah Victims' Names - Hermina Borger." *Yad Vashem.* Accessed April 22, 2016. http://yvng.yadvashem.org/nameDetails.html?language=en&s_lastNa me=borger&s_rstName=hermine&s_place=&itemId=6705895&ind= 76&winId=6418920438816116318.

"Treblinka." *United States Holocaust Memorial Museum.* Last modified January 29, 2016. https://www.ushmm.org/wlc/en/article.php?ModuleId=10005193.

**Max Rubinstein's Biography**

Bacon, Gershon C. "Virtual Jewish World: Danzig (Gdańsk), Poland." *Danzig (Gdańsk), Poland Jewish History Tour.* Date last modified 1980. http://www.jewishvirtuallibrary.org/jsource/vjw/Danzig.html.

"Danzig." *United States Holocaust Memorial Museum.* Last modified January 29, 2016. https://www.ushmm.org/wlc/en/article.php?ModuleId=10005438.

Fry, Michael. "#tbt: Danzig and the Beginnings of World War II." *Nat Geo Education Blog.* Date last modified August 28, 2014.

https://blog.education.nationalgeographic.com/2014/08/28/tbt-danzi
g-and-the-beginnings-of-world-war-ii/.

"German-Soviet Nonaggression Pact." *History.com.* accessed April 22,
2016.
http://www.history.com/topics/world-war-ii/german-soviet-nonaggr
ession-pact.

"Kritallnacht." *United States Holocaust Memorial Museum.* last modified
January 29, 2016.
https://www.ushmm.org/wlc/en/article.php?ModuleId=10005201.

Rubinstein, Max. "My Life, Max Rubinstein." Typescript. 2002.

Shirer, William L. *The Rise and Fall of the Third Reich; a History of Nazi
Germany.* New York: Simon and Schuster, 1960.

"The Avalon Project: The Versailles Treaty June 28, 1919." *Yale Law School.*
Accessed April 22, 2016. http://avalon.law.yale.edu/imt/partiii.asp.

"The Central Database of Shoah Victims' Names - Isser Rubinshtein." *Yad
Vashem*, accessed April 22, 2016,
http://yvng.yadvashem.org/nameDetails.html?language=en&itemId=
9348274.

"The Central Database of Shoah Victims' Names - Vera Rubinshtein." *Yad
Vashem.* Accessed April 15, 2016.
http://yvng.yadvashem.org/nameDetails.html?language=en&itemId=
9348275.

Whittaker, H. A. *Abraham, Father of the Faithful.* Birmingham: The
Christadelphian Magazine and Publishing Association, 1966.

Whittaker, Harry. "Max and Pauline." Typescript. No date.

World Jewish Relief case files for Max Rubinstein.

**Elfriede Ransome's Biography**

"Einstein on Arrival Braves Limelight for Only 15 Minutes." *The New York
Times* (New York, NY), December 12, 1930.

Mason, Kevin. "Building an Unwanted Nation: The Anglo-American Partnership and Austrian Proponents of a Separate Nationhood, 1918–1934." PhD diss., University of North Carolina at Chapel Hill, 2007.

Nye, Ilse. In *We Came as Children; a Collective Autobiography*, edited by Karen Gershon, 25, 47. New York: Harcourt, Brace & World, 1966.

Ransome, Elfriede. In *We Came as Children; a Collective Autobiography*, edited by Karen Gershon, 66, 114–115. New York: Harcourt, Brace & World, 1966.

Ransome, Elfriede. "Israel and Their Land." *The Christadelphian*. February 1989.

Ransome, Elfriede. "The Prayers of Hannah and Mary." *The Testimony*. May, 2003.

## Susanne Woodin's Biography

"Adolf Cohn." *Stolpersteine in Berlin*. Accessed April 22, 2016. http://neu.stolpersteine-berlin.de/en/biografie/978.

"Alice Türk." *Stolpersteine in Berlin*. Accessed April 22, 2016. http://neu.stolpersteine-berlin.de/en/biografie/3221.

"Antisemitic Legislation 1933–1939." *United States Holocaust Memorial Museum*. Last modified January 29, 2016. https://www.ushmm.org/wlc/en/article.php?ModuleId=10007901.

Carter, Raymond. "The Brotherhood Near and Far." *The Christadelphian*. March 1972.

"Clara Cohn." *Stolpersteine in Berlin*. Accessed April 22, 2016, https://www.stolpersteine-berlin.de/en/biografie/977.

"Eva Cohn." *Stolpersteine in Berlin*. Accessed April 22, 2016. https://www.stolpersteine-berlin.de/en/biografie/979.

"Examples of Antisemitic Legislation 1933–1939." *United States Holocaust Memorial Museum*. Last modified January 29, 2016. https://www.ushmm.org/wlc/en/article.php?ModuleId=10007459.

Ford, Paul. "The Brotherhood Near and Far." *The Christadelphian.* November 1977.

"Julius Schlome." *Stolpersteine in Berlin.* Accessed April 22, 2016. http://neu.stolpersteine-berlin.de/en/biografie/1094.

"Paul Schlome." *Stolpersteine in Berlin.* Accessed April 22, 2016. http://neu.stolpersteine-berlin.de/en/biografie/1095.

"Minsk." *United States Holocaust Memorial Museum.* Last modified January 29, 2016. https://www.ushmm.org/wlc/en/article.php?ModuleId=10005187.

"Ruth Schlome (geb. Türk)." *Stolpersteine in Berlin.* Accessed April 22, 2016. http://neu.stolpersteine-berlin.de/en/biografie/1096.

"Therese Türk (geb. Kantorowicz)." *Stolpersteine in Berlin.* Accessed April 22, 2016. http://www.stolpersteine-berlin.de/de/biografie/3222.

Woodin, Susanne. "My Childhood Memories." Typescript. February 2010.

**Suse Rosenstock's Biography**

"Adolf Hitler Is Satisfied by German Troubles; Writes He Has Never Been in Such High Spirits." *The New York Times* (New York, NY), July 31, 1931.

Cassis, Youssef, and Jacqueline Collier. *Capitals of Capital: The Rise and Fall of International Financial Centres, 1780–2009.* Cambridge: Cambridge University Press, 2010.

Ferguson, J. David., and Thomas E. Hall. *Great Depression: An International Disaster of Perverse Economic Policies.* Michigan: University of Michigan Press, 1998.

Fohlin, Caroline. *Finance Capitalism and Germany's Rise to Industrial Power.* Cambridge: Cambridge University Press, 2007.

"German Jews' Passports Declared Invalid." *United States Holocaust Memorial Museum.* Accessed April 16, 2016.

https://www.ushmm.org/learn/timeline-of-events/1933-1938/reich-ministry-of-the-interior-invalidates-all-german-passports-held-by-jew.

Lange, Brenda. *The Stock Market Crash of 1929: The End of Prosperity*. New York: Chelsea House, 2007.

Nadler, Marcus, and Jules I. Bogen. *The Banking Crisis; the End of an Epoch*. New York: Dodd, Mead &, 1933.

Pagelson, Edith Lucas. *Against All Odds: A Miracle of Holocaust Survival*. Rockland: Maine Authors Publishing, 2012. Electronic.

Rosenstock, Suse. *USC Shoah Foundation Institute Testimony of Suse Rosenstock*. USC Shoah Foundation Institute, January 19, 1996.

Stackelberg, Roderick. *Hitler's Germany: Origins, Interpretations, Legacies*. London: Routledge, 1999.

"Young Plan." *Encyclopedia Britannica Online*. Accessed April 16, 2016. http://www.britannica.com/event/Young-Plan.

**Rella Adler's Biography**

Adams, P. H. "Messiah in the Prophets." *The Testimony*. April 1939.

Adler, Rella. *USC Shoah Foundation Institute Testimony of Rella Adler*. USC Shoah Foundation Institute, August 24, 1998.

Hardy, Walter. "The Brotherhood Near and Far." *The Christadelphian*. May 1971.

"The Central Database of Shoah Victims' Names - Josefine Hodes." *Yad Vashem*. Accessed April 22, 2016. http://yvng.yadvashem.org/nameDetails.html?language=en&s_lastName=hudes&s_firstName=josephine&s_place=&itemId=4921261&ind=1&winId=-7234554289528559526.

"The Central Database of Shoah Victims' Names - Mirjam Hodes." *Yad Vashem*. Accessed April 22, 2016. http://yvng.yadvashem.org/nameDetails.html?language=en&s_lastName=hudes&s_firstName=miriam&s_place=&itemId=722841&ind=3&winId=-5564477282211710703.

**Glossary**

Excerpted with permission from the Glossary in *Echoes and Reflections Teacher's Resource Guide* (New York: Anti-Defamation League, 2005, 2014), www.echoesandreflections.org. All rights reserved.

# ACKNOWLEDGEMENTS

The biographies in this book were a collaborative project between the author, the refugee and their family, and the Christadelphian family who housed them. Each of these biographies, after they were written, were then reviewed for accuracy by the refugee, or their family members, or both. They have been double checked, and were not published until all parties involved were satisfied with what had been written. A "thank you" needs to be said to the refugees and their families, and the Christadelphian families. For some, going through this process brought back difficult memories—but they did so because the stories needed to be told and the history needed to be remembered by future generations. It has been an honor and a privilege to work with all of you. Thank you to Charles and Elisabeth Ohlenberg and family, along with Elisabeth Briley; Ingrid and Henry Wuga, Hilary Hodsman, and Gilian Field; Ursula Meyer and Maureen Blotnick, along with Mark Sawyer; Hana Holman, Susan Waite, and David Holman; Charles Borger and family, along with George and Gill MacDonald and Simon Foster; Max and Esther Rubinstein, along with Mark Whittaker; Susanne Woodin; Elfriede Ransome, Margaret Baines, Helen Collard, and Susi Morris, along with Eric Marshall; Suse Rosenstock, Elaine and Alan Peizer, Deborah Rosenstock, and Edith Pagelson, along with John Parry; and Rella Adler, Hilary and Rachel Mentkow, and Debra Stein, along with Sybil Dawson.

This book was born out of two professional development experiences. First, the Belfer Conference for Educators at the United States Holocaust Memorial and Museum, and the online pilot program of Echoes and Reflections, put together by the Anti-Defamation League, the USC Shoah Foundation, and Yad Vashem. Special thanks goes to Jennifer Goss and Dr.

## Acknowledgments

Mark Gudgel, my instructors at the Belfer Conference, and Deborah Batiste, my instructor with Echoes and Reflections.

The Holocaust Studies class consistently provided inspiration and encouragement in this process, along with my local ecclesia, and the Christadelphian community in general.

Thank you to Heather Rothman, who served as the main editor for the entirety of the manuscript, Miriam Reichman who did supplemental editing on a few of the biographies, and Robin Boiko, Wendy Cipriotti, Pat Hampson, Gordon Hensley, Rebecca Laben, Bethany Robinson, Rachel Robinson, and Colleen Uiga who together, proofread the book. Rachel Robinson also helped to format the endnotes and bibliography. Dr. Stephen Snobelen read through the manuscript and offered insightful and helpful comments. Jason Robinson designed the cover.

Perhaps most of all, thanks should go to my loving wife and two daughters. We have one more child on the way—due in July!—and throughout all of this, my wife Ruth read through the manuscript with me, gave feedback, and helped to smooth out some of the rocky bits. Adding to that, she created all of the maps used in this publication. More than anything else, though, their love—both my wife's and my daughters'—provided major motivation for this project.

# INDEX

# PHOTOGRAPHIC CREDITS

**Christadelphians and the Jews**

Page 4: public domain

Page 10: public domain

Page 12: public domain

Page 20: (top) by Abdullah brothers (Bibliothèque nationale de France) [Public domain], via Wikimedia Commons

Page 20: (bottom) public domain

**Charles Ohlenberg's Biography**

All photographs courtesy of Charles Ohlenberg and family.

**Ingrid Wuga's Biography**

Page 114: (top and bottom) photographs courtesy of Robert Burns, as a gift to the Wuga family.

All other photographs courtesy of Ingrid Wuga and family.

**Ursula Meyer's Biography**

Page 137: photograph courtesy of Maureen and Alec Blotnik.

All other photographs courtesy of Mark Sawyer and family.

**Hana Holman's Biography**

Page 150: photograph courtesy of David Holman.

Page 151: (top and bottom) photographs courtesy of David Holman.

All other photographs courtesy of Susan Waite.

**Charles Borger's Biography**

Page 173: (top and bottom) photographs courtesy of Simon Foster. Taken from Ernest Foster's 1939 cine film.

Page 178: photograph courtesy of Simon Foster. Taken from Ernest Foster's 1939 cine film.

Page 180: (top and bottom) photographs courtesy of Charles Borger.

**Max Rubinstein's Biography**

Page 206: photograph taken by the author.

All other photographs courtesy of Max Rubinstein and family.

**Elfriede Ransome's Biography**

All photographs courtesy of Elfriede Ransome and family.

**Susanne Woodin's Biography**

All photographs courtesy of Susanne Woodin.

**Suse Rosenstock's Biography**

Page 304: photograph courtesy of Elaine Peizer.

Page 325: (top and bottom) photographs courtesy of Elaine Peizer.

Page 332: (top) photograph courtesy of Deborah Rosenstock.

Page 332: (bottom) photograph courtesy of Elaine Peizer.

All other photos courtesy of Deborah Rosenstock.

**Rella Adler's Biography**

Page 346: photograph courtesy of Sybil Dawson.

Page 364: photograph courtesy of Sybil Dawson.

# Photographic Credits

Page 365: photograph courtesy of Simeon Pratt.

All other photographs courtesy of Rella Adler.

**A Note about the Author**

Page 403: photograph courtesy of the U.S. Holocaust Memorial Museum

Photograph courtesy of the U.S. Holocaust Memorial Museum.

## A Note About the Author

Jason Hensley, M.Ed, is the principal of a small private school in California. At school, he teaches religious studies and a senior-level course on Christianity and the Holocaust. The material for this book has served as the backbone for the curriculum in the latter course. He frequently lectures on this and related topics throughout North America. Find him on Facebook, and at iwaspartofthefamily.com

Made in the USA
Middletown, DE
14 June 2016